Psychoanalytic Psychology

The Development of Freud's Thought

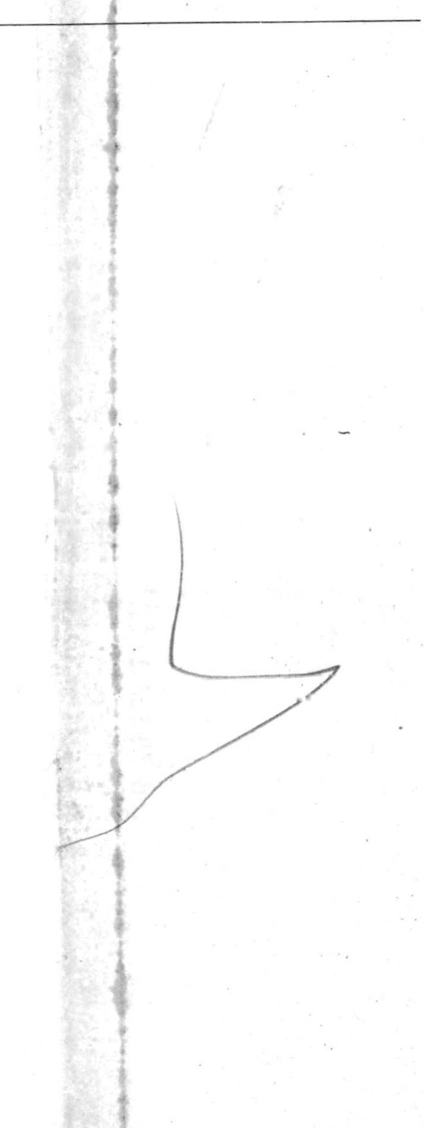

ALSO BY RAYMOND E. FANCHER

Pioneers of Psychology

The Intelligence Men:
Makers of the I. Q. Controversy

Psychoanalytic Psychology

The Development of Freud's Thought

Raymond E. Fancher

W · W · NORTON & COMPANY
New York · London

W. W. Norton & Company, Inc., 500 Fifth Avenue, New York, N.Y. 10110
W. W. Norton & Company Ltd., 10 Coptic Street, London, WC1A 1PU

Library of Congress Cataloging in Publication Data

Fancher, Raymond E
Psychoanalytic psychology.

Bibliography: p.
1. Psychoanalysis. 2. Freud, Sigmund, 1856–1939.
I. Title. [DNLM: 1. Psychoanalytic theory.
WZ 100 F889FW 1973]
RC504.F32 1973 616.8'917'0924 73–1273

ISBN 0-393-09356-5

PRINTED IN THE UNITED STATES OF AMERICA

1 2 3 4 5 6 7 8 9 0

FOR MY PARENTS

Raymond Elwood Fancher, Sr.

Doris Crose Fancher

Contents

1 Introduction:
The Background of Freud's Thought 1

2 The Early Data:
Hysteria and Hypnosis 30

3 First Model of the Mind:
"Project for a Scientific Psychology" 63

4 Dreams 98

5 Sexuality 134

6 Psychoanalytic Psychotherapy
and the Theory of Instincts 165

7 Freud's Final Model of the Mind
and the Implications of Psychoanalysis 195

Index 235

Preface

The approach to Freud adopted in this book originated in my experiences teaching courses on personality theory a few years ago. I found that students were often particularly skeptical about Freud's psychoanalytic theory, sometimes even questioning the usefulness of studying it at all. Their attitude reflected a growing trend in the field of psychology today. While they were ready to grant that Freud was a genius, they qualified this praise by defining his genius as "literary" and thus as irrelevant to the scientific study of behavior. Thus I found myself cast in the role of devil's advocate, and I was prodded to study Freud more closely than I ever had before.

I came away from that study aware for the first time of the scientific base from which psychoanalytic theory developed. By going back to the very earliest psychoanalytic works and then following the chronological development of Freud's thought, I discovered that psychoanalytic theory evolved in a completely proper scientific manner from a matrix of assumptions, hypotheses, observations, experimental manipulations, and logical deductions. Freud's major works were written over a span of almost fifty years, during which his views became increasingly complicated and sophisticated. His early works constituted the foundation upon which the later works were constructed. Thus a reader whose first exposure to Freud is through one of the later works, or through an introductory description that does not adequately deal with the first stages of his theory, is likely to find—as my students did—that the material seems rather dogmatic and unscientific. To begin with Freud's conclusions—his last-developed models of the mind, theories of the instincts, etc.—is to see psychoanalysis apart from the empirical facts that accounted for its growth and power.

Accordingly, the chapters in this book take up Freud's major ideas and work in generally chronological order, building on one another. Readers are encouraged to read the chapters in sequence, though anyone who is eager to plunge immediately into the body of Freud's work might wish to skim over the biographical section of Chapter One. It is hoped that by taking the chapters in order readers will be able to put themselves in Freud's place—to see things through his eyes and in general to develop a feel for the way psychoanalytic theory developed.

While the aim of this book is to present Freudian theory as a properly *scientific* product, no specific claims will be made about its validity. The terms "scientific" and "true" are far from synonymous, and to respect Freud's thought as scientific theorizing does not obligate one to accept all its tenets as true. Scientific theories are always subject to disconfirmation by subsequent observation and analysis, and psychoanalysis is no exception. I hope that readers of the present volume will come to share my view of Freudian theory as an inspired though tentative conceptualization of human nature, worthy of respect and attention but at the same time subject to modification, or even replacement, by new discoveries about human psychology. Such an attitude is fully consistent with the spirit of Freud's own pioneering investigations.

Many people assisted me in the conception and writing of this book, and I would like to express my appreciation to them here. An obvious debt of gratitude is owed to my students, both graduate and undergraduate, who initially inspired my approach to teaching Freud and who have helped me to refine it over the past few years. Several colleagues have been extremely helpful by reading and commenting on various portions of the manuscript. I would especially like to acknowledge the contributions of Allen Adinolfi, David Bakan, Emory

Cowen, Morris Eagle, Jay Efran, David Elkind, Jarold Ramsey, Milton Strauss, Malcolm Westcott, and Melvin Zax. The book is stronger for their efforts. I also wish to acknowledge the excellent editorial assistance rendered by Donald S. Lamm and his colleagues at W. W. Norton & Company, Inc. My wife, Lynn Cogburn Fancher, has assisted at virtually every stage in the preparation of this book; I cannot adequately express my appreciation to her.

Raymond E. Fancher

Toronto
October, 1972

Psychoanalytic Psychology
The Development of Freud's Thought

1

Introduction: The Background of Freud's Thought

An Illustrative Incident

One day in the summer of 1900, Sigmund Freud held a casual conversation with a younger acquaintance. Freud himself was a middle-aged physician at the time, and though he had already achieved a rather controversial reputation with his scholarly colleagues, he had not yet attracted widespread public notice. Thus the young man did not realize that he was talking to one of the great men of his time; he probably regarded Freud as simply an interesting but eccentric academic physician. In spite of this lack of recognition, however, most of the essential aspects of psychoanalytic theory had already been developed by Freud, or were in a state of rapid germination, and within a few years these ideas were to create a revolution in the way human beings thought of themselves. Some of these revolutionary ideas quite fortuitously crept into the conversation between the two men.

The young man was feeling pessimistic and bitter about the state of the world, particularly the prospects it offered for himself and his generation of young men. He was well educated, and at one point in the conversation he wanted to emphasize his bitterness by quoting a line from Virgil's poem *The Aeneid:* "Exoriare aliquis nostris ex ossibus ultor," which means, literally, "Let someone arise from my bones as an avenger." But in quoting the line he forgot to include the word *aliquis* ("someone"). Immediately he experienced that common discomfiting sensation of realizing that one has made a mistake but not knowing specifically what the mistake is. After a moment of embarrassed silence the young man asked Freud whether he could correct the error. Freud provided the missing word.

The young man then attempted to overcome his embarrassment by taking the offensive. He recalled having heard a rumor that Freud had constructed a theory capable of providing a meaning for all sorts of "mistakes," so he challenged the older man to account for his apparently meaningless lapse of memory. Freud, happy to take up the challenge, replied that all he required was the complete cooperation of the young man. First, the young man would have to concentrate his complete attention upon the word *aliquis* and report whatever thought came into his mind in association with that word. Then he was to report his associations to the association, and so on, until the mystery was solved. The only essential rule was that he make no attempt to censor any of his associations, or his reports of associations. *Everything* that came to mind, however fleetingly, was to be reported, even if it seemed ridiculous or unpleasant. The young man agreed to this rule and proceeded to relate his train of thought, beginning with the word *aliquis,* as follows:[1]

"There springs to my mind, then, the ridiculous notion of dividing up the word like this: *a* and *liquis.* What comes next is *Reliquien* (relics), *liquefying, fluidity, fluid,* . . .

"I am thinking," he went on, "of *Simon of Trent,* whose relics I saw two years ago in a church at Trent. I am thinking of the accusation of ritual blood-sacrifice which is being

[1]All of the quotations in this conversation are taken from Sigmund Freud's "The Psychopathology of Everyday Life," included in *The Standard Edition of the Complete Psychological Works of Sigmund Freud* (London, Hogarth Press, 1953–). Hereafter this edition of Freud's works will be referred to simply as *Standard Edition.* Quotations cited in the present instance may be found in Vol. VI, pp. 9–11.

brought against the Jews again just now, and of *Kleinpaul's* book in which he regards all these supposed victims as incarnations, one might say new editions, of the Saviour. . . .

"My next thoughts are about an article that I read recently in an Italian newspaper. Its title, I think, was 'What *St. Augustine* Says about Women.' . . .

"I am thinking about a fine old gentleman I met on my travels last week. He was a real original, with all the appearance of a huge bird of prey. His name was *Benedict,* if it's of interest to you. . . . Now it's *St. Januarius* and the miracle of his blood that comes into my mind—my thoughts seem to be running on mechanically."

At this point Freud broke in to note that the names of several saints had come up in the associations, including two (Augustine and Januarius) who are named on the calendar. The real purpose of his interruption, however, was to inquire about the miracle of St. Januarius' blood, a story with which he was unfamiliar.

"Surely you have heard of that?" remarked the young man. "They keep the blood of St. Januarius in a phial inside a church at Naples, and on a particular holy day it miraculously liquefies. The people attach great importance to this miracle and get very excited if it's delayed, as happened once at a time when the French were occupying the town. So the general in command—or have I got it wrong? was it Garibaldi?—took the reverend gentleman aside and gave him to understand, with an unmistakable gesture towards the soldiers posted outside, that he *hoped* the miracle would take place very soon. And in fact it did take place. . . ."

At this point the young man's face darkened noticeably, and he hesitated in his narrative. When Freud asked what was the trouble, he replied: "Well, something *has* come into my mind . . . but it's too intimate to pass on. . . . Besides, I don't see any connection, or any necessity for saying it." Freud's face must have brightened at this disclosure, for he now was confident that his theory was to be confirmed again. He replied that certainly he would not force the young man to reveal his thought, but that if a fair test were to be made of the theory it was necessary to be absolutely candid.

The young man relented partially and made the beginning of an admission: "Well then, I've suddenly thought of a lady from whom I might easily hear a piece of news that would be awkward for both of us."

Upon hearing this, Freud immediately astounded the young man by breaking in and suggesting that the particular bad news he was afraid of receiving was that the young lady's periods had stopped, and that she was pregnant.

"How could you guess that?" gasped the young man.

"That's not difficult any longer," replied Freud. "You've prepared the way sufficiently. Think of *the calendar saints, the blood that starts to flow on a particular day, the disturbance when the event fails to take place, the open threats that the miracle must be vouchsafed, or else*. . . . In fact, you've made use of the miracle of St. Januarius to manufacture a brilliant allusion to women's periods."

The young man confessed that Freud's hypothesis was correct, and added that the lady in question was Italian, and that he had been with her in Naples, the repository of St. Januarius' relics. Thus still more connecting links were established between the associations and the unpleasant thought.

Thus the "meaning" as well as the mystery of the young man's mistake were revealed. The forgotten word was shown to be connected in the young man's mind, by a peculiar but compelling train of associations, with the fear that his woman friend might be pregnant. Since the young man did not want to think about that distressing possibility, he was motivated also not to think about related ideas that might threaten to call it to mind. The word *aliquis* was therefore "forgotten."

Although no more than a conversation on a summer afternoon, this incident illustrates several characteristic aspects of Freud's approach to understanding human behavior. For example, in seeking the explanations for simple mistakes (which have come to be popularly called "Freudian slips") Freud made use of a technique that was to have great importance in the development of his thought. This technique, known as *free association,* was to Freud what the microscope had been to an earlier generation of biologists, enabling him to see and comprehend things that had previously been the sources of great mystery. Free association was simply the mental exercise that the young man in the example performed. To free associate one first turns one's attention to the idea or thought that is to be the subject of analysis, and then allows his thoughts to run freely from there. Careful attention must be paid to every idea that comes to mind, and special care must be taken to avoid censoring, modifying, or omitting anything. This sounds simple, but in practice it is a very difficult exercise to carry out since inevitably something will happen to interfere with the appropriate free-floating state of consciousness. In the example, the young man quickly came upon a highly disagreeable thought and wanted to terminate the process prematurely. In other cases, something that seems simply ridiculous might come to mind, and the free associator will be tempted to give up on that account. It is precisely these kinds of distractions that must be overcome if free association is to be a useful technique, however, and Freud learned that he must do whatever he could to keep the process going; thus he encouraged the young man to continue with his associations even when they came to entail unpleasant subject matter, until the hidden meaning of his mistake was revealed.

Just as Freud was able to use free association to uncover the hidden meaning of an apparently unimportant lapse of memory, so was he able to use the technique to study a wide variety of human behaviors. The things that he learned enabled him to create a theory that revolutionized the way men think about themselves. Few theories have had so profound an effect on our intellectual climate; the example of the worried young man illustrates three of the revolutionary principles that Freud developed.

First, note that an apparently random and meaningless event—the forgetting of a word—was found to have a definite meaning and to have been "caused" by a specific set of psychological factors. The young man's forgetfulness was not in the least accidental or random, but instead was strictly determined both by his present state of worry and by the fact that his experience had led him to relate the word *aliquis* to the thought of possible pregnancy by the particular train of associations described above. When Freud used his techniques of analysis on still other apparently meaningless or random events—dreams and certain symptoms of mental illness are good examples of these—he discovered that they too seemed to be caused or *determined* by similar psychological factors. Freud generalized from these basic findings and asserted that it must be the same with *all* psychological events; that is, he held that there is no such thing as a "random" or "accidental" psychological act. Everything that one thinks and does is strictly determined by potentially discoverable antecedents. This general principle is referred to as *psychic determinism.*

A second important Freudian principle illustrated by the example is that many of the determining causes of psychological events are not immediately accessible to conscious awareness. The young man initially found himself in a situation in which he was unable consciously to comprehend his own behavior. After he had misquoted the line, he was immediately aware that he had made a mistake, but he could not recall precisely what his mistake had been. He was even more in the dark about the reasons for the mistake. Freud's analysis, of course, not only revealed a discernible cause but showed that the cause lay very clearly in the young man's personal experiences. Until the analysis by free association had been completed, all the conscious thinking in the world was incapable of explaining the young man's behavior to himself. The determining causes of the mistake, though psychological, were beyond the realm of immediate consciousness. Since Freud discovered that many other psychological activities were also incapable of being consciously "explained" until analyzed by free association, he came to recognize the importance of *unconscious determinants* of human behavior.

The third general characteristic of Freud's thought illustrated by the example is the unconventionality of its subject matter. Freud chose to confront and discuss issues that aroused anxiety in people, and that therefore often aroused their resentment as well. Much of the notoriety and opprobrium that Freud endured in his lifetime can be traced to the heavy emphasis he placed on sexuality as an influence on human psychology. In the example, he discerned that the young man was troubled by a thought that was not openly acknowledgeable in polite society. Even today the discussion of pregnancy sometimes arouses some uneasiness, and in the Victorian era, when Freud began his practice, the taboo on discussing sexual matters was far stronger than today. The fact that a subject is embarrassing to discuss, however, does not mean it is without profound effect on human behavior. Freud, in penetrating beyond the bounds of the socially acceptable in his effort to understand psychological phenomena, revealed many uncomfortable truths and forced people to cast aside some cherished illusions about themselves.

As Freud's views on psychic determinism, unconscious motivation, and the role of sexuality in human behavior became widely known, he joined that very small handful of individuals who upset tradition in the search for truth. Freud himself remarked that he, Copernicus, and Darwin struck "narcissistic" blows at man's pride by forcing him to take a less grandiose view of himself. Copernicus, in demonstrating that the earth does not lie at the center of the universe, administered the *cosmological* blow to human pride. Darwin administered the *biological* blow by showing that *homo sapiens* must be closely related to other animal species. It remained for Freud to strike the *psychological* blow when he shattered illusions about the infallibility of human reason and consciousness, the existence of free will, and the essential "purity" of human nature.

Of course, thinkers who achieve the stature of Copernicus, Darwin, or Freud do not come along very often; when they do, it is of great interest to know precisely how it was that their ideas came about. Intellectual historians have suggested two ideal kinds of explanations. The first, labeled the *great man theory,* asserts that intellectual progress, particularly when rapid and dramatic, is the result of almost singlehanded efforts by great men. According to this view, great advances in science stem primarily from the work of just a few geniuses whose discoveries are relatively independent of the knowledge of the past. Directly opposed to the great man theory of intellectual change is the *Zeitgeist* theory. *Zeitgeist* is a German word meaning "spirit of the times," and the *Zeitgeist* theory asserts that intellectual progress occurs when the times are ripe for a particular change, and only then. In essence, this theory suggests that progress of a particular kind becomes inevitable when there is something "in the air" that enables men to see things in new ways. According to this view, someone else would soon have discovered the laws of gravitation if Newton had never existed, and the Copernican, Darwinian, and Freudian theories would all have been essentially duplicated by others if their originators had never been born.

Of course both theories of intellectual change, standing alone and in their purest forms, are straw men. It is obvious that the most brilliant person in the world will achieve nothing unless he is in an environment in which he *can* do something, and it is equally clear that even when the times are ripe for change someone must have the ability to capitalize on the opportunities they present. Thus great intellectual progress is always the result of some combination of *Zeitgeist* and great man. Such certainly was the case with Freud. There is no question that Freud was a brilliant and original thinker—in short, a great man. But there is also no doubt that Freud's theories were greatly influenced by his times and his personal background. Psychoanalytic theory did not just come readymade into his head, with no preparatory work. Freud was very much a child of his time who both benefited and occasionally suffered from the theories and trends that were alive in the scientific world at the time of his major discoveries. He was a great man who lived at a particularly propitious moment in history.

The Early Life of Sigmund Freud

One of the important tenets of mature psychoanalytic theory, accepted almost as a commonplace today, holds that if one wishes to understand fully the creative products of an individual, one must know something about his life and personality. That holds as true for Freud himself as for anyone. The following brief biographical sketch describes influences and events from Freud's early life that seem to have been especially important in determining the course of psychoanalysis. The sketch is necessarily fragmentary, and the interested reader is encouraged to read further in the excellent full-length biographies of Freud listed at the end of the chapter.

Sigmund Freud was born in Freiberg, Moravia—then a part of the Austro-Hungarian Empire but now in Czechoslovakia—on May 6, 1856. His father, Jakob, was a lower-middle-class Jewish wool merchant. The Freud family constellation was rather unusual. Sigmund's mother, Amalia, was Jakob's second wife, his first wife having died after giving birth to sons in 1832 and 1836. Amalia was much younger than Jakob; in fact, she was younger than his first son. When she gave birth to Sigmund, her first child, she was twenty-one; her stepsons were twenty-four and twenty, and her husband was forty-one. Sigmund thus had two half-brothers who were contemporaries of his mother, and the situation was further complicated by the fact that the elder half-brother had a son of his own in 1855, so that Sigmund had a nephew who was a year older than himself.

The family did not stop growing with Sigmund—far from it. In the nine years after Sigmund's birth Amalia had seven more children. Jakob Freud sired ten children, the first when he was seventeen years old and the last when he was fifty-one!

It is difficult, of course, to specify the effect of this unusual family constellation on Sigmund as he was growing up. One thing that seems likely is that in the large family, living in modest quarters, there must have been a great deal of competition for the attention of the parents. In view of the special peculiarities of the generational relationships in this family, much attention must have focused on defining role relationships within the family, and Freud must have become sensitive at an early age to family structure and relationships. It is therefore not surprising that psychoanalytic theory places heavy emphasis on familial relationships and emotions, especially as they are perceived by a child. The famous *Oedipus complex*—one of the most socially unconventional of all Freudian ideas, in which the young boy is postulated to harbor strong lustful feelings toward his mother and aggressive feelings toward his father—was perhaps partially inspired by Freud's having had a young and attractive mother who was of an age with his half-brothers, together with an older and therefore especially forbidding father.

None of this should suggest that Freud's family was more conflict-ridden than other families, however. As shall be seen later, the Oedipal situation was theorized to be an *inevitable* result of a small child's existence in a family where he is cared for lovingly by a warm mother, and where there is also a strong father present to act as a rival for the mother's affections. In fact, it is precisely in warm families that the conflicts are assumed to be greatest. All of the available evidence indicates that the Freud household was a happy one. Occasional misfortunes occurred, as in 1858, when Sigmund's one-year-old brother died, but in general the home atmosphere seems to have been healthy and harmonious.

In 1860 the Freud family moved to Vienna, and there Sigmund was to reside until very close to the end of his long life. It was in Vienna that he entered school for the first time. He was something of a prodigy, winning several academic awards and qualifying for Gymnasium (roughly equivalent to high school) at age nine. He was graduated from it at seventeen. Freud's family was delighted with his intellectual prowess, and they encouraged him in every possible way to succeed academically. He surpassed his brothers and sisters academically without any trouble, and as a result he was provided with a luxury that no one else in his family had: he was given his own room with a gas lamp in it, so that he could study undisturbed and without straining his eyes late at night. The room remained his private sanctuary until he was in his middle twenties. Still another privilege that Freud was given because of his intellectual gifts was the opportunity to charge books to his father's account at a local bookstore. In later life Freud confessed that this was one of the few privileges he had ever blatantly abused, since he occasionally ran up bills that were beyond his father's ability to pay comfortably. Nevertheless, it seems that Jakob did not complain about this, but continued to support his gifted son in every possible way. Given this kind of family background and support, it is not difficult to see how Sigmund —highly talented to begin with—was pushed along the path to an intellectual career.

During his youth Freud combined a lively curiosity with diligence in study. He was especially interested in the humanities —history, philosophy, and literature—and he was a voracious reader. Some of the casual reading he did during his youth was ultimately reflected in psychoanalytic theory. For example, as a teenager Freud became greatly interested in a German writer named Ludwig Börne (1786–1837); he read an essay by Börne written in 1823 and entitled "The Art of Becoming an Original Writer in Three Days." Börne gave the following instructions: "Take a few sheets of paper and for three days write down, without any falsification or hypocrisy, everything that comes into your head . . . and when the three days are over you will be amazed at what novel and startling thoughts have welled up in you." This passage was undoubtedly one of the early sources of the idea of free association, although Freud himself did not consciously recognize its contribution for many years. When Freud was in his sixties, one of his colleagues called his attention to Börne's essay and pointed out its anticipation of free association. Freud had completely forgotten about the essay, and he realized with a shock that he had absorbed and used its major ideas without consciously acknowledging their source. He concluded ironically that forgotten and unacknowledged events are likely to be the true sources of all "original" ideas.

Another source of the free association technique may have been Freud's cultural heritage as a Jew. There are numerous meditational and exegetical techniques employed in Jewish mysticism that bear striking similarity to free association. In this mystical tradition, for example, one of the ways to comprehend the "true" meaning of sacred writings is to engage in a certain kind of wordplay with the text. Key words become the objects of concentrated attention, and by altering the order of their letters, as in the game of anagrams, their hidden meaning may become apparent. This process would seem to be remarkably similar to the way in which the word *aliquis* was analyzed by Freud's young friend. Freud never explicitly acknowledged the contribution of the Jewish mystical tradition to his work, though his library included a number of key books on that subject. He may have purposely obscured his study of Jewish meditational techniques out of fear of anti-Semitic rejection of his work as a whole.

Another important influence on Freud's theory was a psychology textbook which he used during his last year of Gymnasium. The book propounded a point of view taken from the works of Johann Herbart (1776–1841), an influential philosopher of the early nineteenth century. According to Herbart, not all ideas must be conscious in order to affect mental life. Ideas can vary in intensity or energy, and only those with a certain level of intensity can become conscious. The unconscious ideas can still possess some energy, however, and thereby affect the course of mental events. The specifics of Herbart's theory are not of particular interest here; what *is* of interest is that at an early age Freud was exposed to a line of psychological argument that explicitly postulated the existence of unconscious processes. The idea of an unconscious was thus not original to Freud. What *was* original was the way he ultimately developed this idea that was already in the wind.

Although Freud was exposed to psychological thought in his early student years, he did not immediately become interested in the subject; in fact, his chief intellectual interests underwent many changes before he finally settled on psychology some twenty years later. Between the ages of approximately twelve and seventeen, Freud had planned on a career in law or politics—most likely a combination of the two. From an early age Freud had wanted to become a leader, and, consistent with his interest in the humanities, law and politics seemed natural fields of endeavor. Had he pursued these fields, it is likely that he would have done well; the persuasiveness of his later written works indicates that he probably could have become a superb courtroom advocate.

During his last year in Gymnasium, however, Freud underwent an experience that was to alter permanently his occupational ambition. The experience itself was an innocent-seeming one: he heard a public reading of an essay on nature, written by the poet Goethe, who himself had been an excellent amateur naturalist and scientific observer. This essay was inspirational for the young Freud, who described its effect in a letter to a friend: "The urge to understand something about the mysteries of the world and maybe contribute somewhat to their solution became overwhelming." Almost on the spur of the moment, Freud decided to make a career in natural science, an area that in Gymnasium had not been as interesting to him as history and philosophy. In the service of his newly found scientific interest and newly redirected ambitions Freud entered the medical school of the University of Vienna in 1873, at the age of seventeen.

During his early days in the medical school it seemed that his radical change in plans had been a mistake. Freud was not inspired by much of his curriculum, and in several important subjects, including chemistry and zoology, his record was mediocre. One of the few bright spots of his early university career was a reading seminar taught by the famous philosopher and psychologist Franz Brentano (1838–1917). Though Brentano did not influence Freud in any direct or dramatic way, he certainly won the young student's esteem. Freud took his courses as electives for four semesters.

As time went by, Freud found his niche in the scientific aspect of his medical school program and began to demonstrate his talents in research. The University of Vienna, as one of the leading universities of Europe, provided ample opportunities for students to work on ongoing research at its many laboratories, as well as to attend lectures and take courses. Freud eagerly availed himself of these research opportunities, with the result that he took considerably longer than the average student to pass his final medical examinations. He made up for that, however, by publishing several highly respected scientific papers while he was still a student.

Freud's first research effort, conducted in a laboratory of marine zoology, consisted of a search for the sexual organs of the male eel. Up until that time (1876) no one had observed a mature male eel, and therefore the sexual activity of eels was a biological mystery. In the course of his investigation Freud dissected over four hundred eels, and finally provided an important bit of evidence that helped lead to the definite identification of the eel's testes. Thus the first formal scientific effort of the future founder of psychoanalysis—who was later to place so much emphasis on the hitherto overlooked influences of sexuality on human behavior—was directed toward the discovery of the elusive sexual apparatus of the eel.

Freud's work on the sexual anatomy of the eel proved to be only a brief research diversion. Later in 1876, Freud's third year in medical school, he entered the university's Physiological Institute and embarked on some work that was to become his consuming passion for the next several years. The institute was directed by Ernst Brücke (1819–1892), one of the pre-eminent European physiologists of the time and a man whom Freud always revered as his greatest and most influential teacher. Under Brücke's tutelage, Freud became passionately interested in physiology, particularly that of the nervous system. As he became increasingly involved in his work, he was exposed to, and became an advocate of, a particular orientation toward physiology that was to have considerable influence on the later development of psychoanalysis. This orientation was then referred to as the "new physiology," and Brücke was one of its leading exponents.

The new physiology had begun in the 1840s with the work of four brilliant young physiology students. One of them was Brücke; the others were Emil du Bois-Reymond (1818–1896), Hermann Helmholtz (1821–1894), and Carl Ludwig (1816–1896). These four were the favorite students of Johannes Müller (1801–1858), who was regarded as the greatest physiologist of *his* day. Ironically, the four students were to establish themselves as Müller's successors precisely by rejecting one of his most firmly held ideas: the idea that biological processes as they occur in nature are of a qualitatively different nature from the inorganic processes studied by disciplines such as chemistry and physics. That is, Müller and most of the other leading physiologists of the time believed that living matter was animated by forces completely unlike ordinary physical or chemical ones. They postulated a "life force," or *élan vital,* that coursed through organic objects and thereby caused them to live; accordingly, their general position was referred to as *vitalist.*

The four young rebels, however, came to believe that the vitalist position was wrong. They believed—and time has proven the general validity of their belief—that there was no such thing as a qualitatively distinct life force. Brücke and du Bois-Reymond were so strongly opposed to vitalism that in 1842 they pledged the following remarkable oath to each another:

> No other forces than the common physical chemical ones are active within the organism. In those cases which cannot at the time be explained by these forces one has either to find the specific way or form of their action by means of the physical mathematical method,

or to assume new forces equal in dignity to the physical chemical forces inherent in matter, reducible to the force of attraction and repulsion.[2]

Helmholtz and Ludwig were in firm agreement with the spirit of this declaration, and the four became known as *mechanists*, from their belief that all physiological processes must be ultimately reducible to the purely mechanical forces of attraction and repulsion. The application of this belief to experimental physiology was to yield important and valuable dividends of knowledge.

In many respects the mechanist movement in physiology was a simple outgrowth of the more basic revolution that had been wrought in physics by Sir Isaac Newton a century and a half earlier. Newton, in showing that the entire cosmos was governed by the same set of basic laws—that massive and widely separated bodies like planets and stars interact with one another according to the same laws as those which govern the interaction of small bodies on earth, for example—made possible the conception of a "billiard ball universe," a theoretical universe in which all components are thought of as material objects that interact with one another in completely predictable ways, according to the laws of mechanics. The interactions of perfectly spherical balls on a perfectly flat billiards table provide a good analogy to such a universe. The mechanists asserted that all life processes were also subject to purely mechanical laws, thereby suggesting that analogies from the concrete physical world would assist in conceptualizing physiological function. Adoption of the mechanist viewpoint meant that experimental physiologists could be encouraged to use the methods of the physical sciences in conducting their own experiments and constructing theories.

Hermann Helmholtz, the greatest of the four founders of the mechanist movement, epitomized its spirit in 1847 when he formulated the famous law of the *conservation of energy*. The

[2] Quoted in S. Bernfeld, "Freud's Scientific Beginnings," *American Imago*, 6 (1949), p. 171.

law, simply put, held that energy can be neither created nor destroyed, but only transformed from one type to another. Thus the total amount of energy in any closed system must remain constant at all times. This law placed *all* of the forces of nature in close relationship with one another—on a continuum, as it were. It also allowed for the postulation of energy exchanges between living and nonliving matter, thus bringing all phenomena—including the biological—into the same arena of investigation.

In a brilliant application of this principle—indeed, in one of the most brilliant scientific experiments ever conducted—Helmholtz in 1850 succeeded in accurately measuring the speed of the nervous impulse along the nerve fiber of a frog. Using the apparatus of the physicist and chemist, he discovered that nervous transmission was a kind of electrical impulse that traveled along the nerve fiber at a rate of about ninety feet per second—much more slowly than anyone had previously imagined. Of course, if Helmholtz had not believed that the "living" nerve impulse must be mechanical in nature, he would never even have thought to try the "physical" methods of experimentation he used.

It was in this field of neurophysiology—the study of nervous processes—that the new mechanist movement had perhaps its greatest impact. The nervous system had been correctly identified as the locus of much of the "higher" activity that characterizes the more complex forms of life, and widespread efforts were made to account for nervous processes in mechanist terms. The first steps in this direction were the discoveries of the essential structural properties of the nervous system. It was early discovered that there existed at least two kinds of nervous components. There were cell-like structures called ganglion cells that contained nuclei and in general bore resemblances to other kinds of cells that had been discovered in nonnervous tissues; and there were elongated, fiber-like structures. The nervous impulse was known to travel along the nerve fibers, as Helmholtz's experiment had conclusively demonstrated, and was assumed to originate and end in the ganglion cells. At the time that Freud was a student it was not yet known that both the ganglion cells and the fibers were different parts of single cells that are now known as *neurons,* but work was progressing in that direction. In fact, some of Freud's own early research was to have a bearing on this particular discovery.

In general, even before the discovery of the neuron, the most basic units of the nervous system were considered to be structures capable of receiving and transmitting excitation of an electrical nature. The greatest concentration of nervous structures was observed to be in the brain; indeed, the brain was found to be nothing more than an incredibly complex mass of interconnected nervous tissue. It was assumed that the transmitting apparatus of one ganglion cell was connected with the receiving apparatus of another via the fiber, and thus the entire nervous system was viewed as a vastly complex network of interconnected cells.

Though some experiments, like Helmholtz's, could be performed to assess the actual characteristics of individual nervous structures, the structures were generally too small and too difficult to isolate for much work to be done on them individually. Therefore another essential scientific strategy was to draw inferences about what the minute components of the nervous system must be like based on observation of the gross behaviors of the organism. This was a legitimate strategy since it was assumed that all behaviors were mediated and in a sense "caused" by the activity of the nervous system. A good example of this kind of reasoning is provided by Brücke's theory of the "summation of stimulation," a theory Freud was to incorporate several years later in his first psychoanalytic model of the mind.

Brücke noticed that when a small morsel of food is lodged in the esophagus, periodic swallowing reflexes occur until the food is removed. What particularly impressed him was that although the *stimulus* was constantly present (the pressure of the morsel against the esophagus remained constant until the time that it was dislodged), the *response* (swallowing) was not. The response was periodic, occurring at intervals of time. Brücke conceptualized this as an example of the *summation of stimulation,* where a mild but constant irritation like the pressure of the morsel against the esophagus introduces a constant stream of excitation into the nervous system. The nervous system, argued Brücke, must then somehow "sum" this excitation until a certain amount accumulates and a single reflexive behavior like swallowing is released. When the reflexive behavior is released, the nervous system discharges its accumulated, or summed, excitation. If the reflexive behavior fails to remove the source of irritation—as when the morsel is still lodged against the esophagus instead of swallowed—the whole process is begun again. When sufficient excitation has accumulated again, swallowing occurs again, and so on until the morsel has been dislodged and swallowed.

The actual accumulating, or summing, mechanism in the nerve cells had never been directly observed, but Brücke felt that the only way to account for the observed behavioral data was to postulate the existence of such a mechanism.

Thus the intellectual climate that Freud walked into when he entered Brücke's Physiological Institute was an invigorating one. He correctly had the sense of being at the forefront of academic physiology by participating in the mechanist movement which had recently revolutionized the field. The movement was suffused with a sense of intellectual optimism, since it suggested that all phenomena, including biological and neurological processes, were potentially comprehensible under the same terms as physical phenomena. It offered hope that even the most obscure and complex of problems were ultimately capable of scientific explanation and prediction. This movement was not in the least constricted in its methods; speculation and "grand theorizing" abounded, restricted only by the proscription that it not be inconsistent either with observed data or the basic tenets of the mechanist doctrine. Such speculation could and did go beyond its data, however, as in Brücke's formulation of the summation of stimuli.

Given this intellectual background, it was not surprising

that Freud eventually developed his principle of psychic determinism. Psychic activities, after all, clearly took place within the boundaries of individual organisms, and the mechanists had emphatically stated that the only forces active within the organism are common physical or chemical ones, or new ones equal to them in "dignity" (i.e., lawfulness). It was easy for Freud to assume that psychic activities were simply the consequences of neurological activities, and that the neurological activities were demonstrably electro-chemical in nature. When Freud put forth the principle of psychic determinism, then, he was simply extending the most basic doctrine of his most influential physiology teacher into the realm of psychology.

Freud's concern with psychological problems, however, still lay far in the future when he was a student in Brücke's Institute. The problems he worked on there were purely physiological and anatomical ones. For several years he concerned himself with the microscopic investigation of the nerve cells of some primitive organisms, including the crayfish. A meticulous and accurate observer, he contributed substantially to the knowledge of the tissue structure of nerve cells. One of his studies, on the nerve cells of a primitive fish, clearly suggested that nerve fibers and ganglion cells were actually connected in single cells, or *neurons*. Thus he anticipated the discovery that the neuron is the simplest functional unit of the nervous system.

Freud was completely happy at the Physiological Institute and stayed there for six years, during which time his most cherished ambition was to pursue a university career in experimental physiology. He developed rather a casual attitude toward the orthodox practice of medicine, and it was almost incidentally that he took and passed his final doctoral examinations in medicine in 1881.

Circumstances were not propitious in the nineteenth century for a young man who wished to pursue an academic scientific career, however, and for Freud they were even less so than usual. In the first place, academic physiology was not a lucrative profession. In our present era of subsidized science it is difficult to comprehend some of the difficulties under which scientists labored in Freud's day, but one may get some picture of the situation by realizing that Brücke, one of the most famous physiologists in the world, had to settle for a laboratory that was housed in an abandoned and unheated gun factory. He was one of the lucky ones; at least he had a laboratory.

Furthermore, academic positions were few in number and poorly paid. It was said with considerable justification that one really had to be independently wealthy to pursue a serious career in science. During the years he was at the Institute, Freud continued to live at home, relying completely on the generosity of his father for his upkeep. His prospects of advancement were slight because he had the ill fortune to rank very low on the seniority ladder. There were a number of other workers at the Institute who were senior to Freud by margins of less than ten years, and so as long as they stayed there Freud could not hope to rise to a position of authority.

Finally, there was the simple yet brutal fact that Freud happened to be a Jew living in a time and place that were notably anti-Semitic. In the Austro-Hungarian Empire Jews did not even achieve *legal* equality in matters of rights of ownership and residence until 1867, when Freud was eleven. Anti-Semitism was a popular and expedient stand for politicians to take; Karl Lueger, one of the leading political figures in Vienna throughout much of Freud's life, habitually spouted an especially vicious stream of anti-Semitic invective. Jews were commonly subjected to personal humiliations and expected to bear them silently. One of Freud's own most vivid childhood memories, for example, was of his father telling about a gang of Gentile hoodlums who had knocked his hat into the mud. When the young Sigmund breathlessly asked his father what he had done to avenge the insult, the devastating reply was that he had simply put his hat back on and proceeded down the street. In this climate, of course, Freud's chances to advance in an already difficult vocation were even less than usual.

It was inevitable that such discrimination would have personal as well as practical consequences for Freud. One clear effect was a sense of being one against the crowd, of having to do battle against the odds and an overwhelmingly negative public opinion. Freud's sense of being a lonely crusader, defending truth against the forces of hypocrisy and conventionality, was to be a great solace to him later in life, when the sexual aspects of psychoanalytic theory were subjected to vigorous popular abuse. But in the early 1880s the practical consequences of his Jewishness must have seemed only extremely negative to Freud, since they contributed to his already poor prospects for a future at the Physiological Institute he loved so much.

In 1882 two events occurred that caused Freud to abandon reluctantly his ambition of remaining at the Institute. First, Brücke had a friendly but frank talk with him, spelling out in detail the nature of the practical difficulties he would have to face if he persisted in his ambition. Secondly, and probably much more importantly, Freud became engaged to Martha Bernays, a twenty-one-year-old native of Hamburg. At the time of his engagement his income from physiology was so meager that he was still reliant upon the generosity of his father for his own maintenance. It was an absolute necessity for him to make considerably more money if he were to support a wife and family. Thus Freud reluctantly decided that he must enter the field of clinical medicine in order to improve his financial prospects. In 1882 he left the physiological laboratory to embark upon the practice of medicine.

Even then his financial situation did not immediately brighten. Any ambitious young physician—and Freud was certainly ambitious—was expected to undergo a prolonged training period in clinical medicine before establishing himself in private practice. Thus Freud spent the years 1882 through 1885 in training at the Vienna General Hospital, at a very low salary. During that time, however, he was exposed to a wide variety of training experiences in several branches of medicine, under some of the most eminent physicians of the period.

One of these physicians was Theodor Meynert (1833–1892), the director of the hospital's psychiatric clinic. Meynert was one of the leading brain anatomists and pathologists of his day, and therefore his interests represented a medical specialty reasonably closely related to Freud's beloved neurophysiology. Meynert, in fact, espoused a theory highly compatible with the mechanist view of neurophysiology. He believed that specific physical locations within the nervous system—i.e., specific nerve cells or groups of associated nerve cells—"represent" specific mental contents or ideas. For example, seeing a dog results in the excitation of the nerve cells that stand for "dog." If on a later occasion the same nerve cells are excited in the absence of a real dog, the memory of that stimulus is aroused. Thus Meynert believed that both the perception of an event and the subsequent recollection of it in memory resulted from the excitation of the same neural centers. Under this system a "train of thought" could easily be conceptualized *neurologically* as the transmission of excitation from one specific neural center to another. The *psychological* result of such a process was assumed to be the recollection of a series of specific ideas or memories.

Meynert's theory was clearly compatible with the mechanist doctrine since it assumed that psychological processes were caused by the underlying neurological events, and those events in turn were believed to be explainable by ordinary physical and chemical laws. The mechanist movement had made it fashionable to speculate about the existence of relatively simple neural mechanisms to account for the existence of complex psychological phenomena, and Meynert's work was a prime example of this approach. In the course of his training at the hospital Freud became increasingly interested in Meynert's ideas, and finally became a specialist himself in neuropathology (the study of diseases of the nervous system).

As this interest was developing, Freud was also occupied with the task of making a name for himself so that he could set up a private practice as quickly as possible. He distinguished himself as an ambitious and enterprising young physician, and twice came close to achieving fame before even leaving the hospital. In 1883 he devised a new method employing gold chloride to stain specimens for microscopic study. The method at first seemed to offer great promise for neuroanatomical research and aroused considerable professional enthusiasm. But it turned out to be a difficult procedure to perform properly, producing widely varying and therefore unreliable results. After an initial flurry of interest, the technique was quickly forgotten.

Freud's second premature brush with fame occurred a year later, when he investigated a new drug that had come to his attention. The drug was cocaine, and Freud was among the first to discover its anesthetic and mood-altering properties. One of his colleagues, acting upon a hint from Freud, first used cocaine as an anaesthetic for eye surgery and thereby achieved great professional recognition. Freud himself became extremely enthusiastic about the drug as a kind of wonder cure, and prescribed it frequently to patients, friends, and himself for numerous medical complaints. Unfortunately, he did not at first recognize that the drug was addictive. When it became tragically clear that it was, Freud quickly dropped his interest in it. This whole "cocaine episode" was a bitter experience for Freud. Not only did he narrowly miss attaining the professional fame he so eagerly sought, but he also had to face up to the fact that he had become dangerously and unprofessionally enthusiastic about an untested chemical.

By 1885 things began to look up considerably for Freud. By that time his interest in neurology and neuropathology was fully awakened, and he wanted to expand his background in those fields. He decided he would like to study under Jean Charcot (1825–1893), director of the neurology clinic at the Salpêtrière asylum in Paris, and at that time the most famous neurologist in the world. An imposing personality, Charcot was physician and confidant to a list of individuals that read like a *Who's Who* of royalty and aristocracy. His views on neurology were somewhat unorthodox—particularly different from those of the German and Austrian authorities under whom Freud had studied—but he was widely respected nonetheless. In 1885 Freud applied for a traveling grant from the Vienna Hospital to allow him to join Charcot. Competition for the grant was stiff, but mainly because of strong support from Brücke, Freud won it. The amount of the grant was approximately $250, and with this munificent sum Freud travelled to Paris and supported himself for six months while he worked under Charcot. Though he bore excruciating poverty, he was exposed to some important ideas that will be discussed in the next chapter.

The prestige that Freud earned by winning the grant and studying with Charcot finally made it feasible for him to leave the training position at the Vienna General Hospital. After his stay with Charcot, Freud put in a brief stint as an army physician and then returned to Vienna to become director of neurology in a small children's hospital. At the same time he began a small private practice. Thus in 1886 he finally was in a position to earn enough income to marry Martha, after an engagement of more than four years.

As Freud was getting established in his marriage and private practice, he was helped inestimably by another Jewish physician named Josef Breuer (1842–1925), who had befriended him several years before. Breuer was fourteen years Freud's senior, and by the time Freud was beginning at the Vienna General Hospital Breuer had already achieved a fine reputation as a medical practitioner and researcher. Breuer took a strong, almost fatherly interest in Freud and helped him get started both financially and professionally. He proffered a substantial loan when Freud was in financial difficulty, and he was instrumental in getting Freud set up in private practice. Even more important, Breuer subsequently collaborated with Freud in some of the earliest work leading directly to psychoanalysis. These contributions will be detailed in the next chapter.

Freud's major psychoanalytic ideas did not emerge suddenly or spontaneously, but developed gradually over the first fifteen years or so of his private practice. During that time yet another physician emerged to stand beside (and eventually to replace) Breuer in sharing Freud's ideas. Wilhelm Fliess (1858–1928) was a Berlin doctor two years younger than Freud. On a visit to Vienna in 1887 he was called in to consult on one of Breuer's patients, and at that time he met Freud. Following Fliess's return to Berlin, Freud wrote to him about the case. The first sentence of Freud's letter indicated the initial attraction he had felt for Fliess: "I have a strictly business motive for writing to you today, but I must start with the confession that I hope to remain in contact with you, and that you made a deep impression on me." The sentence was prophetic, for it began an extensive correspondence between the two men that was to last for almost fifteen years, during the most creative period of Freud's life. Fliess became friend and confidant to Freud, and in their correspondence and occasional meetings Freud conveyed to Fliess the first tentative formulations of his most important ideas. Fliess reciprocated by sharing his own theories with Freud.[3]

In many ways the relationship between the two men was a strange one. Freud's biographer Ernest Jones has called the relationship the only truly extraordinary event in Freud's personal life because of the extreme reliance that Freud seemed to place on Fliess's judgment and ideas, which were frequently extremely implausible and bizarre.

Fliess was a highly speculative thinker who concocted a number of theories that today seem downright silly. He believed, for example, that there were strong interrelationships among various illnesses, sexuality, and the nose. Deviations of the bodily processes, especially of a sexual nature, were assumed to be caused by disturbances in the mucous membranes of the nose, a condition he labeled the "nasal reflex neurosis." These illnesses were treated by Fliess by performing various operations on the nose. He once performed a nasal

[3] Fortunately, Fliess had the foresight to preserve the letters and manuscripts he received from Freud (Freud destroyed the ones he received from Fliess), and their publication in 1950 provided Freud scholars with an extraordinarily rich source of information about the beginnings of psychoanalytic theory.

operation on one of Freud's patients to relieve her of menstrual symptoms. The symptoms were not improved, but since the patient was a "bleeder" she almost died of complications. It was an index of Freud's peculiar devotion to Fliess that he did not blame him or see the case as discrediting Fliess's theory. Indeed, Freud went out of his way to make excuses for him.

Still another unusual aspect of Fliess's theories was the numerological flavor he gave them. He believed that human experience was determined by two basic cycles: a "feminine" one of twenty-eight days, and a "masculine" one of twenty-three days. The major vicissitudes of life were said by Fliess to be determined by interactions of the two cycles. Each individual was assumed to be *bisexual* to a certain extent, and therefore governed to differing degrees by the masculine and feminine cycles. Fliess found that by carefully manipulating his twenty-three- and twenty-eight-day cycles he could *post*dict the ups and downs of anyone's life—so long as that life had already been lived. In matters of *pre*diction, however, the system did not work so well. Thus he was able to map perfectly the events of the poet Goethe's life, including his death, which occurred at a time when the cycles interacted in a particularly unhappy way. The same system yielded the prediction that Freud would die at the age of sixty-one. Though there is some evidence that Freud worried about this prediction for a while, he nevertheless went on to achieve the age of eighty-two.

Why did Freud, a man of undoubted genius, ever take up with a person who propounded such peculiar theories? There were undoubtedly many good reasons. In the first place, though Fliess's work has been justifiably downgraded by modern scholars, he was far from unintelligent. Part of the act of being truly creative is often the willingness to go beyond the obvious and entertain new ideas. Fliess was excellent at that. It was only in the other part of the truly creative act—the rigorous testing of a novel idea to see if it is valid—that Fliess was notably deficient.

We have already seen that one of the striking characteristics of Freud's own thought was that it frequently went beyond the bounds of the conventional, and he therefore must have found Fliess a congenial partner in unorthodoxy during his own most creative period. Fliess, like Freud, defied Victorian morality and asserted the importance of sexual matters in many human concerns. His speculation about the involvement of the nose in sexuality anticipated the broadening of the definition of the term "sexuality" that Freud was to achieve so fully a few years later. The notion of bisexuality, stripped of its numerological trappings, was also incorporated by Freud into the ultimate body of psychoanalytic theory.

It is likely that Fliess's influence on Freud was, all things considered, a positive one. He tacitly encouraged Freud to engage in creative speculation that went far beyond the conventionally obvious, he provided a sympathetic audience for Freud's first attempts to articulate his own ideas, and he may have made some minor but nevertheless real contributions to the body of psychoanalytic theory. As Freud developed his own theory, of course, and it came into increasing conflict with Fliess's ideas, the strength of the relationship between the two men waned. But for several of the most creative years of his life, Freud thought of Fliess as his best and most talented friend. As things turned out, he was not the worst kind of friend that Freud could have had. When their relationship ceased in 1902, psychoanalytic theory was fully developed and Freud was a great man.

SUGGESTED FURTHER READINGS

The "*aliquis* slip" described in this chapter was taken from Freud's work *The Psychology of Everyday Life* (New York, Norton, 1965).[4] This work was first published in 1901, and

[4] In the text itself, all reference to Freud's works are taken from *The Standard Edition of the Complete Psychological Works of Sigmund Freud*, (London, Hogarth Press, 1953–). In these suggested further readings, however, references are made, when possible, to separately bound, paperback editions of Freud's individual works.

since it contains the analysis of scores of slips and mistakes it is an excellent introduction to Freud's method and general line of thought. It has consistently been one of the most popular of Freud's books.

The early life of Freud is minutely described in Volume 1 of Ernest Jones's monumental biography *The Life and Work of Sigmund Freud* (New York, Basic Books, 1953). A good but briefer account is also found in the first part of *Sigmund Freud: A Short Biography,* by Giovanni Costigan (New York, Macmillan, 1965).

The possible influence of Freud's Jewishness on his thought is discussed by David Bakan in his book *Sigmund Freud and the Jewish Mystical Tradition* (New York, Schocken Books, 1965). The best succinct description of Freud's early scientific training in the mechanistic school of neurophysiology is provided in the journal article by Siegfried Bernfeld entitled "Freud's Scientific Beginnings" (*American Imago,* 6 (1949), 163–196).

2

The Early Data: Hysteria and Hypnosis

When Freud first began to establish himself as a private practitioner of medicine in 1886, his choice of a specialty followed naturally from his long-standing interest in academic neurology. His area of special interest, neuropathology, represented the smallest possible deviation within the field of clinical medicine from his reluctantly abandoned neurophysiology. As a neuropathologist, Freud encountered patients who were suffering from symptoms presumed to be the result of damage to the nervous system. In many cases the relationships between obvious neurological damage and debilitating physical symptoms were clear-cut and explainable according to established neurophysiological laws. In other cases, however, these relationships were not at all obvious, since overt neurological damage was hard to find. It was an interest in the first type of situation that attracted Freud to his specialty, but his sense of puzzlement over the second type inspired the original development of psychoanalysis.

The first category of symptoms, resulting directly from actual physical damage to the nervous system, constituted the classical subject matter of neuropathology. Freud quickly established himself as an expert in this field, writing major works on two important types of classical symptoms within five years of the beginning of his practice. He wrote an authoritative chapter for a medical dictionary on paralyses in children that result directly from organic neurological damage, and a highly regarded book on a group of neuropathological conditions collectively known as *aphasia*. Aphasias, like organic paralyses, are caused by direct physical damage to part of the brain, and they result in severe deficits in the utilization of language. The ability to speak, listen, read, and write may be adversely affected in aphasia, either singly or together.

Conditions like organic paralyses and aphasias were of great theoretical interest to scientific investigators of the nervous system in Freud's day, partly because they were useful in "mapping" the functions of different parts of the brain. When damage to a specific area of the brain was found to be consistently associated with a specific disability, the inference drawn was that that area of the brain must be somehow "responsible" for the impaired function.[1] The relationships discovered in this way did not always follow a simple one-to-one pattern, but in general it did become possible to associate certain parts of the brain with specific functions; a "speech area" of the cerebral cortex came to be identified, for example, by noting which parts of it were most frequently damaged in cases of aphasia. This whole approach, "explaining" behavioral phenomena in terms of underlying neurophysiology, was of course highly consistent with the ideas of the mechanist movement.

This task of mapping the brain was a prestigious one in the late 1880s, though the specific *therapies* that neuropathologists could offer for these cases were not very effective. But at least the conditions were made understandable, if not necessarily curable, and close study promised more exact knowledge about the anatomy and physiology of the nervous system. Freud contributed substantially to that knowledge in his works on organic paralysis and aphasias.

That body of knowledge was *not* advanced by the study of

[1]In many cases the damaged brain areas were specifically and conclusively located only by autopsies following the deaths of the patients.

another type of patient who frequently consulted neuropathologists, but who did not suffer from obvious physical damage to the structures of the nervous system. These patients, labeled *neurotics,* experienced unpleasant symptoms ranging from anxiety attacks and states of lethargy to physical complaints that outwardly resembled aphasias and organic paralyses. Neurotic symptoms were assumed to be the result of some sort of nervous condition, but because they could not be connected with any physical disability or disease process they were baffling to the mechanistically oriented physicians of Freud's time. Most of the better-established neuropathologists preferred to devote their time to patients with classical symptoms, and avoided seeing neurotics altogether. Such "undesirable" patients were thus left to physicians of lesser reputation. Freud himself undoubtedly would have preferred to treat only organically damaged patients, but as a young and struggling private practitioner he had to take what patients he could get; consequently a major segment of his clientele was neurotic.

Unlike many of his contemporaries, however, Freud came to regard the neurotic problems presented by his patients as challenges rather than burdens. Instead of dismissing neurotic symptoms simply as manifestations of degeneracy or poor character, as was commonly done by his colleagues, Freud attempted to study neurotic symptoms scientifically, even though his strenuously acquired expertise in neural physiology and anatomy was of slight help to him in the process.

Among the neurotic patients seen by Freud in the early days of his practice, one major type turned out to be especially intriguing. These patients, called *hysterics,* suffered from a bewildering variety of both physical and psychological complaints. Freud's investigation of hysteria led him to develop a number of concepts that became the groundwork for much of psychoanalytic theory. The remainder of this chapter will show how these ideas developed, beginning with detailed descriptions of the hysterical neuroses and the ideas about hysteria that were prevalent when Freud was a young physician.

The Early Data: Hysteria and Hypnosis

Hysteria

Hysteria was a frequently observed condition in the upper-middle and upper classes of Victorian society. The most common and dramatic types of hysterical symptoms were peculiar afflictions of the musculature or of the senses that could not be traced to underlying pathology of the organ systems involved. Superficially, these symptoms frequently were similar to the results of neurological damage: paralyses, anaesthesias (losses of feeling), uncontrollable and convulsive trembling, loss of the power of speech, and blindness. An experienced physician could easily differentiate between hysterical and organic symptoms, however. Freud himself wrote an important paper early in his career in which he summarized the major ways in which some of the differentiations could be made. He noted, for example, that in cases of paralyses initiated by damage to the brain (as in a stroke, for example), it is usual for an entire side of the body to be afflicted. Thus, if the damage is severe, it is likely to result in paralysis of the face, arm, and leg on one side of the body. If the damage is moderate, the paralysis is likely to be severe in one part of the body, and less severe in areas adjacent to that part. Thus, a patient might suffer a complete paralysis of the left arm, and slight paralysis or impairment of the left leg and the left side of the face. If the damage is slight and only one limb is afflicted, the paralysis varies in severity at different points of the limb; a patient might have a completely paralyzed hand and wrist, but the shoulder of the same arm might retain partial mobility.

Freud pointed out that these "rules"—completely inviolable in organic paralyses—were almost never followed in the paralyses of hysterical patients. An hysterical patient might complain of a paralysis of the arm, for example, but inevitably this hysterical paralysis would differ in important dimensional respects from an organic one. It might extend completely from fingertips to shoulder and then abruptly cease. Instead of shading into the leg and face, or varying in its intensity in the arm itself, this hysterical paralysis would be completely confined to the arm. Similar anomalies were found in other hysterical symptoms that seemed superficially to resemble organic symptoms. Loss of speech due to hysteria was frequently complete, whereas a true aphasia usually permitted the patient at least to utter a few simple words like *yes* and *no*. In Freud's words, hysterical symptoms tended to demonstrate "precise delimitations" and "excessive intensities" that were not characteristic of simple neural damage. Since Freud assumed that organic symptoms were the logical result of anatomical relationships in the nervous system, he concluded that hysterical symptoms represented anatomical nonsense. He summarized the situation by stating that "in its paralyses and other manifestations hysteria behaves as though anatomy did not exist or as though it had no knowledge of it."[2]

In still other cases, hysterical symptoms made even less neurological sense. It was not unusual, for example, to discover an hysterical patient who complained of complete paralysis of his legs and yet was a regular sleepwalker in spite of the "paralysis." Contradictions of this type made it abundantly clear that the symptoms could not be the result of underlying physical damage or disease. Freud's medical colleagues regarded hysterics as malingerers and nuisances scarcely worth the attention of a respectable physician. Indeed, it was hard to take seriously the plight of a sleepwalking paralytic. Yet there was evidence that hysterical symptoms did cause genuine discomfort. Hysterical symptoms had a *subjective* reality for the patients, even if they could be proven *objectively* to be fictions. Thus an hysterical anaesthesia of the hand might be subjectively real enough to allow a patient to withstand needle pricks or heat without showing any sign of pain. If such a patient were merely faking, he would have to be an extraordinarily good faker to ignore stimuli that would cause a normal individual to react strongly.

In addition, hysterics frequently suffered from a class of symptoms even more mysterious than these anomalous physical

[2] *Standard Edition*, Vol. I, p. 169.

complaints. Known as *dissociative reactions,* these symptoms are the source of much fascination among the public at large. Dissociative symptoms may vary greatly in their severity, but they all involve disruptions of memory and the associative processes. The term *dissociation* is used to describe these states because a certain store of memories has become "dissociated" or "detached" from the normal or current store. A normal individual gains access to the contents of his memory by means of a train of associations. For example, the question "What did you do last night?" normally initiates a train of associations leading quickly to the recollection of last night's activities. This does not happen in the case of an hysteric who is amnesic for last night's activities: the memories are dissociated, and the train of associations triggered by the question is unable to reach them.

States of *amnesia,* if not caused by epilepsy or physical injury to the head, are usually classified as hysterical dissociative symptoms. Amnesias of this sort range from brief and simple periods of blackout for which the individual retains no memory, to extensive and dramatic *fugue states,* in which an individual may completely "forget" all those aspects of his past that have to do with his sense of personal identity, such as his name, address, and occupation. Occasionally, such individuals adopt completely new identities to replace their forgotten ones, with new names, acquaintances, skills, and hobbies. One such individual suddenly disappeared from his home in Florida one day, and after a few months he was believed to be dead by his family. Then, six years after his disappearance, he called his family and reported that he had just remembered his proper name. He had been working as an orderly in a Louisiana hospital for the six years under an assumed name.

The most spectacular and intriguing of all the dissociative conditions is the rare *multiple personality.* The defining feature of a multiple personality is that two or more "personalities," with distinctive traits and memories, coexist in the same individual. The case of "Eve," presented in the book and film *The Three Faces of Eve,* has received a good deal of public attention. Eve was a young housewife who entered psychotherapy because of headaches and periods of blackout that she could not account for. She was a very quiet and conscientious individual, shy in her relations with other people. One day as she was talking with her psychotherapist, she suddenly complained of a headache, and a moment later she was transformed into a completely different personality. The new personality—labeled "Eve Black," in contradistinction to the shy and conscientious "Eve White"—was flirtatious, vivacious, and irresponsible. A while later, with the help of hypnosis, the patient reverted to her Eve White personality once again, with no recollection of her experiences since the headache. She eventually learned that her periods of blackout marked times when the Eve Black personality was dominant, and that although Eve White had no knowledge of Eve Black, Eve Black was aware of everything that Eve White did and said. To confuse things still further, *a third* distinct personality, referred to as "Jane," emerged during a further course of treatment. Jane seemed to be a kind of compromise between the other two personalities, more outgoing than Eve White but less irresponsible than Eve Black. Jane was aware of both Eve White's and Eve Black's experiences, but neither of them knew anything of her. The case was finally successfully resolved, with Jane becoming the dominant personality.[3]

Still another kind of hysterical symptom, closely related to dissociation, is *somnambulism*. Somnambulism occurs when an individual goes into a trancelike state during which contact with external reality is either nonexistent or highly tenuous. While in a trance, a somnambulistic patient is likely to say or do things that seem bizarre to an observer. Sleepwalking and sleeptalking are varieties of somnambulistic behavior, though in patients suffering from severe hysteria the trance may be achieved directly from a waking or semi-waking state.

These, then, were the major symptoms of hysteria that Freud frequently observed during the early days of his medical

[3] The complete story of Eve may be found in C. H. Thigpen and H. Cleckley, *The Three Faces of Eve* (New York, McGraw-Hill, 1957).

practice: physical disabilities that were subjectively real to the patients but for which no underlying physical causes could be found (paralyses, anaesthesias, sensory deficiencies), mysterious lapses and alterations in the functions of memory (amnesias, fugue states, multiple personalities), and peculiar trance-like states in which patients said and did bizarre things (somnambulism). In individual patients these sometimes appeared singly as isolated symptoms, and sometimes in complicated and spectacular combinations with one another. Since the symptoms were neither amenable to orthodox neurological explanation nor explicable in "common sense" terms of human motivation, the easiest response for a physician was to dismiss them as chicanery on the part of the patients. Freud chose the more difficult approach of looking carefully and objectively at the symptoms, and trying to construct a new theory that could explain them. In doing so, he placed himself among a small minority in his profession.

Though in the minority, Freud was far from the first physician to take an interest in hysterical phenomena. The symptoms themselves had been recognized by some medical men since antiquity; indeed, it was the ancient Greeks who had named them. The choice of name tells us something about the early Greeks' conception of the illness, since it is derived from the word *hystera*, meaning uterus. Greek physicians believed that hysteria was a condition exclusively confined to women, and that it was caused by a "wandering uterus." The uterus of an hysterical woman was supposed to have the perverse tendency of spontaneously wandering—physically moving!—from its appropriate place in the abdomen and taking up residence in another part of the body. Its new resting place became the site of a physical hysterical symptom. Thus a woman with hysterical arm paralysis was viewed as suffering from a uterus that had invaded her arm.

One of the primary therapies for hysteria prescribed by Greek physicians was fully consistent with their conception of the condition. It consisted of applying a foul-smelling substance to the afflicted area of the body, in the belief that the odor would drive the uterus away. To ensure that the uterus proceeded in the proper direction once it had been set in motion, a pleasant-smelling substance was applied to the abdomen as a positive attraction. Ludicrous as it might seem today, this therapy was sometimes successful in bringing about an alleviation of the symptoms. Though the Greeks did not realize it, they had discovered that hysterical symptoms can sometimes be treated by the power of *suggestion.*

By the time Freud began to practice medicine, the commonest therapies for hysteria were not great improvements over the Greek procedures. Two popular treatments were called "electrotherapy" and "hydrotherapy," the former consisting of the passage of mild electrical currents through the afflicted organs, and the latter involving the prescription of various kinds of baths. These treatments also occasionally resulted in success, even though their permanent *physical* effects were nil. As with the Greek method, the effective therapeutic agent in these treatments was suggestion. Any cure effected, therefore, had a psychological rather than a physical basis, though this fact was not recognized by most doctors.

Since most physicians refused to take hysterical phenomena seriously or to treat them at all, those few who did were not held in the highest esteem by the medical establishment. Like their patients, they were regarded as somewhat suspect. Some of them became even more suspect in the eyes of their colleagues when they began using *hypnosis* to treat hysteria, for hypnosis was even less respectable than hysteria as a scientific interest. Nonetheless, these investigators were really in the vanguard of their profession. Recognizing that in successful cures of hysteria the cause was usually suggestion, they reasoned that hypnosis would provide a more efficient and perhaps more effective cure by maximizing the therapeutic power of suggestion. Freud was to join this small group of unorthodox physicians.

However, hypnosis became much more than just a simple therapeutic tool for Freud; it became a major source of data itself, taking its own place along with hysteria as a scientific puzzle. The solutions that Freud finally proposed formed the cornerstone of psychoanalytic theory. In order to understand the precise nature of the puzzle with which hypnosis confronted him, we must first describe the kinds of hypnotic phenomena with which he was familiar and the way they were regarded by most members of the scientific and medical fraternity of his day.

Hypnosis

Hypnotic phenomena have undoubtedly occurred ever since the earliest stages of human civilization, but they did not begin to receive systematic attention until the late eighteenth century, when a Swabian physician named Franz Anton Mesmer (1734–1815) recognized and publicized widely a number of hypnotic effects. Though it was Mesmer who first caused the public to recognize hypnosis as an important human phenomenon, he was also responsible for its being called into question and then disrepute. His story was a bizarre one that ended in his being considered a charlatan and formally disowned by the medical profession. Unfortunately, there was much in his character to justify such harsh treatment, in spite of his genuine accomplishments.

Mesmer began his medical career by plagiarizing most of his doctoral dissertation, which was about the influence of the planets on human health. One of the few original ideas that Mesmer put forth in this dissertation was that a force called "animal gravitation" is responsible for the peculiar ways in which heavenly bodies exert influences on human behavior.

He received his degree and for several years conducted an orthodox practice in Vienna. In 1774, however, he undertook the treatment of a young woman who suffered from a bewildering array of symptoms, including convulsions, chronic vomiting, toothaches, periodic lameness, fainting fits, and inflammation of the bowels. Though she would undoubtedly have been regarded as an hysteric if she had lived a century later, that diagnosis was not a popular one in Mesmer's time, and her symptoms were diagnosed individually. All standard treatment procedures completely failed to help her. Finally, acting on a suggestion from a Jesuit astronomer who also happened to make magnets, Mesmer tried a "magnetic treatment," which consisted simply of applying magnets to the soles of her feet and other parts of her body. When Mesmer did this, the young lady went into an extended "crisis state," characterized by sweating, twitching, and intense painful sensations in the joints and in the loci of the various symptoms. These magnetic treatments were continued over several days, at the end of which the patient was completely cured of her symptoms. Mesmer had discovered his new stock in trade, which he immediately began to publicize as the revolutionary therapeutic technique of *animal magnetism*.

The acceptance of Mesmer's technique by the scientific community was not enhanced by the fact that he immediately became involved in an acrimonious dispute with the Jesuit astronomer over credit for the discovery. In the argument Mesmer claimed that he had clearly anticipated this mode of treatment as far back as his medical dissertation, when he postulated the concept of animal magnetism. What he *had* postulated then, of course, was animal *gravitation*, not *magnetism*.

While the dispute was raging, Mesmer went ahead and treated several more patients with his new method. He reported stunning successes with all of his cases, including a blind girl whose sight he supposedly restored. While some of his treatments were undoubtedly successful, this last case raised a major controversy in medical circles. Some physicians believed he actually had effected a cure; others did not. A final decision was not possible, however, because shortly after the "cure" the patient suffered a "relapse" and became blind again. Shortly afterward Mesmer moved his practice from Vienna to Paris.

Once in Paris, Mesmer lost no time in gaining real notoriety; it was as if his Viennese escapades had been a mere rehearsal. No longer content to treat patients one at a time,

Mesmer began to give mass treatments in Paris by means of his famous *baquet* (French for "tub"). The *baquet* was a large wooden vessel filled with iron filings and placed in the center of Mesmer's treatment room. Patients entered the room in groups and grasped iron handles that protruded from the tub. The lights in the room were dim, and Mesmer played soft music on a glass harmonica from an adjoining room. After this period of stage-setting, Mesmer and his assistants entered the treatment room dressed in flowing, lilac-colored robes. They dramatically pointed iron rods or their fingers at the patients. Usually some of the patients responded immediately by falling into a "crisis state" like that of Mesmer's first patient to receive the magnetic treatment. As if by contagion, many other patients in the room would quickly follow suit. At the conclusion of these crisis states the patients who had experienced them generally reported an improvement in their symptoms.

To account for his successes, Mesmer concocted a wildly implausible theory about the alignment, ebb, and flow of magnetic like forces within the human body. Though he repeatedly petitioned the various medical and scientific societies of Paris to investigate his theory and treatment procedures, he was ignored by these bodies for years. The general populace, however, flocked to his *baquet* in ever-increasing numbers. Finally he achieved such popularity that he could no longer be ignored by the scientific establishment, and two royal commissions were appointed to investigate the scientific and medical merits of animal magnetism. Both commissions found that Mesmer's theory was absolutely worthless. Once having made this judgment, the commissions apparently neglected even to consider Mesmer's "cures," reasoning that if the theory was worthless the phenomena and cures on which the theory had been based must be suspect as well. The scientific orthodoxy of Mesmer's time had thrown out the baby with the bath water by suggesting that *everything* Mesmer did must have been fraudulent or muddled because *some* of it was. For decades this verdict hindered the investigation of hypnotic phenomena by respectable scientists.

Nevertheless, Mesmer did not lack for enthusiastic and dedicated followers, even though most of them were without accepted scientific credentials. One of the most important was the Marquis de Puysegur, a wealthy French aristocrat who conducted many important experiments on phenomena that were beginning to be known as *mesmerism*.[4] Puysegur learned how to induce the crisis state but was upset by the apparent discomfort it created in his subjects. He therefore tried to keep them as calm as possible during the induction of the state. One day, while mesmerizing a young servant boy and trying at the same time to keep him calm, he noted that the boy went into a sleeplike state instead of crisis. In this state, the boy was able to respond to questions and follow suggestions that Puysegur put to him. Puysegur also noted that when the boy came out of his sleeplike state he had no recollection of what had occurred. Once the state was re-induced, however, the boy immediately recalled everything that had happened. Thus it was learned that the crisis state was not necessary to mesmeric phenomena and that certain individuals could be induced to enter directly into a trancelike state of somnambulism. The somnambulistic trance became an essential part of almost all subsequent mesmeric investigations and demonstrations.

Puysegur believed that subjects who had been placed in a trance possessed almost miraculous powers of clairvoyance, and vastly increased physical and intellectual capabilities. Modern research has disproved most of these notions, but they persisted as part of the popular image of mesmerism for many years. Such beliefs were undoubtedly encouraged by the fact that subjects in a mesmeric trance did in fact demonstrate some unusual behaviors. Amnesia for mesmeric experience and its recollection upon subsequent trance induction occurred in

[4] "Animal magnetism" rapidly became unfashionable as a name both because of the commission's unfavorable reports and because it was discovered that actual magnets or magnetized materials were not necessary to produce the crisis-like states. "Mesmerism" was introduced as a substitute name. The mesmerist could induce crisis states simply by making passes with his hands over and around of the bodies of his patients.

later subjects, just as it had in Puysegur's servant. It was also quickly established that many mesmerized subjects could demonstrate apparent paralyses, anaesthesias, and hallucinations. Though the powers of mesmerized subjects were not increased beyond their capabilities in other states of high concentration, the subjects could be influenced to display peculiar symptom-like phenomena upon the suggestion of the mesmerists.

The vast majority of respectable physicians and scientists remained skeptical about these phenomena, regarding them as hoaxes perpetrated by charlatans. This did not deter the growth of a population of traveling stage mesmerists, however, who did a thriving business putting on shows for large audiences of amazed laymen. A typical performance consisted of the induction of a trance in a professional subject, followed by the demonstration of suggested paralyses ("You will be unable to move your left arm"), anaesthesias ("You will feel no pain in your hand, even though I pierce it with a needle"), hallucinations ("You had better run away from the bear that is coming after you"), amnesias ("You will remember nothing of this after you awaken"), and post-hypnotic suggestions ("After you wake up you will remove your shoes but will forget that I told you to do so"). The subject invariably responded to these suggestions in a convincing way, even undergoing actual needle pricks without betraying indications of pain. The audiences were usually convinced of the genuineness of the performances.

With the widespread public attention that was being attracted to mesmeric phenomena throughout Europe, it was inevitable that at least a few respectable scientists would begin to demonstrate some interest in the subject. One such was James Esdaile (1808–1859), an English surgeon practicing in India. Esdaile was impressed with the demonstrations of mesmeric anaesthesia that he witnessed, and in 1845 he began performing operations under mesmerically induced anaesthesia. He succeeded in reducing not only the pain experienced by his patients, but their mortality rate as well. The legacy of Mesmer continued, however, and Esdaile's results were dismissed by his medical colleagues on the grounds that he had used highly suspect "native" patients.

Another English physician named James Braid (ca. 1795–1860) had somewhat more impact on the medical community. In 1841 Braid witnessed a stage mesmerist's performance. Doubting the authenticity of what he saw, he asked the permission of the mesmerist to take the stage and examine the subject. He was surprised when the mesmerist acceded to his request and even more surprised when he found that the phenomenon seemed genuine. The subject seemed truly insensitive to pain, and when his eyes were forced open the pupils remained dilated. Convinced that mesmerism was something more than chicanery, Braid began a systematic scientific investigation of it. Among the important things he discovered was that mesmerism was not a function of some strange "power" held by the mesmerist, but rather the result of suggestibility on the part of the subject. Braid also provided a new name for the phenomenon by suggesting that mesmerism might more appropriately be named "neuro-hypnotism" ("nervous sleep"). Shortened to *hypnotism,* the term has remained with us ever since.

In the mid-nineteenth century, when Freud was born, hypnotism was just beginning to receive systematic investigation by these few individuals willing to brave the scorn of their colleagues. They clearly established the genuineness of a number of hypnotic effects, including amnesias, paralyses, anaesthesias, hallucinations, and post-hypnotic suggestions.

It should be evident by now that there were numerous similarities between hypnotic phenomena and hysterical phenomena. Both were regarded with suspicion by medical and scientific authorities. Both were peculiar conditions of the memory and of the body that could not be explained by somatic factors. Both defied analysis in terms of the predominant mechanistic theories of the nineteenth century, and called for a new set of explanatory principles. Toward the end of the century, a group of men emerged who tried to provide those principles, and who therefore became leading influences on the development of Freud's thought.

Hypnosis and Psychopathology

The most prominent of this small group of investigators was Jean Charcot, the highly respected French neurologist and director of the neurology clinic at the Salpêtrière asylum in Paris under whom Freud studied in 1885–1886. Charcot was unusual among the prominent physicians of his day in that he seriously regarded hysteria as a disease, considering it as the result of degeneration of the nervous system. He was also among the first to note the similarities between hysteria and hypnosis, and he discovered that he could induce, remove, or replace hysterical symptoms by means of hypnosis. Nevertheless, he was not impressed with the potential value of hypnosis as a *therapy* for hysteria, even though it could sometimes cause the symptoms to disappear. Such a view would have been inconsistent with his theory of the degenerative nature of hysteria. Instead, he concluded that hypnotizability and hysteria were essentially the same thing, with the former being one of the symptoms of hysteria. A corollary of that belief, of course, was the opinion that only hysterics could be successfully hypnotized, since only hysterics suffered from the prerequisite neural damage.

Charcot was not without challengers on this issue, in spite of his prestige. A competing school of hypnotism developed in the French city of Nancy under the leadership of a country doctor named Ambrose-August Liébeault (1823–1904) and his colleague, Hippolyte Bernheim (1837–1919). Liébeault had been a simple practicing physician who began experimenting with hypnotism as a means of treating some of his difficult cases. He had some success with this method and soon attracted Bernheim as a colleague. Bernheim quickly assumed authority equal to Liébeault's, and the two of them established a clinic at Nancy. On the basis of their work there they developed a theory of hypnosis that was in sharp contrast to that of Charcot. The major difference was that Liébeault and Bernheim did not believe hypnotic susceptibility was a degenerative symptom equivalent to hysteria. They believed instead that hypnosis was the result of ordinary suggestion and could be attained by individuals with nervous systems completely intact. Thus the Nancy school regarded hypnosis as a "normal" phenomenon, whereas Charcot and his followers regarded it as psychopathological. This particular controversy raged for many years before it was finally resolved in favor of the Nancy school's position. Charcot himself had the good grace to admit his error shortly before his death in 1893.

These theoretical differences aside, Charcot and the Nancy school were not far apart on other ideas. Both, for example, took hypnosis seriously as a legitimate phenomenon, and thereby placed themselves firmly among the *avant garde* of their time. More importantly, the three investigators all perceived a relationship between hypnosis and hysteria. Charcot, viewing hypnotizability as an hysterical symptom, had time and again used hypnosis to produce new symptoms, and then to remove them, in hysterical patients. Liébeault and Bernheim were impressed especially by the hypnotic *removal* of Charcot's induced hysterical symptoms, and found that they could sometimes successfully treat *original* hysterical symptoms by means of direct hypnotic suggestion. They would hypnotize an hysterical patient and then give him the direct suggestion that upon waking from the trance his symptoms would be alleviated. The success of this treatment was attributable to the direct influence of suggestion, as had been the success of previous therapies for hysteria from the Greeks through Mesmer. But Liébeault and Bernheim made their suggestions strongly and explicitly, whereas the older techniques had only implicitly and indirectly suggested that improvement would occur.

Hypnotic treatments of hysteria were not always successful. Sometimes they did not work at all, and often what relief they did provide was short-lived. Nevertheless, hypnosis came to be added to the scanty arsenal of techniques available for the treatment of hysteria. It was clearly better than nothing, and it began to be used experimentally by some of the more broad-minded European physicians of the late 1880s.

One such physician was Freud's older friend Josef Breuer. Breuer was highly respected in Viennese medical circles, and he built up a thriving private practice. Although he did not usually have to treat hysterical patients, he took one on in 1880, primarily as a personal favor to the patient's family. Breuer did not initially believe he could do much to help the patient, a twenty-one-year old girl whom he subsequently called "Anna O.," and his early approaches to therapy consisted simply of waiting and watching over her sympathetically. As things turned out, this was really almost all Breuer needed to do, since his remarkable patient largely provided her own cure. Along with it she provided the clues that led to the first formulations of psychoanalysis.

The beginning of Anna's illness was traced back to July, 1880, when her father became very ill and was confined to his bed. This was a source of great worry to the family. Anna, who doted on her father, was especially distraught. She immediately took upon herself the primary nursing duties that the illness necessitated, and spent many exhausting hours sitting by her father's bedside in a state of vigilant apprehension. But his condition did not improve, and as the months went by Anna became literally consumed with exhaustion from her nursing task. She became weaker and weaker physically, and displayed an increasing number of distressing symptoms. Her condition finally became so severe that she was forced to abandon her nursing duties and take to bed herself. It was at this point, in December, 1880, that Breuer was called in to treat her.

The specific symptom that precipitated the summoning of Breuer was a severe cough, but by that time Anna was also afflicted with a convergent squint that hindered her vision, headaches, paralyses of the neck and arm muscles, anesthesias of the elbows, and numerous other physical symptoms. She also developed a peculiar anomaly of speech: she was always capable of understanding everything that was said to her in her native German, but at various times she could talk or write only in English. Immediately prior to becoming bedridden, Anna had begun to experience distinct alternations of consciousness. In one state she was very lethargic and melancholy but otherwise normal. This state alternated with another—which she called her "naughty state," or her "absence"—in which she was highly agitated, irrational, susceptible to hallucinations, and sometimes uncontrollable in her behavior.

Breuer immediately recognized the hysterical nature of this bewildering array of symptoms. The exact means that he used to try to help her in the first few months of his conduct of the case are not known, but at any rate Anna's condition seemed to improve spontaneously until April, 1881, when her father died. Breuer's work on the case then began in earnest.

Anna's initial response to this newest life crisis was to fall into a deep state of apathy, and subsequently her condition deteriorated seriously. Peculiar trancelike states began to appear periodically. Sometimes these states resembled her earlier "absences," but on other occasions they were almost somnolent and seemed to Breuer to be like self-induced hypnosis. Soon a fairly regular pattern emerged: during the daytime hours Anna entered agitated hallucinatory states, becoming wildly excited and upset. These periods were always followed by relatively tranquil "hypnotic" states in the evening hours. Breuer discovered that if Anna were permitted while in the hypnotic state to recite the contents of all of her hallucinations from the day, then she invariably would leave the trance state and enjoy a period of almost normal tranquility and lucidity during the following late night hours. If, however, she did not describe the hallucinatory contents during the hypnotic period, she suffered from extreme anxiety throughout the night. Anna came to refer to the exercise of reciting her hallucinations as the "talking cure," or, even more jocularly, "chimney sweeping." This talking cure occurred spontaneously the first time, but Breuer quickly came to recognize its importance and to encourage its performance each evening.

This measure provided only temporary relief for the late

evening hours, however, and Anna's daytime hallucinatory stage could not be eliminated. Furthermore, as time went on new physical symptoms kept cropping up. One of these symptoms, no more important than the others in and of itself, was an annoying "hydrophobia": an inability to drink water or any other beverages. The symptom began suddenly and persisted for six weeks, during which time Anna was overcome by a feeling of revulsion, and was unable to bring herself to drink, whenever she brought a glass near her lips. While the symptom lasted, her entire intake of fluids was derived from fruits, and she complained of a constant ravenous thirst. This symptom took on considerable additional importance during one of Anna's hypnotic states when she began describing to Breuer an Englishwoman whom she knew but did not especially like. The woman had a dog that Anna particularly despised. Anna described how on one occasion she entered the woman's room and observed the dog drinking water from a glass. When the event occurred, Anna was filled with strong feelings of disgust and loathing, but out of politeness she was unable to express them. As she recited this account to Breuer, she for the first time permitted herself the luxury of expressing fully and animatedly her negative feelings about the dog's drinking. When she emerged from the trance she immediately asked for a glass of water, which she received and drank without the slightest difficulty. The hydrophobia never appeared again.

After this astonishing event, Breuer learned from Anna that the event with the dog was one that she had completely forgotten up until the moment she recalled it in the hypnotic state. At this point Breuer made his great contribution by hypothesizing that other hysterical symptoms might be "explained" and removed by the recollection of forgotten unpleasant events that had been associated with them. Accordingly, he began to experiment by hypnotizing Anna deliberately and then asking her to recollect what she could about each of her symptoms. To his immense gratification, he discovered that every symptom could be traced back to a traumatic or unpleasant situation for which all memory was completely absent in the waking state. Breuer found that whenever he could induce Anna to recall those unpleasant scenes and, more importantly, to express the emotions they had caused her to feel, the symptoms would disappear.

Thus the origin of Anna's squint and associated visual disturbance was traced back to a time when she was sitting by her father's sickbed, extremely upset about his condition and on the verge of breaking into tears. She did not want to alarm him, however, and fought desperately to hold back her tears. While she was in this state, her father asked her for the time. Because of the tears in her eyes she had to bring her watch close to her face and squint to see it. Her arm paralysis and speech disturbance were associated with another occasion when she had been sitting by her father. Her arm had rested on the headboard of the bed for a long time, when suddenly she thought she saw a black snake dart out from the wall. In terror she tried to recoil, but found that her arm had gone to sleep from resting on the headboard and could not be moved immediately. This increased her terror even more, and when she tried to scream she was so panic-stricken that she was at a loss for words. After desperately trying to think of something to say, she recalled the words of an English prayer that she repeated over and over. Both of the events just described were completely forgotten during her normal waking consciousness. When she recalled them under hypnosis, and expressed fully the terror and sorrow associated with them, the symptoms disappeared completely and permanently.

By means of this new therapeutic technique, which Breuer named the *cathartic method,* he was able systematically to remove all of Anna O.'s symptoms. By the middle of 1882 she seemed completely and dramatically cured. During the course of the treatment, however, it became more and more evident that Anna was becoming strongly attracted emotionally to Breuer, and toward the end she made excessive demands on his time and talents. Finally she went so far as to proclaim openly her love for Breuer, an occurrence that dismayed the completely proper physician greatly, and his wife even more. The situation reached a crisis shortly after he announced to Anna that the treatment would soon be terminated because she was completely well. He was hastily summoned to Anna's bedside, where he discovered that she had concocted one final hysterical symptom: she was in the throes of an hallucinated childbirth. Breuer, who had never even discussed sexual matters with Anna, and who was a true son of the Victorian age, was shocked by this turn of events. He dropped the case immediately, and the next day he left with his wife on a second honeymoon.

It does not seem that Anna suffered much from this abandonment by her physician. She soon recovered from her final symptom and went on to become one of the leading social workers of the day, ultimately being commemorated on a postage stamp for her contributions to the profession. Breuer, however, was so upset by the final turn of events in the case that he could never again bring himself to treat hysterical patients with the cathartic method. He abandoned the ingenious technique worked out in collaboration with his most remarkable patient, and it is likely that his achievement and discovery would have gone unnoticed by the world if it were not for the fact that he spoke of the case occasionally to some of his medical colleagues. Among those colleagues was his young friend Sigmund Freud.

Freud and the Origins of Psychoanalytic Theory

When Freud first encountered hysterical patients in his private practice, he did not immediately use Breuer's cathartic method. In fact, he was initially very conservative, relying almost exclusively on hydrotherapy and electrotherapy. He was disappointed with the results, however, and finally reported that the complicated manuals describing electrotherapy techniques were no more useful than an "Egyptian dream book." He quickly came to believe that the few positive results achieved with this method were due primarily to suggestion.

Freud therefore abandoned the use of electrotherapy altogether and continued to use hydrotherapy only in conjunction with other techniques.

Upon deciding that suggestion was the most important aspect of electrotherapy, Freud sought to maximize its effect by employing direct hypnotic suggestion in the manner of the Nancy school. He found that this method represented an improvement over electrotherapy, and he treated a number of cases successfully with it. One such case was a young mother who was unable to nurse her baby or to take any food herself as long as she was trying to nurse. Freud hypnotized her and suggested that her symptoms would disappear—which they did. Her cure was only temporary, however; when she had a second child her symptoms returned and had to be removed hypnotically once again. Many of the other hypnotic "cures" that Freud effected were even more temporary than this one, and in some cases improvement failed to occur at all. Freud sought still more effective ways of helping his hysterical patients, and it was with hopes of learning some useful new twists to hypnotic therapy that he visited Liébeault and Bernheim at Nancy in 1889. He was disappointed to discover that their techniques were no more effective than his own.

At this point Freud remembered Breuer and his cathartic method, and upon his return to Vienna he began experimenting with the method on his own patients. He hypnotized them and then asked them to recall the very first instances in which their symptoms, or the physical manifestations similar to their symptoms, had appeared. He found that the patients almost always recalled unpleasant events that had been long forgotten. He also found, as Breuer had found with Anna O., that if the emotions appropriate to the events were expressed, the symptoms improved. This process of expressing long pent-up emotion about a previously forgotten event, referred to as *abreaction,* was recognized by Freud to be an important therapeutic agent. If abreaction occurred, relief of symptoms almost always followed.

Only one factor marred Freud's satisfaction with the cathartic method: the necessity of using hypnosis to execute it. He was never completely comfortable in the role of hypnotist, and, even more important, he found that not all of his patients were sufficiently hypnotizable to enter the necessary trance. Thus Breuer's cathartic method was applicable only to a portion of the patients who needed help. Since the most important component of the cathartic method seemed to be the recollection of previously forgotten unpleasant incidents, Freud began to look for a way of helping his non-hypnotizable patients to jog their memories.

The solution he finally devised emerged from the recognition that the hysterics' forgotten painful memories were in many ways similar to the forgotten memories in post-hypnotic amnesia. Both were forgotten during the normal waking state but remembered quite easily under hypnosis. In connection with this train of thought, Freud recalled a particularly startling demonstration that Bernheim had performed for him at Nancy, the significance of which had not been immediately apparent. Bernheim had placed a female subject in a hypnotic trance and suggested to her the "negative hallucination" that he was no longer in the room. The subject went on to act very convincingly as if Bernheim were not there, even when he made overtly threatening gestures toward her. When she came out of the trance she had no memory of what had occurred, manifesting a typical post-hypnotic amnesia. Bernheim then startled Freud by telling him that the subject's memory was only *apparently* lost, and that he could help her to regain it without recourse to hypnosis. Thereupon he placed his hand on the subject's forehead and asserted emphatically that she could remember everything. Much to Freud's surprise, as well as that of the subject herself, she began to recall everything that had happened to her—including Bernheim's threatening gestures, which she had supposedly never experienced at all. Thus Bernheim made it clear that a complete re-hypnosis, with induction procedures and trance state, was not absolutely necessary for overcoming post-hypnotic amnesias.

Freud's recollection of this demonstration led him to speculate that perhaps he could help his hysterical patients to regain their memories by adapting Bernheim's technique. He quickly developed the *pressure technique,* which entailed his suggesting to a patient that a missing memory would spring to mind immediately when he placed his hand on the forehead. He used this technique without hypnosis, instructing his patients simply to try to remember back to the first times their symptoms occurred. When memory lapses inevitably appeared, Freud used the pressure technique and found that forgotten memories were indeed gradually recalled. Thus the cathartic method became feasible for *all* hysterical patients, and not merely the hypnotizable ones. Freud found that his success with the pressure technique was sufficient to permit him to abandon hypnosis completely.

In his initial experimentation with the pressure technique, Freud was quite authoritarian and sometimes arbitrary in his attitudes toward the patient. He had strong ideas about what were appropriate memories and what were not. Thus, if a patient recalled something that seemed nonsensical or implausible to Freud, the memory was dismissed and the pressure technique applied again. Patients began to complain about this arbitrary exercise of authority, and as Freud came gradually to recognize the importance of *fantasy* and *associations* as well as actual memories, he became more tolerant of his patient's verbalizations. Gradually, after several years of painstaking experimentation, the pressure technique became transformed into the *free association method,* where patients freely reported everything that came to mind without censoring or editing. Freud found that free association was even more efficient than the pressure technique in eliciting forgotten material, because if the train of associations continued long enough it inevitably would lead back to the crucial memories. As described in the previous chapter, free association became Freud's most important tool in exploring the mind.

As a result of his non-hypnotic uses of the cathartic method, Freud compiled considerable experience in treating hysterical patients successfully and became convinced that he understood many of the secrets of hysteria. He began a vigorous campaign to persuade Breuer to collaborate with him on a theoretical paper and book about hysteria. Breuer, who had been badly shaken by his experience with Anna O., agreed only with much reluctance. The fruits of their collaboration were published in 1893, a paper entitled "On the Psychical Mechanism of Hysterical Phenomena," and a book that appeared in 1895, entitled *Studies on Hysteria.* In these works they propounded a revolutionary theory of hysteria with vast implications for the understanding of normal as well as psychopathological behavior.

The central thesis of their theory was tersely summarized in their assertion that *"Hysterics suffer mainly from reminiscences."*[5] Their basic conclusion was that hysterics suffered from certain unpleasant memories or ideas that they were unable to bring to consciousness under normal conditions but that nevertheless exerted strong motivational influences on behavior. Breuer and Freud argued that the forgotten memories were of a traumatic or unpleasant nature. Since they could not be brought into consciousness, the negative emotion arising from them could not be expressed openly. Thus emotional energy, referred to as *affect* in psychoanalytic jargon, came to be "dammed up" and deprived of its normal avenue of discharge. The dammed up energy—called *strangulated affect* by Breuer and Freud—was regarded as the immediate source of hysterical complaints. On certain occasions, as when something occurred to remind the patient of the traumatic memory, the negative affect became very strong and could no longer be simply dammed up. Instead of being expressed and dissipated in the normal way, however, it became "converted" into physical sensations and symptoms. The physical symptoms of hysteria, then, were viewed as substitutes for the conscious recollection of painful memories and the corresponding experience of negative affect; these symptoms were labeled *conversions* by Freud and Breuer. The most substantial proof that they put forth to

[5] *Standard Edition,* Vol. II, p. 7.

support their view of hysterical symptoms as conversions of dammed-up affect was that symptoms disappeared after the strangulated affect had been appropriately expressed and discharged.

Having conceptualized hysteria in this way, Freud and Breuer were faced with the problem of explaining *how* the affects came to be damned up or strangulated in the first place. In the early stages of the theory, they argued that there were three different ways in which an affect could remain unexpressed, leading to three major subclassifications of hysteria. The first and simplest of these, labeled *retention hysteria* by Freud, was said to occur whenever external circumstances conspire to prevent the expression of affect. Thus an individual who faces a crisis or very unpleasant situation, but feels that he must maintain a calm and unruffled exterior throughout, may develop hysterical symptoms. A combat soldier who feels that he must not express his fear, or a bereaved person who feels that he must maintain a "stiff upper lip" and suppress his grief, would be especially apt to develop retention hysteria. A retention hysteric may be perfectly conscious of all that happens to him and of the way he feels, but circumstances do not allow him to express his feelings. The damming up of emotion is strictly "voluntary" in a retention hysteric, and therapeutic attempts are aimed directly at inducing him to give up his voluntary inhibition of emotional expression. Thus the condition, and its therapy, were seen by Freud and Breuer as relatively straightforward.

The second subclassification was largely Breuer's idea and was referred to as *hypnoid hysteria.* Breuer felt that some individuals, like Anna O., were especially prone to falling spontaneously into trancelike "hypnoid states" after engaging in monotonous but time-consuming behaviors like sickbed-watching or knitting. Emotionally arousing events occurring during these hypnoid states were likely to be forgotten upon waking, just as in post-hypnotic amnesias. Since memories of such events were not accessible to normal consciousness, the powerful negative affects associated with them could not be discharged normally. Instead they manifested themselves in conversion symptoms. Breuer felt that this concept of hypnoid hysteria drew strong support from the fact that females were much more likely than males to become hysterics. His argument was that females were much more likely than males to engage in the monotonous activities (e.g., needlework or nursing) that were especially conducive to hypnoid states.

Implicit in the description of hypnoid hysteria was an extremely important concept: the *pathogenic idea.* The theory of hypnoid hysteria implied the revolutionary notion that a strictly *mental* entity a memory or an idea—was capable of exerting a direct influence on the physical processes of the body. A forgotten memory was held to be the cause of a physical illness, and the memory was aptly described as "pathogenic" (literally, "disease-creating").

Defense hysteria, the third form of hysterical conversion, was primarily Freud's notion, and the one that he emphasized most strongly in his own writings (i.e., those on which he did not collaborate with Breuer). In retention and hypnoid hysteria, virtually *any* emotionally laden idea was potentially pathogenic, so long as the situation in which it arose prohibited the abreaction of affect. In the case of defense hysteria, however, Freud postulated that there was something so painful or objectionable about the content of the idea itself that the patient actively resisted bringing it into consciousness. In his word, the memory or idea was *repressed* into unconsciousness by a patient because it represented not something that had occurred during a trance state but something that the patient could not bear to think about. The primary evidence that led Freud to this formulation was the fact that frequently his patients, whether under hypnosis, the pressure technique, or free association, seemed actively and openly to resist entertaining these ideas in consciousness. It was only with a good deal of patience, reassurance, and sometimes even outright cajolery that Freud could induce his patients to bring these ideas to mind even tentatively. When they finally were brought to mind, they were often found to have moral or sexual connotations, and their recollection generally led to abreaction and the disappearance of the associated symptoms.

The rationale for using the term "defense" to describe this form of hysteria was obvious. The symptoms, occurring in the full conscious awareness of the patients, were *substitutes* or *symbols* for pathogenic ideas that remained unconscious. As long as the symptom was present, the idea was unconscious; but as soon as the idea became conscious, the symptom disappeared. Since the idea or memory was unpleasant to the patient, the symptom was assumed to occur as a defense against its conscious recognition.

As Freud's experience with defense hysterics increased, it became clear to him that the symptoms did not have a one-to-one relationship with the pathogenic ideas they represented. He found that in almost every case an individual symptom represented not one but a whole conglomerate of pathogenic memories by emphasizing some feature that all the memories had in common. In one of his cases, for example, a woman's minor but troublesome symptom was an uncontrollable jerking and twitching of the hands. Three forgotten unpleasant memories associated with this symptom were uncovered by treatment: a childhood experience in which the woman's hand had been struck as punishment by her schoolteacher, an occasion on which she had been badly startled while playing the piano, and still another childhood occasion on which she had been forced to massage the back of an uncle whom she feared and disliked. By emphasizing activity of the hands, the symptom represented a feature common to all of these memories. Freud's term for this multiple causality was *overdetermination*; the symptom was not caused by a single psychological event, but rather was "overdetermined" by several of them.

Therapy for defense hysteria was more complicated and difficult than for the other two kinds of hysteria because of the factors of defense and overdetermination. The therapist had to assure the patient that he would not himself pass moral judgment on the thoughts that were expressed, and he was obliged to use any means he could think of to ease the patient's resistance. It was especially important that the patient trust the therapist; any factor that might increase his embarrassment or his natural hesitation about confiding his thoughts worked to the detriment of the therapy. The phenomenon of overdetermination presented therapeutic problems too, because patients could not get rid of their symptoms simply by remembering a single pathogenic memory for each. Rather, a whole constellation of memories had to be dealt with and worked through before relief of symptoms occurred.

Within a year or so of the publication of *Studies on Hysteria,* Freud became convinced that defense hysterias were the only ones that really deserved to be taken seriously. He came to feel that retention hysterias were relatively trivial, since they were highly liable to spontaneous abreaction without intervention by a physician. At the same time, he came to doubt seriously the very existence of hypnoid hysteria as a separate entity. The concept of hypnoid hysteria had stemmed primarily from Breuer's experiences with a single patient (Anna O.), and Freud personally had never come across a serious case of hysteria that could not be demonstrated to be of the defense type. He came to believe that if Anna O.'s symptoms had been investigated further in the light of knowledge of the processes of defensive repression, they too would have demonstrated defensive aspects underlying the apparently hypnoid ones.

Freud also came to believe that all defense hysterias had one essential feature in common: the major repressed pathogenic ideas all had important *sexual* connotations. In case after case he found that the repressed memories uncovered by therapy included scenes of childhood sexual experiences—especially seduction by adults. The patient suffering from uncontrollable hand motion, for example, amplified her memory of massaging her uncle's back with an additional recollection of being sexually assaulted by him after the massage. When this kind of material emerged in several cases of hysteria, Freud developed a *seduction theory* to the effect that a childhood seduction or sexual molestation, usually at the hands of a parent or other close relative, was a necessary precondition for the development of defense hysteria. The memory of the seduction was especially painful and was therefore repressed. Once repressed, it became a pathogenic idea capable of causing hysterical conversions. Thus Freud came to believe not only that all important hysterias were defense hysterias, but also that they were initiated by sexual traumas occurring in childhood. The seduction theory itself later proved to be wrong in its details, but it constituted an important step toward Freud's recognition of the role of sexuality in motivating human behavior.

Implications for a General Theory

Undoubtedly the most important idea to emerge from Freud's studies of hysteria and hypnosis was the notion of *unconscious motivation.* The evidence available to Freud indicated clearly that there were situations in which "forgotten" memories or ideas had direct influences on overt behavior. Thus, a posthypnotic suggestion carried out by a hypnotic subject after he comes out of a trance but is amnesic for the trance itself was motivated by a suggestion or idea of which the subject was unconscious. Likewise, hysterical conversions were motivated by unconscious pathogenic ideas.

The concept of "unconscious" that Freud developed did not simply imply "not conscious," however; it specifically included ideas and memories that had been fully present in consciousness before being subjected to some repressing force and that under certain conditions could be brought back into consciousness in their original form. Unconscious ideas had not simply "disappeared" but had been rendered inaccessible to conscious awareness. Since certain conditions like hypnosis or variants of cathartic therapy could help restore the ideas, it made sense for Freud to postulate the existence of a storehouse of memories that are unconscious, but that nevertheless remain intact. Instead of disappearing or fading away, these memories exert definite motivational influences. The concept of unconscious motivation helped to clarify many of the previously bewildering aspects of hypnosis and hysteria.

Once Freud recognized the role of unconscious motivation in such highly unusual or pathological states as hypnosis and hysteria, he saw that the concept could be applied to many facets of "normal" behavior as well. Thus he began to apply the technique of free association to everyday mistakes or slips, like the "*aliquis* example" described in the preceding chapter. He marshaled an impressive amount of evidence demonstrating that these mistakes were not the random, haphazard events that they superficially seemed to be, but rather were purposive, unconsciously motivated, and fully determined behaviors. Freud published an ingenious book in 1901 entitled *The Psychopathology of Everyday Life* in which he argued that all errors—be they slips of the tongue or pen, misreading or mishearing of information, or the simple forgetting of something—contribute toward the fulfillment of wishes. Thus the man who temporarily "forgets" the name of his best friend when an opportunity arises to introduce him to an important acquaintance may be manifesting an unconscious hostile wish toward his friend. The term "Freudian slip" has come to be associated with these motivated mistakes, though the proper word in psychoanalytic terminology is *parapraxis.*

Freud's recognition that many aspects of normal behavior could be accounted for by the principles he uncovered in his study of hysteria was gratifying to him. He had come to believe that any theory of psychopathology was worthless unless it could be usefully related to knowledge about the normal functioning of the nervous system. In accordance with this belief he was especially eager to relate his clinical findings about hysteria and hypnosis not only to parapraxes and similar behaviors, but also to the normal functioning of the human nervous system as he had come to understand it in his career as a neurologist. His attempt to accomplish this integration is the subject of the next chapter.

SUGGESTED FURTHER READINGS

A thorough discussion of hysteria as it has been construed through the centuries is provided by Ilza Veith's *Hysteria: The History of a Disease* (Chicago, University of Chicago Press, 1965). The full presentation of a now-classic case of multiple personality is made by C. H. Thigpen and H. Cleckley in *Three Faces of Eve* (New York, McGraw-Hill, 1957). Good histories of hypnotism are provided in Chapters 7 and 26 of *A History of Experimental Psychology* by E. G. Boring (New York, Appleton-Century-Crofts, 1957), and in F. A. Pattie's "A Brief History of Hypnotism," in *Handbook of Clinical and Experimental Hypnosis*, edited by J. E. Gordon (New York, Macmillan, 1967).

Of Freud's own works, an 1893 paper entitled "Some Points in a Comparative Study of Organic Hysterical Paralysis"[6] is of interest because it illustrates the similarities and differences between organic and hysterical symptomatology. In 1894 he published his pioneering paper on "The Defense Neuropsychoses," setting forth for the first time his views on the defensive nature of many hysterical and obsessional symptoms. The next year he and Breuer published their famous *Studies on Hysteria* (New York, Avon Books, 1966). This book contains several case histories, including that of Anna O., and was the first work to document systematically the existence of unconscious motivation. The best brief historical introduction to psychoanalysis by Freud himself is "Five Lectures on Psycho-Analysis" (1910), published under the title *The Origin and Development of Psychoanalysis* (Chicago, Gateway Editions, 1955).

[6] This and all subsequent short papers by Freud that are suggested as further readings may be found in S. Freud, *Collected Papers*, ed. James Strachey (5 vols., London: Hogarth Press, 1950–1952) .

3

First Model of the Mind: "Project for a Scientific Psychology"

Throughout most of 1895, the year *Studies on Hysteria* was published, Freud was hard at work on a new and difficult undertaking much in line with the mechanistic inclinations of his teachers. In his own words, his ambition was to write a "Psychology for Neurologists" whose purpose would be "to see how the theory of mental functioning takes shape if quantitative considerations, a sort of economics of nerve force, are introduced into it."[1] His aim, in short, was to employ his knowledge of neurology in constructing a hypothetical "model of the mind" that could account for neurotic as well as normal mental functioning. His task was not unlike that facing an inventor who seeks to design a robot capable of thinking and behaving like a real human being, except that the inventor would probably design a robot composed of inanimate components instead of nerves and muscles.

The construction of this model assumed tremendous importance for Freud. In April, 1895, he wrote his friend Fliess: "On the scientific side I am in a bad way; I am so deep in the 'Psy-

[1] Sigmund Freud, *The Origins of Psycho-Analysis* (New York, Basic Books, 1954), pp. 119–120.

chology for Neurologists' that it quite consumes me, until I have to break off out of sheer exhaustion. I have never been so intensely preoccupied by anything."[2] A month later he was still at the task, as he described in a passage illustrating his mode of work as well as his intensity of purpose: "During recent weeks I have devoted every free minute to such work; the hours of the night from eleven to two have been occcupied with imaginings, transpositions, and guesses, only abandoned when I had arrived at some absurdity, or had so truly and seriously overworked that I had no interest left for the day's medical work."[3] Freud's spirits rose or fell according to his progress on the project for several months. In early October, when he came upon a stumbling block, he wrote: "I have been alternately proud and happy and abashed and miserable, until now, after an excess of mental torment, I just apathetically tell myself that it does not hang together yet and perhaps never will. . . . The mechanical explanation is not coming off, and I am inclined to listen to the still, small voice which tells me that my explanation will not do."[4] A short while later he was much happier, as the project seemed close to success: "Everything fell into place, the cogs meshed, the thing really seemed to be a machine which in a moment would run of itself. . . . I can naturally hardly contain myself with delight."[5]

The result of Freud's labor was a draft manuscript of one hundred hand-written pages that was sent to Fliess in the late fall of 1895. Then, mystifyingly, Freud apparently dropped the whole project. The manuscript, into which he had poured so much of his energy, was never revised for publication or even referred to in any of his later published works. In fact, the very existence of the manuscript was unsuspected until several years after Freud's death, when it was published along with a selection of his letters to Fliess. The original manuscript bore

[2] *Ibid.*, p. 118.
[3] *Ibid.*, p. 120.
[4] *Ibid.*, p. 126.
[5] *Ibid.*, p. 129.

no title—not even the "Psychology for Neurologists" that Freud had suggested in his letter—but the English translators of the manuscript called it "Project for a Scientific Psychology."

While the precise reasons for Freud's abandonment of the manuscript remain obscure, it is clear that many of the ideas first expressed in the "Project" continued to dominate Freud's thinking about human psychology. A number of very important psychoanalytic concepts were first formulated there, albeit in a quasi-neurological, mechanistic terminology that at first seems very different from that of Freud's better-known works. Because of its association with the origins of Freud's psychoanalytic ideas, and because of the light it sheds on Freud's most basic assumptions about the human mind, the "Project" remains a work deserving of serious study.

The following pages will outline the model Freud proposed in the "Project." The arguments and ideas he put forth there are tightly reasoned and sometimes difficult to follow. In fact, the work in general is probably the most complex of all of Freud's writings, partly because the manuscript was never edited and polished for publication and partly because of the intrinsic complexity of its reasoning. But understanding the "Project" is well worth the effort involved.

"Project for a Scientific Psychology": Basic Assumptions and Definitions

As Freud set out to devise his hypothetical model of the mind, he sought to construct it from units that were both plausible from the point of view of neurological knowledge and capable of mechanistic explanation. The *neuron* was a good candidate for such a unit on both counts. First, the neuron had been identified by 1895 as the most basic unit of the nervous system, and since the functioning of the nervous system was assumed to underlie all human behavior it was plausible for Freud to construe the mind as being constituted by a system of neurons.

Second, the work of Helmholtz, Brücke, and their colleagues had demonstrated that the neuron was amenable to study as a mechanistic unit. Thus the neuron was selected as the most basic unit in the "Project."

The nervous system was known to be an incredibly complicated network of interconnected neurons, and Freud followed his teachers in believing that "mental activity" is the psychological result of electrochemical energy moving throughout the neural network. He also followed his teachers in two other important respects. He accepted Meynert's belief that specific neural locations "represent" specific ideas, memories, or perceptions. Both the perception of an event and the subsequent memory of it were assumed to involve the excitation of the same neural location. Within this system, the transmission of excitation from one neuron to another could result psychologically in the recollection of a *series* of specific memories; i.e., in a "train of thought."

Freud borrowed from Brücke as well as Meynert. Brücke, it will be remembered, had demonstrated that the nervous system must be capable of the "summation of stimulation"—of accumulating small increments of excitation within itself until the total reaches sufficient intensity to release a reflexive response. Freud construed the neurons of his hypothetical nervous system as having just such an accumulating device, with logical consequences of the greatest importance.

More specifically, Freud conceptualized each individual neuron as a "receptacle" capable of receiving, holding, and transmitting varying amounts of excitation. He believed that the nature of the excitation was closely akin to electrical or chemical energy, but since his system did not depend on an exact identification of the excitation he simply called it "*Q*", and stated that it was subject to the general laws of physics. *Q*'s most important property was its capacity to "fill up," or *cathect*, an individual neuron. A neuron was said to be cathected to the degree that it was filled up with excitation, or *Q*. At a given moment in time, some neurons are more highly cathected than others, and a given neuron may vary in its degree of cathexis from one time to another.[6]

Freud believed that the amount of *Q* an individual neuron can retain is limited. He assumed that each neuron has a certain threshold capacity, above which it no longer stores new *Q* but *discharges* it instead into the muscular system of the organism. After a neuron becomes cathected above its threshold, or *hypercathected*, it instantaneously releases all of its accumulated *Q* in a dramatic manner. A partial analogy is a balloon, which is capable of accumulating air until its capacity is surpassed and it bursts. The "discharge" of air and consequent emptying of the balloon are analogous to what happens to a hypercathected neuron. A difference between the two situations, however, is that a discharged neuron returns immediately afterwards to its initial uncathected state, whereas the burst balloon has been permanently altered and damaged by the violent discharge of its air.

The consequences of a neuronal discharge are great, according to Freud's model, because each discharge into the muscular system results in the performance of an overt motoric act. Thus neural discharges serve as triggers, releasing muscular reactions. The input of large amounts of *Q* into the nervous system is the neurological prerequisite for a state of "arousal," resulting in the motoric activation of the organism.

This raises a question about the *sources* of *Q* input to the nervous system: where does *Q* come from, and how does it enter the nervous system to begin with? Freud said there were two major sources. *Exogenous* sources are all of the external stimuli that constantly impinge on any organism: light, heat, sound, smell, pressure, and so on. *Endogenous* sources are

[6] The term "cathexis" is actually a neologism coined by Freud's translators. Freud's original German word was *Besetzung*, an everyday term having the general meaning of "filling" or "occupation." Freud was reportedly unhappy with the new English term, derived from the Greek verb meaning "to occupy," since he disliked needless technicality in language. Nevertheless, in the present instance as well as several others to be noted later, the neologism has remained in standard English use.

found in the intracellular processes of the body itself. Hunger, thirst, sexual urges, and other tissue needs create endogenous *Q*. The major difference between the two sources of *Q* was thought by Freud to be one of quantity rather than quality. He believed that the intensity of exogenous *Q* was substantially greater than that of the *Q* emanating from endogenous sources. Once inside the nervous system, however, exogenous and endogenous *Q* were assumed to operate in exactly the same way and to be interchangeable with each other.

Although similar in their essential natures, exogenous and endogenous sources of *Q* present different *practical* problems for an organism. When exogenous stimuli become too intense they can be dealt with by the simple response of flight; endogenous stimuli of great intensity require a more complicated response. One can run away from an external irritant, but not from an internal need.

A prototypical example of the flight response to exogenous stimulation is provided by the *reflex*, believed by many neurophysiologists of Freud's day to be the most basic unit of behavior. For present purposes a reflex may be defined simply as a specific stimulus-response sequence that occurs rapidly, and apparently automatically and involuntarily. The cough is an example of a reflex. Here the stimulus is usually a foreign object that irritates the membranes of the respiratory tract, and the response is the violent expulsion of air referred to as a cough. If the reflex has been "successful" the expulsion of air has removed the irritating stimulus. Thus the reflex has a tendency to shut itself off by separating the irritating external stimulus from the organism.

Freud's view of the neurological events occuring in a reflex like the cough is illustrated schematically in Figure 1. In Figure 1a, *S* represents an external stimulus that has just begun to impinge on the organism from the outside—bombarding it with a certain amount of irritation of energy. The effective part of this energy, from the standpoint of nervous system functioning, expresses itself as a certain amount of *Q*. Thus heavy concentrations of *Q* are present at the boundary of

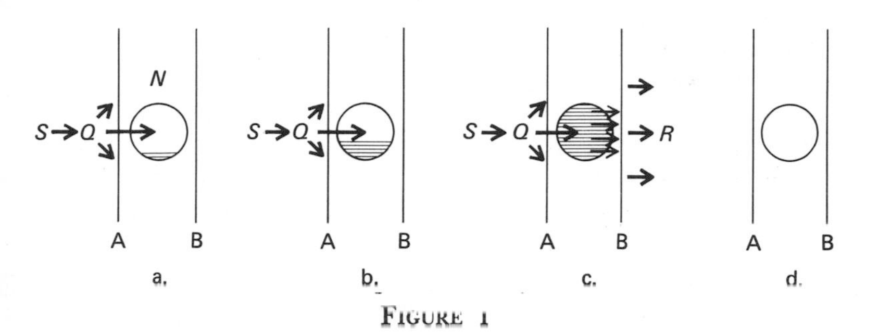

FIGURE 1

the nervous system (A), and some of this *Q* is permitted to enter through a screenlike device into the nervous system proper. In this greatly simplified example, assume that only one neuron (*N*) is involved. The *Q* that enters the nervous system at A therefore cathects the neuron; the dark area at the bottom of the neuron represents the accumulated cathexis. Figure 1b represents the same situation as Figure 1a, except that the stimulus has been present for a longer time and the neuron is therefore more highly cathected. In Figure 1c the neuron has become hypercathected and is in the process of discharge. It releases its energy into the periphery of the muscular system (B), thereby initiating the response component (*R*) of the reflex. If the response is successful, it removes the initial irritating stimulus and the neuron returns to an uncathected and unstimulated resting state, as represented in Figure 1d. If the stimulus has not been removed by the response, conditions revert to the state depicted in Figure 1a, and the cycle begins again. Of course, this whole hypothetical process nicely accounts for Brücke's "summation of stimuli" arguments, described in Chapter One.

It should be noted that the *Q* that actually cathects the neuron (i.e., that enters the nervous system) is of a much lower order of magnitude than the energies on either side of the nervous system. That is, of the total amount of energy generated by *S*, only a small proportion is allowed actually to pass through the screen at A and cathect the neuron, and the total energy of external stimuli is therefore considerably greater than the energy of the nervous system. Similarly, the total muscular energy involved in the response occurring at B is much greater than the discharged *Q* that triggered it. Thus the *Q* in the nervous system is small in magnitude, of a completely different order from the relatively massive energies inherent in the external world. This *Q*, however, is postulated to account for the selectivity in human behavior, and it is the prototype for Freud's concept of *psychic energy,* the fuel that makes the mental apparatus work.

It should also be noted that a reflex uses and disposes of energy in a very efficient way, from an "economic" point of view. The source of *Q* is the energy of the external stimulus itself, and some of that same energy becomes employed in the process of getting rid of the stimulus. The net effect of the reflex is thus to shut itself off. Therefore the reflex, and the pressures of exogenous stimulation generally, does not require the nervous system to have an independent energy of its own. The nervous system can escape from exogenous stimulation by using the *Q* from that very source to energize its escape responses.

The situation with respect to *endogenous* stimulation is considerably more complicated. Freud believed that the intracellular processes of the body give rise to distinct stimuli that impinge upon the nervous system from within, and therefore cause *Q* to enter the system. He felt that the magnitude of this stimulation is less than that of external stimulation, and does not require the screening device suggested in Figure 1 to reduce the magnitude of entering endogenous *Q*. Otherwise, the end result of endogenous stimulation is the same; the cathexis of a neuron or system of neurons. In this case, however, a simple reflexive discharge of the cathexis cannot resolve the problem because the stimulus is not one from which the organism can escape or flee. Thus a discharge into the muscular system activates the organism in one way or another, but does not suffice to cut off the endogenous source of *Q*. What is required in the case of endogenous stimulation is an active and precise manipulation of the environment so as to bring a need-gratifying substance into the grasp of the organism. In the case of hunger, for example, the environment must be manipulated so that food is readily accessible. After food has been provided it can be consumed in a reflexive manner by swallowing. Note, however, that even this very simple situation requires at least *two* discrete motoric acts: one to manipulate the environment so as to provide food, the other to swallow the food. This contrasts with the case of exogenous stimulation, which can be relieved in a single reflexive act.

The necessity for manipulating the environment created by the endogenous sources of *Q* results in two demands upon the nervous system above and beyond those raised by exogenous sources. While exogenous stimuli provide the *Q* that results in their own removal, endogenous sources require extra motoric acts to ensure their termination. Because the *Q* necessary to trigger these extra acts must come from somewhere, an effectively operating nervous system must have at its disposal a reservoir of *Q* which can be employed selectively to trigger appropriate manipulative responses. Thus the first demand raised by endogenous needs is for a reserve supply of energy to be stored within the nervous system.

The second demand arises from the *selectivity* in behavior required to manipulate the environment effectively and meet endogenous needs. For example, the obtaining of food entails specific and well-integrated activities, ranging from the stalking and killing of prey to the ordering of a meal from a waiter. In order to complete these activities successfully, it is necessary not only to perform certain acts, but also to *inhibit* the performance of inappropriate behaviors. The hunter must not only follow the trail of his quarry, but also refrain from actions that would frighten it off. Thus the satisfaction of endogenous needs requires the nervous system to delay or inhibit discharges that would lead to inappropriate behaviors, while at the same time providing an extra supply of *Q* for selective use in the triggering of appropriate responses.

In Freud's model the nervous system is able to accomplish

this under certain conditions because the individual neurons come to act in concert with one another. All of the billions of neurons in the nervous system are interconnected in a vastly complicated network, and Freud assumed that sometimes a neuron may transmit some or all of its accumulated cathexis to one or more of its neighbors. Thus whenever a neuron receives large amounts of Q one of two things may happen: it may accumulate the *Q* until it becomes hypercathected and triggers a discharge, or it may regularly transmit portions of the *Q* to its neighbors, thereby maintaining several neurons at moderate levels of cathexis but inhibiting discharge. Several interconnected neurons, acting together and "sharing" their cathexes, may thus facilitate the effective manipulation of the environment by making unlikely the hypercathexis of any single member and thereby inhibiting discharge. At the same time, however, such a system of neurons contains small amounts of *Q* in several places, and therefore constitutes the reservoir of energy *potentially* available to trigger appropriate manipulative behaviors. Under proper conditions, the system can allow small amounts of *Q* from several different neurons to converge upon a single neuron and trigger an effective manipulative act. Thus both of the demands created by endogenous needs are partially met by the ability of neurons to transmit *Q* from one to another.

Freud held that neurons do not always or universally possess this ability, but that certain conditions are necessary to facilitate the inter-neuronal flow of *Q*. He postulated the existence of a *contact barrier* between every pair of interconnected neurons, setting up resistance against the transmission of *Q* between them. The resistance of contact barriers surrounding a neuron is decreased if that neuron is partially cathected. Thus the contact barrier may be thought of as a kind of valve, regulating the flow of *Q* to and from a neuron as a function of its degree of cathexis. Stated another way, this principle suggests that partially cathected neurons tend to attract still more *Q* to themselves. Figure 2 illustrates the general tendency. In 2a, neither neuron X nor neuron Y is cathected, and there is

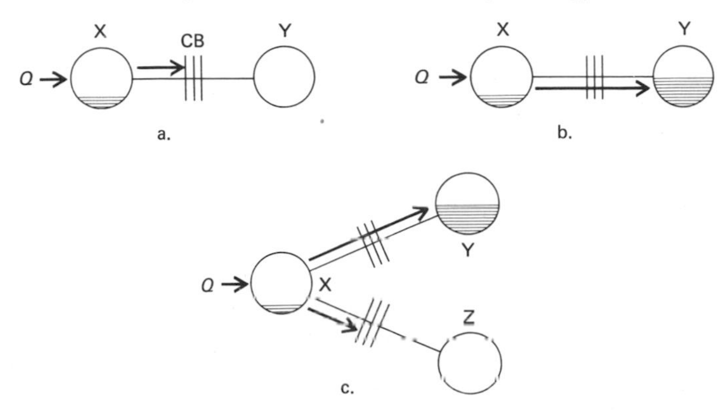

FIGURE 2

accordingly a high degree of resistance at the contact barrier (CB) between them, represented by three vertical lines. This means that new *Q* flowing into X will have a difficult time moving on to Y, and cathexis of X will increase rapidly. In Figure 2b the same situation is represented, except that here neuron Y is partially precathected. The resistance at the contact barrier is decreased accordingly, and the likelihood is increased that some of the new *Q* arriving in X will be passed on to Y. Figure 2c is simply a combination of 2a and 2b, indicating that if neurons Y and Z are both connected to neuron X, and only Y is partially precathected, then new *Q* arriving in X is more likely to be transmitted to Y than to Z, all other things being equal. This illustrates the fact that new excitation entering the nervous system is likely to flow through the system from neuron to neuron in a path determined in part by the degree of precathexis of the individual neurons. Figure 3 represents a very simple network of neurons, with new *Q* entering the network at neuron A. Neurons B and E are moderately precathected, and neurons C, D, and F are uncathected. The most likely path for new excitation to follow in such a system will be from A to B to E, rather than any of the other possibilities open to it.

This principle—that *Q* is more easily transmitted to preca-

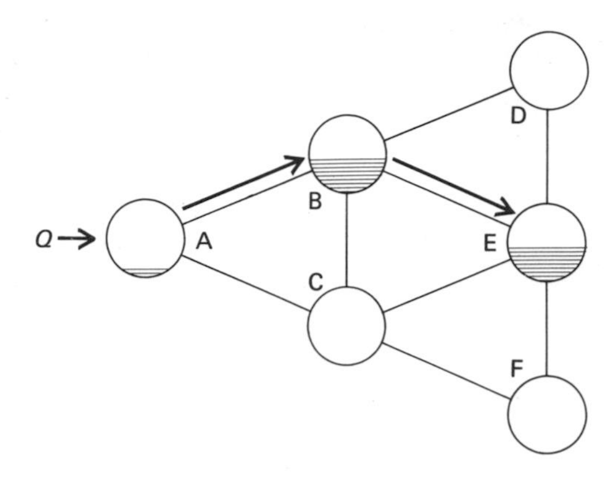

FIGURE 3

thected than to uncathected neurons—has some very interesting implications when it is interpreted on a psychological rather than a strictly neurological level. It will be remembered that an assumption of Freud's was that the flow of excitation from one neuron to another could be conceptualized as the neurological equivalent of a "train of thought." What the above considerations suggest, quite simply, is that a precathected (i.e., pre-activated) neuron has a great organizing influence on the sequence of the train of thought. The connections between the precathected neuron and its neighbors are strengthened (via the weakened resistance at the contact barriers), and therefore it is especially easily "associated to." If we assume, as Freud did, that a cathected neuron represents a particular memory or idea that has been "activated," then we see how that idea has a *motivational effect* on the train of mental events. For example, if an individual is hungry the neurons representing memories of hunger and food are cathected. These neurons are especially likely to attract associations to themselves, and as a result many elements of the individual's train of thought will have to do with hunger and its alleviation.

The transmission of Q between pairs of neurons was believed by Freud to be governed by a second principle: when transmission across a particular contact barrier occurs once, the effect is to lower permanently the resistance at that barrier. The resistance is further permanently lowered with each subsequent transmission. If a transmission occurs once between neurons A and B, the likelihood of another such transmission in the future is increased. As the two neurons transmit back and forth to each other with increasing frequency, the resistance at their contact barrier becomes less and less, until it may finally approach zero. At that point the two neurons are virtually equivalent to one another; with almost no resistance between them they essentially become one large neuron. On a psychological level, this principle is equivalent to the assertion that things that have been associated with one another in the past are likely to be associated again in the future. After many repeated associations the two elements may finally come to be virtually equivalent to one another.

When the two principles governing the flow of Q in Freud's model are examined from a broader perspective, they suggest that the course of a person's mental activity is determined jointly by factors representing his *present* and *past* experiences. The first principle—the tendency of precathected neurons to attract still more Q to themselves—reflects the present state of the organism because the patterning of precathexis is largely dependent upon the specific endogenous and exogenous stimuli that are impinging at a given moment. The nervous system of a hungry man is characterized by a cathexis of those neurons representing memories associated with "hunger," and that of a man who sees a bear by the cathexis of neurons representing "bear." These cathexes represent the individual's present reality situation and attract new Q to themselves. Thus the train of thought is partially determined—or *motivated*—by the representation of present external and internal reality as it is recorded in the nervous system.

The second principle governing the flow of Q in the system reflects the past experience of the organism, since neurons that have exchanged cathexis with one another in the past will be especially predisposed to do so again. Neural activity is therefore governed by *learning* as well as by the immediately present energy relationships in the neurons. Figure 4 illustrates some of the ways in which present state and past history may interact to influence the course of energy flow. In Figure 4a, assume that *Q* transmissions between neurons A and B and between A and C have occurred with equal frequencies in the past. Therefore the predetermined resistances at the two contact barriers are equal, and the transmission of new *Q* from A is determined by the degrees of precathexis at B and C. Since B is more cathected than C, there is much more flow from A to B than from A to C. Figure 4b shows the obverse situation: B and C are equally precathected and exert equal pulls on the *Q* arriving in A. But transmissions in the past have occurred more frequently between A and C than between A and B, and the resistance is therefore less between A and C. More new *Q*

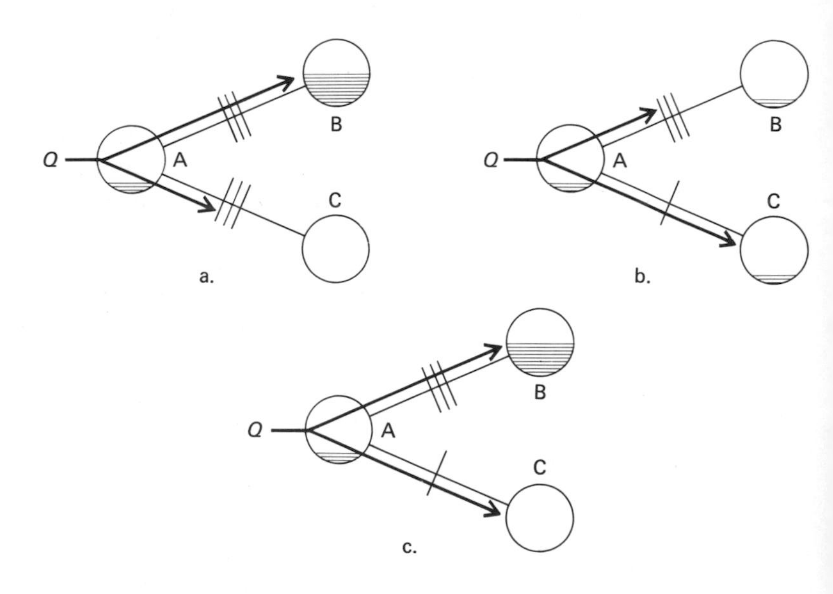

FIGURE 4

from A will therefore go to C than to B. Figure 4c represents a situation in which the two factors counterbalance each other. Transmission in the past has occurred more frequently between A and C, but at the present time B is more heavily cathected than C. Thus *Q* from A may be transmitted in equal amounts to both B and C—to B because of the pull of the present, and to C because of the push from the past.

Differentiation of the Neutral Network: The Phi and Psi Systems

On the basis of the assumptions and principles developed in the preceding section, Freud deduced a set of developmental events which he believed to be characteristic of mental growth for all human beings. He assumed that the nervous system of a newborn infant is almost completely undifferentiated. Before the organism has had any experience, the resistances at all contact barriers in the system are large and approximately equal in magnitude. Only with experience does it develop into a complex and sophisticated network of differential potentials for the transmission and discharge of *Q*. "Experience" means stimulation from within or without, and as soon as that happens some interconnected neurons inevitably become simultaneously cathected. This simultaneous cathexis makes possible the exchange of *Q* between the neurons, and every exchange permanently reduces the resistance at the separating contact barrier. Thus the early experiences predispose the nervous system's responses to later ones. If the later experiences are similar to the early ones, resulting in the simultaneous cathexis of the same neuron groups, these predispositions will be strengthened. If the new experiences are different, the resulting new patterns of simultaneous cathexes will partially offset the predispositions of the contact barriers. This results in a somewhat different pattern of *Q* transmission, and a modified predisposition for the processing of still later experiences. This process repeats itself again and again, until the system becomes highly organized and structured. Then new experience is processed by contributions from the present and the past in such a complex manner as to make it difficult to separate their individual effects.

In addition to these modifications, Freud also suggested that systematic changes occur in various parts of the system because of anatomical considerations. He noted that some neurons lie at or close to the exterior surface of the organism and are therefore in direct contact with exogenous sources of stimulation. He referred to this part of the nervous system as its *sensory end,* because it encounters *Q* directly from the outside and introduces a portion of it into the interior. Freud assumed that these sensory neurons are relatively few, but that they are connected to a large number of neurons in the interior of the system. The first "layer" of interior neurons has connections with a larger number of neurons more interior still, and so on into the center of the nervous system. The entire structure may be visualized as something like Figure 5, in which row A corresponds to the sensory end of the system, and Rows B, C, and D are the first, second, and third interior layers of neurons.

An important consequence of this arrangement of neurons is that relatively large quantities of excitation will enter the system through the sensory neurons in Row A and be transmitted on to Row B. All of this transmission must take place across a small number of contact barriers (four, in the illustration). When that same total amount of *Q* is transmitted from Row B to Row C, there are twice as many channels available to it. Therefore each contact barrier separating B from C will

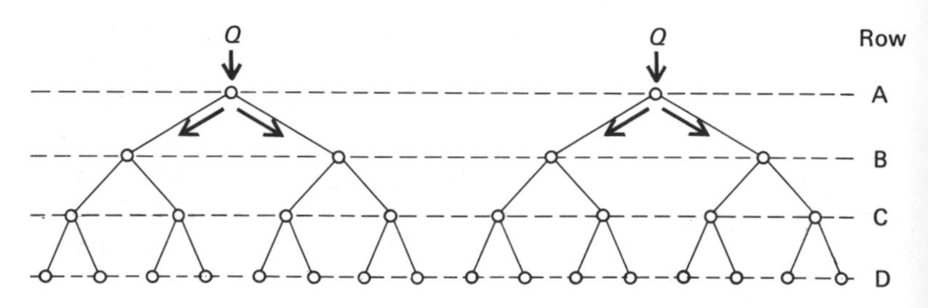

FIGURE 5

be traversed, on the average, only half as frequently as those separating A from B. Still deeper in the system, those separating C from D will be traversed less frequently still.

It is easy to deduce the permanent effect of these circumstances: the contact barriers between Rows A and B, being crossed very frequently, will quickly have their resistances eroded away. Thus the sensory neurons come to be relatively *permeable*, transmitting *Q* deeper into the system with considerable ease. Most of the contact barriers separating neurons deeper in the system are traversed less frequently, and therefore those neurons remain relatively *impermeable* to future excitation.

Freud argued that the terms "permeable" and "impermeable" are especially apt labels for the sensory and interior parts of the nervous system. Sensory neurons are accurately described as permeable because they come to be undiscriminating with respect to the kind of stimulation that they pass on into the system. Those neurons that receive visual stimulation, for example, do not discriminate among different visual stimuli by allowing some to cathect the system while barring others. All visual stimuli that impinge on the sensory neurons produce *Q* that is transmitted into the impermeable portions of the system. In other words, once the permeability of the sensory end is established, the capacity of the nervous system to be excited by Stimulus Y is not altered by the fact that it has already been excited by Stimulus X. As a kind of shorthand expression, Freud referred to the whole system of permeable sensory neurons as the *Phi system*.

"Impermeable" seemed to Freud to be an appropriate adjective to describe the deeper parts of the neural network, because it was obvious that not all neural transmissions are indiscriminate or easily achieved. The fact that human beings have *memory* indicated that some parts of the nervous system must be permanently altered by experience in a way that allows it to respond selectively to stimuli. Thus the psychological equivalent of the cathexis of a particular impermeable neuron—i.e., one that will retain cathexis rather than immediately pass it on—is the arousal of a particular memory. Freud named these interior, impermeable, memory-recording neurons the *Psi system.*

Freud subdivided the neurons of the Psi system into two categories, though the two categories should be thought of as representing end points of a continuum rather than discrete entities. The first category of Psi neurons were said to constitute the *pallium* or *mantle* and were defined as having more or less direct connections with the Phi system. Thus mantle Psi neurons are the first to be steadily cathected as a result of exogenous stimulation, and the pattern of mantle Psi cathexes records the pattern of exogenous stimuli. A cathexis of mantle Psi via Phi, therefore, is referred to as a *perceptual cathexis.*

The second kind of neuron in the Psi system, defined as having relatively direct connections with endogenous sources of stimulation, is referred to as *nuclear.* The relationship of nuclear Psi neurons to endogenous stimulation therefore parallels that of Phi neurons to exogenous stimulation. The cathexis of a nuclear Psi neuron reflects the presence of a certain kind of internal need or tension. Specific somatic needs result in the cathexis of specific nuclear Psi neurons; thus a "thirst neuron" is cathected in a state of thirst, a "hunger neuron" in a state of hunger, and so on. Such cathexes, resulting in nuclear Psi directly from endogenous sources, may be referred to as *need cathexes.* The absolute magnitude of *Q* introduced by these endogenous sources, it will be remembered, is postulated to be much less than that introduced by exogenous sources. Thus the contact barriers surrounding nuclear Psi do not become as permeable as those of Phi. Nevertheless, nuclear Psi comes to be cathected with considerable frequency, resulting in certain regular patterns of transmission whose nature will be made clear shortly.

As the human child develops, his emerging Phi and Psi systems interact in certain patterns that are virtually universal because of experiences that are common to all human beings. These experiences all have to do with complications arising from endogenous stimulation. One example is the state of hunger, and comparable processes are assumed to surround every other recurrent endogenous need as well.

After a human infant is born, he loses the steady supply of nourishment that had previously reached him via the umbilical cord. As a result, he now periodically becomes hungry. His need for food results in endogenous stimuli which impinge upon the nervous system and create a state of cathexis in the "hunger neurons" in nuclear Psi. When the infant is very young his nuclear Psi neurons are very impermeable, and the buildup of cathexes there results in frequent discharges. The discharges create a reflex-like general arousal of the musculature, and the infant kicks, screams, flails, etc. Though these reflexive behaviors are not adaptive in and of themselves, they come to serve an adaptive purpose in a roundabout way by calling attention to the infant's distress. The hungry infant's cries are usually heeded by his mother, who feeds him and thereby terminates the endogenous stimulation.

As more and more feeding experiences occur, part of the infant's nervous system begins to become organized about them. Each time the mother feeds the child, she presents a consistent pattern of exogenous stimuli that is represented by perceptual cathexes in mantle Psi. Thus it frequently happens that a need cathexis representing "hunger" is present simultaneously with perceptual cathexes representing external sources of gratification ("mother," "breast," "bottle," etc.). Since the cathexes are simultaneous, transmissions between the neuron pairs are facilitated. This lowers the permanent resistance separating the involved neurons, and therefore permanent neural associations are established between the nuclear Psi neurons representing hunger and the mantle neurons representing the external stimuli surrounding the presentation of food.

Once the food is presented to the young organism, still newer connections become established within the system. The nourishment is ingested through the usual eating reflexes (sucking and swallowing), and as these effective discharges of Psi cathexes occur the infant undergoes the *experience of satisfaction*. The experience of satisfaction has many components, including the diminution of hunger and a general pleasurable feeling of lack of tension. The diffuse reflexive activity of kicking, screaming, etc., initially triggered by the build-up of need cathexis, ceases as the hunger comes under the control of appropriate sucking and swallowing reflexes, and the infant arrives at a satisfying state of relative quiescence. All of the external components of this experience of satisfaction produce exogenous stimulation and result in the cathexis of a new pattern of neurons in mantle Psi. "Satisfaction" therefore comes to be represented in the mantle Psi simultaneously with the presence of the need-gratifying objects, and associations are promptly formed between these cathected neurons.

This introduces complications into the system as a whole. In the initial condition of the infant, the mantle neurons representing need-gratifying objects or the experience of satisfaction could become cathected only via *Q* input from Phi; that is, only when the stimuli they represent were actually present in the external environment. Now, however, because of the increased potential for transmission between these neurons and the nuclear Psi neurons representing hunger, it is possible for them to become cathected from *endogenous* sources. Nuclear centers, cathected in a state of hunger, may now transmit some of that *Q* to the mantle neurons representing the state of satisfaction. This situation can be described easily from a psychological point of view: hunger tends to elicit *memories* of food and the objects that have provided food in the past; a hungry man thinks of food and its consumption. The cathexis of mantle Psi in this situation was aptly described as a *wishful cathexis* by Freud. Thus the presence of endogenous needs may come to elicit the memory of past situations in which those needs have been satisfied, and these memories are in essence wishes for the present. It is important to note here, however, that there is no functional difference between a wishful and a perceptual cathexis of a mantle neuron, apart from the source of *Q*. A cathected neuron behaves in the same way regardless of whether the original source of its *Q* was exogenous or endogenous.

The implications of this are very important because they lead to a generalization about "spontaneously" produced mental activity. There are only two sources of *Q* input into the nervous system: the external world via the Phi system, and the internal bodily processes via the nuclear Psi system. This means that all mental activity must be initiated and sustained by energy emanating from either the external world or the internal needs of the body. Any mental activity not instigated by the former must originate in the latter, and therefore mental acts that are "spontaneous" (i.e., not elicited by immediately present external stimuli) must be assumed to arise from the internal needs of the body. Such activity is instigated by *Q* that enters the system through nuclear Psi, and the neural paths it follows upon entering the system must be essentially those laid down in the past by experiences of satisfaction. This means that all self-induced mental activity must be initiated by the establishment of wishful cathexes. A deduction from Freud's system, therefore, is that *all self-induced mental activity may be interpreted at one level or another as wishful thinking.*

The Omega System and the Ego

The capacity of the nervous system for wishful cathexis has both positive and negative potential consequences for the survival of the organism. On the positive side, the wishful cathexis provides an indicator of what ought to be sought in the external world to meet the internal need; when one is hungry, the wishful cathexis of "food" indicates that a search for food should be initiated. Thus wishful cathexes reflect past learning about how needs can be satisfied. On the negative side, however, confusion is added by the fact that a mantle Psi neuron may now become invested with *Q* from either exogenous or endogenous sources. Since discharges into the musculature result from *any* hypercathexis, regardless of the source of the *Q* involved, it is now possible for wishful cathexes to build up sufficiently in mantle Psi neurons to initiate inappropriate discharges. The example of eating behavior may be used to illustrate this confusion.

When eating behavior occurs, it is the result of hypercathexes of neurons representing "food," "eating," or the like. Under normal circumstances, the hypercathexes take place because real food is present in the external environment; its *Q* enters the nervous system and results in a perceptual cathexis of mantle Psi. As mantle Psi becomes hypercathected, discharges occur and the specific behaviors appropriate to eating—sucking, chewing, swallowing, etc.—are released. This is an appropriate and adaptive sequence of events. It is not adaptive, however, when the hypercathexes result from a wish for food rather than the perception of food. Yet this result is made possible by the strong associations between nuclear Psi and mantle Psi engendered by prior experiences of satisfaction. The nervous system as described so far has no mechanism for differentiating between external reality and a memory of external reality, and thus eating behavior may be initiated by the presence of real food *or* by the (wishful) memory of food. An example of the latter are the sucking and swallowing movements frequently made by infants who actually have no food in their mouths. They have confused a wishful cathexis with a perceptual one.

To function adaptively, of course, a mature human being must be able to discriminate adequately between his wishes and reality; otherwise he expends so much energy in wishful activity that he accommodates insufficiently to the real world. It is in the interests of an organism to correlate its neural discharges with the presence of both wish *and* reality at the same time. The best time to eat is when one is hungry and food is available at the same time.

Freud postulated two components of the mature nervous system to allow for this kind of adaptation. First, he postulated the existence of a separate system of neurons—the *Omega system*—which responded to exogenous but not to endogenous stimulation. This system provided the indicator of reality necessary to allow the nervous system to differentiate perceptual from wishful cathexes. Second, he postulated the gradual development of an *ego*,[7] a neural agency whose function is to inhibit discharges until perceptual and wishful cathexes are simultaneously present in the same neurons. Acting in concert, the Omega system and the ego allow the organism to adapt its actions to the requirements of its inner needs as well as to external reality.

The problem of conceptualizing the Omega system was a difficult one for Freud, and he himself was not completely happy with the final theory. When he originally began to construct his hypothetical model of the mind he hoped to be able to complete the task by postulating only *quantitative* variables. He was successful in this for the part of the model that has been described so far; all of the differentiations and divisions of labor within the system as it has been described are attributable solely to the presence of differing degrees of cathexes at differing times and locations. When it came time to specify the neurological events necessary for discriminating actual perceptions of events from memories of events, however, it was impossible to do so simply in terms of variations in quantities of *Q*. *Q* originating from both exogenous and endogenous sources had to be functionally identical, since both kinds of *Q* are capable of initiating discharges. The only way Freud could find to get around this impasse was to postulate a new system that registers the *qualitative* aspects of external stimulation. Thus when the nervous system simultaneously records an impression of quality as well as quantity, this serves as an indication that the *Q* is originating in an external source.

Freud assumed that the unique attributes of external stimulation detected by the nervous system are its variable temporal qualities, or *periods*. The exact nature of period is not specified by Freud, but presumably it has something to do with the fact that most external stimuli consist of patterns of vibrations, waves of differing frequencies, etc., and therefore have temporal characteristics that may be detected by certain kinds of

[7] The German term that Freud actually employed was *das Ich*, literally, "the I."

receptor neurons. Period is absent from memories, and this accounts for the difference between a perception and a memory. Freud postulated the existence of a separate set of neurons—the Omega neurons—which become cathected by period rather than *Q*. Their cathexis indicates the presence of exogenous stimulation and on a subjective psychological level results in the phenomenon of *consciousness*.

The Omega system is clearly not the strong point of the "Project" from an esthetic point of view, since it adds little to the elegance of the over-all model. The Omega neurons seem almost an afterthought, and they contrast with the parsimonious and tightly reasoned concepts that constitute the other parts of the model. Freud himself seems to have regarded the Omega system somewhat wryly, since the name "Omega" occurred to him in a humorous way. The first name he had thought of for the system was the "W system," with *W* standing for the German word meaning "perception" (*Wahrnehmung*). He then felt that since the Phi and Psi systems had been provided with Greek names, this new one ought to be similarly dignified. Omega is the Greek letter that most closely resembles a written W, so that was the name Freud chose.

In spite of their lack of theoretical elegance, the Omega neurons nevertheless added an important feature to Freud's model. The ability to differentiate reality from fantasy is unquestionably an important aspect of effective human functioning, and Freud had to account for it. The Omega system was one hypothetical neural mechanism that could do so.

The ego, as a generalized inhibitor of discharge, is more easily conceptualized within the prior framework of the "Project." The ego is constituted by several neural mechanisms that have in common the attribute of facilitating frequent transmissions of small amounts of *Q* throughout the nervous system. Thus the ego tends to disperse *Q* evenly throughout the network, preventing the build-up of hypercathexes in isolated areas. A hypothetical example will illustrate the functioning of an ego.

Assume the existence of a very rudimentary nervous system,

consisting only of three neurons that are separated from one another by strong resistances at their contact barriers. New quantities of excitation arriving in the system will thus tend to concentrate in the single neurons they enter, rapidly hypercathecting them and initiating discharges. If each neuron is capable of retaining one unit of *Q* before becoming hypercathected, then one unit of *Q* input into a single neuron of the system may be sufficient to initiate discharge. Now, by way of contrast, assume a system whose three neurons can freely transmit *Q* among themselves. In this system new *Q* will not simply accumulate in the neuron that receives it but will disperse evenly among the three neurons. No single neuron will approach a state of hypercathexis until both of the others do as well, and the system will be able to contain almost three units of *Q* before it permits a discharge to occur. The first system, with its minimal ability to inhibit discharge, is described in Freud's terminology as having a "weak ego." The second system, maximally able to delay discharge, has a "strong ego."

It is now possible to specify the characteristics of a normal human nervous system that make for a strong ego. First, a system that is precathected evenly and in moderate amounts will tend to disperse new inputs of *Q* evenly throughout itself. As new *Q* enters a particular neuron, the precathexes in adjoining neurons pull some of it toward themselves. Thus if cathexis becomes substantially greater in a single neuron than in its moderately cathected neighbors, some of its excess *Q* can be transmitted to them. An evenly distributed pattern of *Q* throughout the nervous system is therefore one component of a strong ego. In general, the strength of the ego is directly proportional to its total amount of evenly distributed *Q*, since greater precathexes will produce lessened resistances between neurons.

A second factor determining the strength of an ego is the pre-existing pattern of resistances at the contact barriers. If a nervous system has had considerable and varied early "experience," in which transmissions occurred between many different pairs of neurons, then that system is maximally predisposed to disperse new *Q* inputs along the previously used pathways. Such dispersals will prevent *Q* from concentrating in individual neurons, and therefore discharge will be inhibited.

In summary, the two factors that contribute to a strong inhibiting ego are 1) a pattern of excitation that is evenly distributed in moderate amounts throughout the system, and 2) a past history of frequent transmissions between many different pairs of neurons. It should be noted that if the latter condition is met, its consequence is to assure that new *Q* entering the system will distribute itself in general conformity to the first condition. Thus the two factors are interrelated, and the ego is created by the systematic interplay of the two general neuronal tendencies cited earlier as enabling the organism to meet its endogenous needs by manipulating the environment effectively. This similarity is no coincidence, for *ego* is simply the formal term Freud provided for the neural organization that makes possible adaptive, realistic functioning.

The Primary and Secondary Processes

It is important to note that the strength of an ego may vary considerably. First and most obviously, it varies in a developmental sense. An immature nervous system has virtually no ego because it has had little prior experience to wear down resistances at selected contact barriers and thus open itself up to the even distribution of cathexes. As the system matures it becomes increasingly capable of dispersing *Q* through the prefacilitated channels created by past neural transmissions. Generally speaking, then, the ego of a mature system is stronger than the ego of a young one.

But even the ego of a mature nervous system may vary in strength, depending upon the amount of *Q* it contains. If there is no *Q* in the ego, the only reduced resistances are those due to previous transmissions. If there is much evenly dispersed *Q*, the resistances are further decreased and the inhibiting power of the ego is increased. Thus a mature system's ego may be "cathected" and strong at one moment but "uncathected" and weak at another, depending on the total amount of *Q* at its disposal.

An extremely important part of the "Project" was devoted to working out the implications of strong and weak egos for mental functioning in general. Freud hypothesized two ideal modes of mental activity: the *primary process* is characteristic of a system with a weak ego, and the *secondary process* is made possible by a strong, inhibiting ego. The choice of names was dictated by the fact that the primary process occurs first in time, since immature organisms are incapable of the secondary process. Freud cited four major dimensions on which the primary and secondary processes contrast with one another. It should be noted that these are all *continua* rather than absolute categories, and that "pure" primary or secondary process functioning is rarely observed in reality. But mental activity may be classified as "more primary process" or "more secondary process," depending on where it falls on these dimensions.

The first and most obvious dimension is that of immediacy of discharge. A strong ego is capable of inhibiting indiscriminate or inappropriate discharges, whereas a weak one is not. Therefore the primary process is generally characterized by *immediate discharge,* the secondary process by *delayed discharge.* Psychologically, this distinction may be translated into a tendency toward impulsive action and a need for immediate gratification in the primary process, and a tolerance for delay of action or gratification in the secondary process.

The second dimension involves the orientation of the nervous system toward reality. If the ego is strong, discharges are generally inhibited. Thus action by the organism may be postponed until the nervous system receives a signal that a response is both desirable (as indicated by a wishful cathexis of mantle Psi) and realistically possible (as indicated by an indication of quality in the Omega neurons). If the ego is weak, however, the indications of reality have no significance because the system is unable to delay discharge. Wishful cathexes will be permitted to accumulate and initiate numerous discharges. Thus the primary process tends to be dominated by wishful considerations, while the secondary process is strongly oriented to the demands and constraints of external reality. Though Freud did not use these specific terms in the "Project," in later writings he was to say that the primary process is governed by the *pleasure principle*, the secondary process by the *reality principle*. The logic of these terms is obvious. Freud regarded the orientation toward reality as the single most important criterion of primary or secondary process in the "Project," and he frequently used the term "a primary process" to denote any action unattuned to reality.

The other two dimensions defining primary and secondary process modes of functioning concern the economics of energy flow and storage within the nervous system. The principal energic fact about the secondary process, of course, is that it is made possible by a highly cathected ego. This means that a relatively large total amount of energy, or *Q*, is present in the nervous system, though it is spread evenly throughout. Most of this *Q*, moreover, is *bound* or *quiescent* within the system; that is, it does not move about the system itself, but instead remains stored within individual neurons. Its being bound facilitates the spreading about and subsequent binding of still newer *Q* to enter the system. The situation is very different in the primary process, which occurs when the ego is weak. Since the ego is not cathected, there is very little *Q* stored within the system, and the total amount of energy involved in primary processes is therefore less than in secondary processes. Of the total energy that is present, however, a much larger proportion is *mobile* than in the secondary process; the *Q* does not tend to stay long in any one place, but quickly moves along the pathways laid down by past experiences of satisfaction (thus converting need cathexes into wishful cathexes) and out of the system entirely via discharge.

It is also important to note that the size of individual energy transmissions is likely to be greater in the primary process. In the secondary process, the strong ego ensures that any new *Q* entering the system has *several* available channels along which it may be transmitted and dispersed. Thus Q from an individual neuron may be sent out in several different directions at once, with each individual transmission being relatively small. In the primary process, a weak ego provides few if any channels for the dispersal of new Q, and such transmissions as do occur are likely to be relatively massive ones. Thus in the secondary process energy transmissions are frequent but small in magnitude, whereas in the primary process they are relatively less frequent but very large. Table 1 summarizes all of these major formal differences between the two processes.

PRIMARY PROCESS	SECONDARY PROCESS
1. Presses for immediate discharge.	1. Tolerates delay of discharge.
2. Responds to wishes (the pleasure principle).	2. Responds to reality (the reality principle).
3. Has proportionately large amounts of mobile cathexes.	3. Has proportionately large amounts of bound cathexes.
4. Transmits Q in large amounts.	4. Transmits Q in small amounts.

TABLE 1

Freud believed that the "normal" mental activity of a mature human being was secondary process. All the acts of perceiving, judging, planning, anticipating, and calculating that people perform every day are examples of realistic, ego-controlled functioning. From an adaptive point of view such functioning is highly desirable. A substantial portion of the "Project" is given over to the description of precise neurological interactions among the ego, Phi, Psi, and Omega that could account for such sophisticated and complicated behaviors. Freud's speculation is ingenious, and represents a *tour de force* of secondary process functioning itself. Over the long term, however, such speculation has not retained its interest, and Freud himself seldom returned to such considerations after the "Project." What was of much more enduring interest was a consideration of "abnormal" mental events—those hiatuses in secondary process functioning that bedevil everyone from time to time, and some people consistently. In general Freud interpreted these abnormal behaviors as reversions to the primary process, following a weakening or decathexis of the ego. He was especially interested in interpreting hysteria in this way, thus integrating his clinical insights into the illness with his knowledge of neurology.

Hysteria and the Primary Process

Freud saw three major attributes of hysteria that he wished to account for in terms of his neurological model. First, there was the fact that the symptoms invariably seemed to be caused by *pathogenic ideas,* by thoughts and memories that managed to express themselves physically as conversion symptoms in spite of the absence of organic pathogens. Second, there was the tendency of the conversion symptoms to bear *symbolic* but indirect relationships to the pathogenic ideas, with the result that the pathogenic ideas themselves remained unconscious. That is, the symptoms seemed to be substitutes for conscious recognition of the pathogenic ideas. And third, the specific symbolic relationship of a symptom to its pathogenic ideas seemed *overdetermined.* Each symptom seemed to represent several different pathogenic ideas at the same time.

At a purely descriptive level, it is evident that the model in the "Project" was very appropriate for explaining these hysterical characteristics. To begin with, hysterical conversions are obviously primary process mechanisms because they are created by ideas and memories and bear no logical relationship to the contingencies of external reality. Thus the symptoms must be the results of discharges initiated by large components of endogenous stimulation. This implies that some subversion of the inhibiting capacities of the ego takes place in hysteria, allowing these primary process discharges to occur.

The symbolic nature of the conversion symptom was easily translatable into the terminology of the "Project" as an automatic and immediate *displacement* of cathexis from the neurons representing the pathogenic idea to those representing its substitute. As an example, consider Anna O.'s hydrophobia, which resulted from her observing a dog drinking from a glass. Presumably, every time Anna saw a glass of water it reminded her of the pathogenic experience and therefore resulted in the cathexis of the neuron representing her memory of the dog drinking from a glass. This neuron did not retain its cathexis, however, but immediately transmitted it—"displaced" it—to another neuron representing her feeling of disgust. This displacement was instantaneous because, in a sense, the original neuron had become permeable and unable to retain cathexis. The displaced cathexis collected in the second neuron until it initiated discharge, resulting in the muscular constrictions that made it impossible to drink. Anna became *conscious* of the memory represented by the second neuron (the memory of feelings of disgust and tightness in the throat), and not of that represented by the first (the pathogenic idea), because only in the former did *Q* ever come to rest. The *Q* was displaced so rapidly from the first neuron that consciousness could never be directed there but was deflected instead to the second, symbolic neuron.

All this seems perfectly reasonable at a descriptive level, since a rapid displacement of cathexis is a plausible mechanical explanation for the unconscious symbolic aspects of hysteria. However, the model does not suggest any immediate reason *why* this displacement should take place at all. That is, no property of the nervous system has been suggested in the model to explain why a pathogenic neuron should so automatically displace its cathexes. Since it is the rapid displacement that renders the pathogenic idea unconscious, the previous statement is tantamount to the assertion that the model has not explained the causes of repression. Unfortunately, Freud never was able to specify a neural mechanism that would satisfactorily explain the reasons for the displacement of consciousness. He simply assumed that it must occur, though he could not supply a neural rationale for it. It was on this point, more than any other, that the "Project" failed in its mechanistic ambitions.

For the phenomenon of overdetermination, however, Freud was once again able to offer a complete and adequate neural explanation. Consider as an example the patient described in the preceding chapter, whose symptom of hand twitching was found to be overdetermined by a group of memories involving her hands. Assume here for simplicity's sake that there were only two pathogenic ideas: the memory of rubbing her uncle's back, and the memory of being hit on the hand with a strap. In Figure 6, these memories are represented by the neurons marked "uncle" and "strap," respectively. Each of these memories has a number of closely associated ideas, indicated in the figure by connected neurons. Since both memories involved the hands in some way, a memory involving hands is a *common associate* for the two memories. The neuron marked "hands" represents it in Figure 6. Assume now that the memories of "uncle" and "strap" both begin to become cathected and to transmit their Q to their associates. In this condition, "hands," as the common associate of both ideas, receives a double dose of Q. In the absence of a strong inhibiting ego its cathexis may rapidly increase until it discharges. The result of the discharge is the muscular contraction of the hand that constitutes the symptom.

It is now easy to see that overdetermination is another common consequence of a weak ego; i.e., of the primary proc-

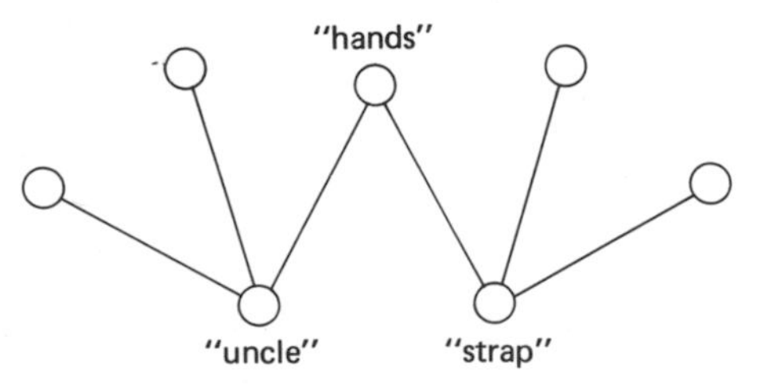

FIGURE 6

ess. In the absence of a general inhibitor of hypercathexis, neurons with many associates will frequently discharge because they receive *Q* from many sources.

Assessment of the "Project"

Freud's stated goal when he set out to construct his model of the mind was to integrate his clinical and neurological knowledge, specifically by accounting for both normal functioning and hysteria in neurological terms. Although he constructed an ingenious model that was fully consistent with the neurological knowledge of his day, he was only partly successful in achieving his stated aim. The major flaw in his hypothetical system was probably its failure to deal adequately with repression. It did not provide a mechanism to account for the automatic and immediate displacement of *Q* from one neuron to another. The "Project's" explanation of hysteria also undoubtedly suffered because Freud in 1895 still accepted the clinically erroneous "seduction theory" of the genesis of hysteria.

In assessing the "Project" today, of course, it must be remembered that it was a highly speculative work based on a turn-of-the-century conception of the nervous system. Some of Freud's assumptions about the nature of the nervous system are regarded as suspect by present-day neurologists, and this obviously bears on the truth value one should assign to the "Project." Experiments attempting to "locate" specific memories in specific single neurons, for example, have not met with complete success, and thus it may be that Freud's key assumption about the nature of memory storage was incorrect. On the other hand, it also appears that Freud may have correctly anticipated in his speculations certain qualities of the nervous system that were not conclusively discovered until many years later. His hypothesis about the variable cathexis of individual neurons, for example, has been described by one prominent modern neurologist as "one of those strokes of luck or genius which in retrospect appears uncanny,"[8] since it has been recently discovered that such a phenomenon probably actually occurs. To summarize, then, it must be said that the literal accuracy of Freud's model as a representation of the nervous system has not been established. It is undoubtedly incorrect in many respects, but perhaps prophetically accurate in others.

Its literal inaccuracy and explanatory failures notwithstanding, the "Project" was a highly productive venture for Freud for two reasons. First, in the course of constructing the model Freud developed several concepts that seemed correct in their *psychological* implications, quite apart from their accuracy on a neurological level. These concepts, including cathexis, primary and secondary processes, the ego, bound and mobile psychic energy, displacement, and the basic notion of the mind as an energy processing organ, retained major importance in his theory for the rest of his life. Second, the "Project" was important for Freud because in the course of its construction he became seriously concerned for the first time about the nature of *dreams*. Only a few pages of the "Project" were given over to dreams, but they provided the starting point for a series of investigations that five years later culminated in Freud's masterpiece, *The Interpretation of Dreams*. These investigations, as well as the ideas from the "Project" that inspired them, are described in the next chapter.

SUGGESTED FURTHER READINGS

The "Project for a Scientific Psychology" is included in Freud's *The Origins of Psycho-Analysis* (New York, Basic Books, 1954). This fascinating work consists of extensive excerpts from the correspondence with Fliess, including letters and notes as well as manuscript drafts. The volume as a whole provides an insider's view of the development of psychoanaly-

[8] Karl H. Pribram, "The Neuropsychology of Sigmund Freud," in A. J. Bachrach, ed., *Experimental Foundations of Clinical Psychology* (New York, Basic Books, 1962), p. 445.

sis, since it includes the first, tentative statements to a friend and confidant of many ideas that were later to become well-known components of Freud's theory.

A thorough investigation of the influence of Freud's neurological teachers on the development of the "Project" is provided by Peter Amacher in *Freud's Neurological Education and Its Influence on Psychoanalytic Theory* (New York, International Universities Press, 1965). An up-to-date assessment of the "Project" by a neurologist is Karl H. Pribram's "The Neuropsychology of Sigmund Freud," in A. J. Bachrach, ed., *Experimental Foundations of Clinical Psychology* (New York, Basic Books, 1962).

4
Dreams

When Freud finished writing the "Project," he had carried his attempt to account for psychological phenomena in neurological terms almost as far as it would go. Ingenious though the neurological model was, Freud found that it was simply impossible to provide a completely mechanistic explanation for everything that happens in the mind. Freud undoubtedly had the "Project" in mind when he wrote in 1915, "Every endeavour to think of ideas as stored up in nerve-cells and of excitations as passing along nerve-fibres, has miscarried completely."[1] This did not mean Freud had abandoned his mechanist belief that physiological processes must *ultimately* be responsible for psychological events, but it did mean he had decided that not enough was yet known about neurophysiology to work out the precise relationships. Attempts to speculate on such relationships led to blind alleys, so Freud turned his attention to the construction of a "psychological" model of the mind—one whose components were defined in purely psychological terms bearing no necessary relationships to anatomically distinct parts of the nervous system.

Freud's transition from a neurological to a psychological level of analysis did not occur abruptly. It was a gradual change that developed over a period of several years. The most important factor in this transitional and crucial phase of

[1] *Standard Edition*, Vol. XIV, p. 174.

Freud's career was the development of a theory about the nature of dreams. The study of dreams helped him to bridge the gap from a neurological to a psychological point of view in conceptualizing human behavior.

The Origin of the Dream Theory

Freud's theory of dreams was unique among his major theoretical works in that its most important components emerged suddenly and almost spontaneously, in a kind of "Eureka" experience. The principal idea that arose in such a sudden manner, and that he later referred to in a letter to Fliess as the "Secret of Dreams," was the notion that *all dreams represent the fulfillment of wishes.* This "secret" occurred to Freud one day in July 1895, when he successfully interpreted one of his own dreams.

In the summer of 1895 Freud's major intellectual effort was the construction of the "Project." It seems that in the course of his very intense speculation and theorizing about neurological processes and their relationships with psychological functioning, he found himself irresistibly drawn into the consideration of many topics that had initially been without particular interest; among them, as was noted in the previous chapter, were sleep and dreams.

The discussion of sleep and dreams in the "Project" is prefaced by the description of three crucial assumptions about the essential nature of sleep. First, Freud noted that the onset of sleep usually presupposes the minimization of exogenous stimulation. The common preparations one makes for going to sleep all serve this tendency: the bedroom is darkened, extraneous noises and distractions are minimized, a constant and comfortable temperature is established, and in general the would-be sleeper closes himself off from the external world and its stimulation. A consequence of this for the sleeper's nervous system, of course, is that the input of exogenous Q is greatly reduced if not eliminated altogether. Any energy activating the nervous system during sleep, then, must consist mainly of *Q* that was stored in the ego prior to sleep, or that arises during the night from the endogenous sources of stimulation.

But even that *Q* is reduced during sleep. The second major assumption Freud made about the state of sleep was that it is characterized by a depleted ego. The evidence supporting this assumption consisted primarily of the observation that the performance of highly satisfying consummatory acts tends to be conducive to a state of sleep. Thus an individual who has just copulated or who has just eaten a large and satisfying meal is likely to feel sleepy. Such satisfying activity must be triggered by the discharge of significant amounts of *Q* from the system, and when it is performed it temporarily shuts off endogenous sources of *Q*. Consummatory activities thus serve both to deplete the ego *and* to inhibit endogenous stimulation. The line of reasoning surrounding Freud's second assumption may be summarized as follows: sleep follows consummatory activity; consummatory activity creates a state of relative depletion of the ego; therefore sleep takes place when the ego is depleted. This formulation, though having some face validity, does not take into account those occasions when consummatory activity is not followed by sleep, or when sleep is not preceded by consummatory activity.

A more substantial body of data supports Freud's third major assumption: that during the state of sleep the muscular system of the sleeper is in a state of inhibition, as evidenced by the obvious immobility of most sleepers. In Freud's neurological system, this inhibition was conceptualized as the result of a blockage of the normal paths of discharge from the neurons into the musculature. That is, the neurons were viewed as being physically incapable during sleep of discharging into the motor apparatus and thereby initiating overt movements.[2]

Freud's earliest dream theory was made up of the logical con-

[2] Recent research has shown that large muscle movements do occur during sleep, but never during that stage of the sleep cycle most frequently associated with dreaming. Thus Freud's assumption is still reasonable insofar as it pertains to his theory of dreams.

sequences of these three assumptions, deduced in the following manner. In the period immediately after an individual falls asleep, mental activity in general is reduced to a minimum. This is because the external sources of *Q* have been shut off, the endogenous needs have been temporarily sated, and even many of the stored-up cathexes in the ego have been discharged. Thus there is little energy available to activate the nervous system. As the night proceeds, however, this state of quiescence gradually comes to an end because endogenous sources of stimulation have not been shut off as effectively as external ones. One cannot "turn off" an internal organic process as one can a light or other potentially distracting external stimulus. Internal needs can be satisfied only on a temporary basis, and they recur periodically.

Thus as the night of sleep proceeds, endogenously originating *Q* gradually begins to enter the nervous system and to cathect nuclear Psi. Furthermore, once these cathexes occur they cannot be dealt with and restrained in the usual manner. Since the ego was largely decathected just before the onset of sleep, the transmission of new endogenous *Q* to other neurons is not facilitated by simultaneous cathexes. The only paths that the newly accumulating *Q* can follow are therefore the pre-existing ones established by previous experiences of satisfaction. Thus the need cathexes in nuclear Psi are rapidly converted into wishful cathexes, because the only open paths of transmission are those connecting the neurons representing the needs with those representing the memories of satisfaction of the needs.

Since mental activity during sleep must follow the paths of wishful cathexes, and since dreams are the most vivid kind of somnolent mental activity, it follows that, as Freud put it, "Dreams are *the fulfillments of wishes*."[3] Here was the rationale for the monumentally important "Secret of Dreams" that Freud described for the first time in the "Project."

But this is not the whole story of mental activity during sleep. The wishful cathexes, once they occur, have very little

[3] *The Origins of Psycho-Analysis* (New York, Basic Books, 1954), p. 402.

opportunity to disperse themselves throughout the nervous system because of the decathected state of the ego. Thus *Q* is destined to build up in considerable concentrations in the neural centers representing memories of past satisfactions. Since the *Q* is endogenous in origin, and therefore incapable of being fled from, primary process discharges become inevitable when cathexes build up beyond the thresholds for discharge. That is, with the ever-increasing accumulation of wishful cathexes, and without the presence of a strong inhibiting ego, the thresholds for discharge into the musculature are quickly surpassed.

A theoretical dilemma arises here, however, because of the muscular immobility characteristic of the state of sleep. Freud assumed that the normal paths of discharge from the neurons into the musculature are closed off during sleep. Thus the hypercathected neurons representing the satisfaction of wishes cannot activate the large muscles of the body by their discharge, in spite of the fact that the economics of the nervous system demand the occurrence of primary process discharges. To resolve this dilemma, Freud proposed an ingenious hypothesis. He suggested that the discharges in sleep, instead of following the normal, "progressive" direction from Psi into the musculature, follow a "retrogressive" path back into Phi and the perceptual apparatus. This retrogression is made possible by the state of sleep. The large quantity of exogenous stimulation that almost constantly flows into the system via Phi in the waking state has been shut off, and thus the channels connecting Phi with Psi—normally occupied by *inwardly* flowing *Q*—are largely dormant. The normal effect of inwardly flowing *Q* is to inhibit retrogressive discharge, because any retrogressive flow would have to "swim against the current." In sleep this inhibition is absent and retrogression can occur more easily.

The result of this retrogressive flow and eventual discharge into the perceptual apparatus, said Freud, is a subjective experience identical with the real perception of an object in the external world. That is to say, the result is an hallucination, and the sleeper undergoes the vivid perceptual sensations that we know as a dream. A retrogressive discharge thus produces a realistic perceptual experience, instead of the motor activation that derives from progressive discharge.

It is especially important to note that according to this formulation dreams are the direct results of primary processes, first and foremost because they are almost exclusively the result of internally originating wishes rather than external reality. Since exogenously originating *Q* has been barred from the nervous system during sleep, external reality cannot possibly be attended to, and secondary processes are therefore impossible. In addition, the enfeebled state of the ego during sleep means that the energy that is present in the system tends to be mobile, transmitted in relatively large units, and therefore productive of a large number of discharges. All of this, of course, means that there must be a basic similarity between the formal characteristics of dreams and psychopathological symptoms, since both are the results of primary processes.

A brief example taken from one of Freud's own dreams will suffice to illustrate some of these similarities. A small part of the dream as Freud described it went as follows: "O. [a colleague and friend of Freud's] has given Irma [a patient of Freud's] an injection of propyl. I then see 'trimethylamin' very vividly before me and hallucinate its formula."[4] This brief dream fragment is typical in a number of ways of adult dream experience. First, its content was patently nonsensical. The injection of propyl was a ridiculous medical procedure; it certainly was not something that Freud had ever had occasion to observe in his real-life medical practice. The second element of the dream fragment—the hallucination of the word *trimethylamin* and its chemical formula—was even more bizarre from the standpoint of waking consciousness. It represented an abrupt change in the dream narrative, bearing little logical relationship to the first dream element. The only possible logical connection lay in the fact that both propyl and trimethylamin are organic chemical compounds, but this fact obviously did not satisfactorily explain the dream sequence. Abrupt and

[4] *Ibid.*, p. 403.

apparently nonsensical changes in the sequence of experience are common characteristics of many dreams, of course.

Freud discovered that his dream made considerably better sense after he had free associated to it in much the same manner that his hysterical patients free associated to their symptoms. Using the dream fragment as a starting point, Freud soon came up with two important associations. The first was that Irma's illness, undiagnosed in the actual dream, must have been of a sexual nature. The second was the recollection of a conversation about sexual chemistry that he had recently had with Fliess, in which his attention had been drawn to the role of trimethylamin. Both of these ideas had great personal significance for Freud, since they represented concerns and personal relationships that were very important to him; they seemed infinitely more important and relevant to his life than the overt dream content taken by itself. He therefore concluded that these two ideas should properly be considered to be part of the total dream content.

Thus the dream fragment was found to consist of two elements that were initially conscious and two that were initially unconscious. The conscious elements were A) the injection of Irma with propyl, and B) the hallucination of trimethylamin; the unconscious elements were C) the thought about the sexual nature of Irma's illness, and D) the recollection of the conversation with Fliess about sexual chemistry. As Freud thought about these four elements, he realized that the one that by itself possessed the least personal significance, and which seemed oddest in the overall dream context, was B, the hallucination of trimethylamin. Its only importance was that it was a *common associate* of the unconscious elements C and D, as well as the conscious thought A, because it too concerned an organic chemical compound.

If each of the four elements is thought of as being represented by a specific neuron, the neurological state that Freud assumed to underlie his dream can be reconstructed. B was initially an indifferent idea, so it began in an uncathected state. In the course of the dream, however, A became hypercathected and C and D also became excited, though not to the point of discharge. B, however, as a common associate of all three of the others, was capable of receiving transmissions from three sources. It was then a simple matter for its "borrowed" cathexis to surpass the threshold for discharge, resulting in the hallucination of trimethylamin. Thus "trimethylamin" became a part of the dream because it bore a faint relationship to the notion of the propyl injection, and especially because it conveniently "symbolized" two other ideas that were very important to Freud.

This whole configuration of relationships greatly resembled the phenomenon of *overdetermination* that Freud had observed in hysteria. Hysterical symptoms were said to be overdetermined when they bore symbolic relationships to several pathogenic memories at the same time. In much the same way the conscious dream thought "trimethylamin" was overdetermined by the number of important but unconscious dream thoughts of which it was a common associate. Freud suggested that many apparently bizarre components of dream ideation in general could be accounted for by the mechanisms responsible for overdetermination.

In the "Project" itself, Freud did not go beyond this brief analysis of dreams. He simply established that they are wish fulfillments, follow the primary process, and have certain structural similarities to psychopathological symptoms. His primary accomplishment was his discovery that dreams, like symptoms, possess a peculiar kind of "illogical logic" that renders them potentially interpretable and meaningful.

The Influence of Dream Theory on Psychopathological Theory

In the years immediately following the completion of the "Project" Freud found himself increasingly preoccupied with the nature of dreams. Having discovered that dreams were interpretable in much the same way that neurotic symptoms were, he began to subject large numbers of his own dreams as well as his patients' dreams to analysis by free association. As he did this, a number of new conclusions about the dream processes began to occur to him, and these conclusions were to have major significance in shaping his emerging new theories about psychopathology and human nature in general.

In the first place, it quickly became apparent that the wish fulfillment in dreams is not always obvious. In fact, a considerable number of dreams (such as nightmares and anxiety dreams) seemed on the surface to represent the very opposite of a wish fulfillment. But Freud discovered that if only the free association process goes on long enough, wishful ideas are bound to emerge and reveal themselves as the true motivators of the dreams.

Often the wishful ideas did not emerge easily, however, even after extensive free association. Just as hysterics put up resistance to the remembering of the traumatic scenes underlying their illnesses, so dreamers did not seem to want to acknowledge the important wishful thoughts responsible for their dreams. Only with persistence, patience, and often the experiencing of extreme anxiety could they express many of the wishful ideas indirectly symbolized by the conscious dream content.

As resistance of this type was overcome in large numbers of cases, Freud made an even more astonishing discovery. It seemed that in every case the resisted wish related to sexual ideas dating from childhood, such as incestuous wishes towards parents or siblings, or "perverted" sexual acts involving the mouth and anus as well as the genitals. No wonder the dreamers were loath to admit such wishes! In time Freud came to believe that these childhood sexual wishes lay behind virtually *every* dream, and that they could inevitably be uncovered if the free association process were carried out long enough and persistently enough.[5]

[5] One of the most frequent criticisms of Freud's theory centers around this point. Critics have noted—with some justification—that if a person free associates long and persistently enough, virtually anything is likely to appear. Thus *any* hypothesis that one might have can be "confirmed" by

Freud's discovery that childhood sexual wishes lay behind dreams was one more bit of evidence leading to the conclusion that the basic mechanisms of dreams and hysterical symptoms were similar. There were *some* differences, of course, the most obvious being that symptoms were relatively long-lasting, while dream experiences were transient; and that symptoms involved primary process discharges into the musculature, while dreams were the result of retrogressive discharges into the perceptual apparatus. These differences notwithstanding, Freud concluded that the really basic structural and defensive aspects of the two phenomena were sufficiently alike that dreams could be regarded as miniature but authentic models of neurotic processes. Once this conclusion was reached, the study of neurosis was greatly facilitated because dreams could be regarded as appropriate "laboratory samples" of the subject. Dreams were much more abundant than neuroses, and therefore more accessible for study. And since Freud himself was a frequent recaller of his dreams, he could serve as his own best subject.

It seems likely that Freud's discovery of the essential similarity between dream processes and neurotic processes contrib-

---

the free association method; if one believes that dreams or symptoms are caused by ideas about birdbaths, to take a ridiculous example, one only has to allow the free association process to go on until birdbaths are mentioned—as inevitably they must be if the process lasts long enough—and the hypothesis will seem to be confirmed.

Freud was aware of this kind of criticism, and he attempted to deal with it in a number of ways. To begin with, he pointed out that *initially* he had not hypothesized that free associations of a sexual nature would turn out to be important. He simply noted that such associations arose spontaneously with much greater frequency than would be expected by chance, and without any suggestion by him to the patients that such *should be* the case. Second, and more important, he noted that when the sexual associations emerged, dramatic consequences were likely to follow. In his hysterical patients, for example, abreaction and subsequent symptom relief were more likely to follow associations to childhood sexuality than associations to, say, birdbaths. In the case of dreams, sexual associations were more likely to be followed by a "shock of recognition" or some other dramatic indicator of significance than would be expected by chance.

uted to a major change in his theory of psychopathology. When the dream theory began to develop in 1895, Freud still strongly believed that hysteria was the result of childhood sexual traumas, usually at the hands of close relatives. Freud gradually became suspicious of this "seduction theory," however, for three general reasons. First, he noted that often his patients' difficulties did not cease completely upon recollection of the seduction scenes. Sometimes their symptoms persisted, although perhaps with diminished intensity, and their resistance to further free association increased. If the memories of seduction had been truly at the heart of the neuroses, then these nagging after-effects should not have occurred. Second, through other investigations Freud was becoming aware of the general unreliability of memories dating from early childhood. What seem to be very vivid memories of real occurrences in childhood often turn out to be contradicted by clearly established facts. The subjective certainty manifested by his patients in the reality of their seduction scenes could no longer be regarded as positive evidence. Finally, the seduction theory was ultimately unplausible. If it were true, it indicated the existence of a much higher frequency of perversion among fathers and uncles than one could reasonably expect, even granting the fact that sexual activity in general was much more common than good Victorians were wont to admit.

Thus the weight of evidence against the seduction theory gradually built up, and in the summer of 1897 Freud felt compelled to abandon it completely. In a remarkable letter to Fliess[6] he vividly described the curious mixture of feelings that the abandonment of the theory inspired in him. On the one hand he was very disappointed, since he had hoped to make his name as the solver of the riddle of hysteria. "Now I do not know where I am," he wrote, "as I have failed to reach theoretical understanding of repression and its play of forces." In spite of such understandable feelings of disappointment, however, he also wrote about his sense of intellectual pride and a vague optimism for the future:

[6] *Ibid.*, pp. 215–218.

Were I depressed, jaded, unclear in my mind, such doubts [about the seduction theory] might be taken for signs of weakness. But as I am in just the opposite state, I must acknowledge them to be the result of honest and effective intellectual labour, and I am proud that after penetrating so far I am still capable of such criticism. Can these doubts be only an episode on the way to further knowledge?

It is curious that I feel not in the least disgraced, though the occasion might seem to require it. Certainly I shall not tell it in Gath, or publish it in the streets of Askalon, in the land of the Philistines—but between ourselves I have a feeling more of triumph than of defeat.

Freud even seemed dimly aware of a possible source for his future triumph. Though his clinical theory of hysteria had failed, other components of his work still seemed worthwhile: "In the general collapse only the psychology [the attempt to construct a general model of the mind, as begun in the "Project"] has retained its value. The dreams still stand secure, and my beginnings in metapsychology have gone up in my estimation. It is a pity one cannot live on dream interpretation, for instance."

Freud's words were prophetic, because his developing dream theory contained a key to the eventual solution of his difficulties with the seduction theory. He had concluded that dreams were motivated by wishes. All wishes, of course, must have *some* basis in reality (one cannot wish for ice cream without having had some real experience to suggest what ice cream is), but at no point did Freud believe that the wishes expressed by dreams represent literal re-creations of real events from the past. Instead he interpreted dream-motivating wishes as *fantasies*—as imaginative productions that are *based* on real experiences, but that twist and weave them into wishful patterns far exceeding anything that has actually occurred in reality.

In 1897, then, Freud's views on hysteria and dreams resembled each other in the following ways. Dreams were exactly like hysterical symptoms in that they were primary process products, they were often overdetermined, they represented in a peculiarly symbolic way sexual ideas of a childish nature, and they were motivated by ideas that were normally unconscious. The only major difference, apart from the more innocuous consequences of dreams, was that the unconscious ideas motivating dreams were wishful fantasies, whereas the unconscious ideas responsible for hysterical symptoms were supposed to be memories of actual experiences. And it was precisely on that point of difference that the theory of hysteria was demonstrably wrong! Here then was the key to the dilemma: *why not regard the pathogenic ideas underlying hysteria as wishful fantasies also?* Then the traumatic events related by hysterics could be interpreted as associations to childhood wishes of a sexual nature, or as disguised representations of the wishes themselves. By 1898 Freud had adopted this new view of hysteric pathogenic ideas. The task of treating hysterical patients now became one of bringing childhood wishes, rather than memories, to consciousness.

Freud's new conception of hysterical pathogenic ideas emphasized one of the most important implications of the "Project." Since energy from *either* exogenous or endogenous sources can cathect neurons and result in their discharge, it follows that the nervous system does not respond only to what is "real" from an objective, external point of view. "Reality," for the nervous system, consists at varying times of varying proportions of exogenous and endogenous excitation. When the organism is functioning adaptively, according to the secondary process, more or less accurate distinctions are made between the two sources, but nevertheless all cathexes are equally "real" regardless of their origins. When the ego is weak and the primary process dominates, wishes take on what Freud called *psychic reality* and dominate the behavior of the organism. The results, be they the hallucinations of a dreamer or the conversion symptoms of an hysteric, take on a sense of subjective reality for the individual comparable to the psychic reality that initiates them. Freud came to believe that this understanding—that the deepest of human wishes and fantasies have a psychic reality just as compelling as the reality of anything experienced in the external world—was one of his greatest discoveries.

The Psychology of Dreams

The years from 1897 to 1900 were marked by great achievement for Freud. He revised and refined his theory of psychopathology along the lines already indicated, he subjected himself to the most searching and painful scrutiny in a self-analysis, and he conducted an exhaustive study of the psychology of dreams. The fruit of all this labor was *The Interpretation of Dreams*, a massive book published in 1900 that is generally regarded as Freud's masterpiece. In that work Freud not only presented a brilliant elaboration of his theory of dreams, but he also used that theory as the basis for a revised model of the mind. The new model was constructed in completely psychological terms, and as such it represented the culmination of his drift away from the neurologically oriented style of the "Project." Most of the major ideas expressed in *The Interpretation of Dreams* underwent little or no modification in Freud's lifetime, in marked contrast to other major aspects of psychoanalysis, which underwent almost constant revision as long as Freud lived. These enduring ideas will be outlined in the remainder of this chapter.

The most essential of Freud's discoveries about dreams, of course, was that while dream content taken by itself is meaningless and often ridiculous, it yields a surprising number of ideas that make very good sense indeed when made the subject of free association. In Freud's view, then, there is one dream content consisting of very basic and elemental wishes that give the dream its real meaning, and a disguised or transformed content constituted by the perceptual experience of the dream per se. The latter content—the raw dream experience taken by itself—was labeled the *manifest content* by Freud. The hidden but more significant content, consisting of the ideas behind the dream, was called the *latent content*. A large and important part of *The Interpretation of Dreams* is devoted to an examination of the precise relationships that exist between the manifest and latent contents. That is, the book attempts to explain why and how the latent content comes to be translated into the peculiar language of the manifest content. This entire process of translation was referred to by Freud as the *dream work,* and it was assumed to take place quite automatically and beyond the conscious volition of the dreamer.

One of the major characteristics of the dream work has already been described: namely, that the manifest content differs from the latent content for reasons of defense. Thoughts and wishes of an infantile and sexual nature were found to underlie dream imagery; in the terminology just introduced, the thoughts and wishes are the latent content and the dream itself the manifest content. Thus the latent content is frequently repugnant and difficult to acknowledge consciously, and the manifest content is a disguised, less unpalatable representation of it. Dreams, like hysterical symptoms, permit the covert and disguised expression of ideas too obnoxious to be acknowledged openly.

The technique by which the dream defends against the latent content is also already familiar: the manifest content *alludes* indirectly to the latent content. Thus in Freud's dream about Irma's injection, the apparently innocuous idea of "trimethylamin" was found to allude to more emotion-laden and taboo thoughts about sexuality and sexual illnesses. The technical term Freud used to denote this defensive use of allusion was *displacement.* He assumed that the energy that normally would be used to invest and activate the latent dream thought (the sexual idea) becomes *displaced* to some other idea ("trimethylamin") standing in a symbolic relationship with the latent thought. This, of course, is identical with the process of displacement postulated to occur in hysteria, in which the energy from the pathogenic idea becomes displaced onto the conversion symptom.

The process of displacement accounts for one of the most popularly known of all psychoanalytic concepts, the so-called "Freudian symbol." Freud held that because of certain commonalities in the experience of all human beings, a certain small number of images are inevitably symbols for specific latent ideas when they appear in dreams. Thus any manifest dream objects that are elongated in shape and/or capable of penetrating—e.g., swords, poles, blimps, guns, etc.—are said to be symbolic of a penis. Objects capable of acting as receptacles, like boxes, purses, caves, or pockets, for example, are symbols of the vagina. In the course of interpreting hundreds of dreams Freud compiled a miniature "dictionary" of dream symbols of this type, most of them alluding to sexual matters.

Even though a considerable number of these common dream symbols are cataloged in *The Interpretation of Dreams*, Freud warns that the majority of displacements in dreams are not susceptible to such universal interpretation: ". . . the peculiar plasticity of the psychical material (in dreams) must never be forgotten. Often enough a symbol has to be interpreted in its proper meaning and not symbolically; while on other occasions a dreamer may derive from his private memories the power to employ as sexual symbols all kinds of things which are not ordinarily employed as such."[7] Thus displacements usually derive from the idiosyncratic experience of the dreamer. "Trimethylamin," for example, could symbolize sexual thoughts only for an individual like Freud, whose experience provided associative links between sexuality and organic chemistry. Freudian symbols, then, provide simple *examples* of the results of displacement in dreams, but they constitute only a small proportion of the total number of displacements. One could never interpret an entire dream simply on the basis of Freud's miniature dictionary.

Besides displacement, Freud noted yet another "defensive" aspect of dream phenomena. He discovered that if an individual is asked to provide *two* accounts of the manifest content of the same dream, there are inevitably changes in the second version. Some changes are blatant, involving the dropping off or adding on of entire passages, while others are very subtle, con-

[7] *Standard Edition*, Vol. V, p. 352.

sisting perhaps of the simple substitution of one word or phrase for another. After observing this phenomenon many times and then going on to interpret the dreams, Freud concluded that such changes were not random, but rather were attempts to cover up "weak spots" in the dream's disguise. They went even further than the dream work in hiding the nature of the latent thoughts. If a patient omitted a certain passage when reciting a dream for the second time, for example, Freud felt sure that the omitted passage contained particularly important and "dangerous" allusions to the latent thought.

On the basis of these observations, Freud concluded that there probably is *another* point at which manifest content gets changed and distorted in a defensive way, when the dreamer tries to verbalize the dream for the first time. When a person is asked to describe the content of his dream he must translate his purely perceptual dream experience into words that will communicate its nature. This is often a difficult task, and the dreamer may grope ineffectively for words. Freud believed that changes in the essential nature of the manifest content are introduced here, just as they are between the first and second verbal accounts, and that they also serve defensive purposes. This whole process of changing and elaborating the manifest content after the actual occurrence of the dream was referred to by Freud as *secondary revision.*

Freud drew an important inference from the phenomenon of secondary revision. Since each succeeding version of the manifest content differs more widely from the latent content than the one preceding it, Freud concluded that in the waking state even the pure manifest content is too dangerous to be openly acknowledged. That is, even though the manifest content is a "censored" version of the latent content, making its points only by allusion, it has to be revised even more in the waking state to make it acceptable. Freud used the very term *censorship* to denote the psychic agency responsible for these changes, and on the basis of the above facts he concluded that its workings were as follows. The censorship clearly must be operative during the dream work itself, since the latent thoughts undergo defensive distortion as they become the manifest content. Since the manifest content itself undergoes further defensive changes via secondary revision in the waking state, however, it appeared that the censorship must be stronger in the waking state than in sleep. Therefore Freud concluded that the censoring agency *is operative but somewhat relaxed* during the state of sleep. It exercises *some* defensive control over the dream work but is lenient enough to allow at least partial and disguised expression of the latent thoughts. In the waking state the repression of the latent thoughts is more complete, indicating more effective operation of the censorship.[8] Thus the state of sleep, with its condition of relaxed censorship, provided a kind of window into the unconscious that was of inestimable value to Freud.

Returning to his consideration of the dream work proper, Freud described a phenomenon he called *condensation*, whereby two or more diverse latent dream thoughts are represented in the manifest content by a single dream symbol. Thus condensation is directly parallel to the mechanism of overdetermination in hysteria, since in both cases several unconscious ideas come to be represented by a single conscious symbol. The image of "trimethylamin" from the dream of Irma's injection provides an example of condensation as well as displacement since it was symbolic of *two* latent dream thoughts: the notion that Irma's illness was a sexual one and the recollection of a conversation with Fliess. Another example of condensation frequently employed by Freud in his lectures on dreams was the "composite figure"—a single dream object with individual characteristics reminiscent of several different objects. Thus a character may appear in a dream with the face of one person, the clothing of another, and the mannerisms of yet another, symbolizing all three persons at the same time.

One consequence of condensation is that the manifest con-

[8] Note that the censorship here is largely equivalent to the "ego" as it was postulated in the "Project"—strong and inhibiting in the waking state, and relaxed and permissive of the primary process in sleep.

tent of dreams can achieve great economy of expression, with many different ideas symbolized by few dream images. Even a short dream fragment may therefore be packed with significance. At the same time, this economical quality runs counter to the "normal" tendencies of the waking state and thus may account for some of the bizarreness of dreams. In the waking state it is generally necessary to achieve *precision* in the use of symbols, in order that they may accurately reflect external reality. No such constraint hinders the dream work, however. Whereas in normal waking thought symbols (words) tend to be precisely defined and denotative, in dreams they tend to be extremely general and connotative.

A final point about condensation is that though it does not *necessarily* serve a defensive function, it often does so. A dreamer may become aware consciously only of a seemingly harmless condensation, while in reality the condensation was manufactured in the dream work to represent several different *threatening* thoughts. That is, a dream image may be the result of both condensation and displacement at the same time.

Besides displacement and condensation, there is one other mechanism that Freud believed was responsible for the dream work, deriving from what he called *considerations of representability*. This aspect of the dream work occurs because manifest dreams are almost exclusively *perceptual* experiences, while the latent thoughts that they represent have major *conceptual* components. Most "thoughts" do not have immediate perceptual aspects as they are experienced, and yet the task of the dream is to translate these conceptual thoughts into the perceptual images of the manifest content. The problem is directly analagous to that faced by an artist who wishes to represent an abstract concept in a painting. If he wishes to convey the notion of "justice," for example, he may create an image of a blindfolded figure holding a pair of scales.

It is an interesting fact that dreams often demonstrate a great deal of ingenuity and creativity in the way they concretely represent abstract thoughts. The processes involved were very well illustrated by an early student of Freud's who tended when he was very tired to go almost directly from a waking state into a state of light dreaming. Sometimes he experienced the peculiar phenomenon of having the contents of his consciousness change abruptly from an abstract, imageless train of ideas into a vivid and graphic perceptual representation of that train of ideas. He lay awake one night grappling with the problem of how to revise an uneven and awkward passage in an essay he had written. Suddenly, he found himself no longer thinking abstractly but instead vividly imagining almost hallucinating—a scene that clearly symbolized the problem: he saw himself planing a piece of wood. Freud assumed that a process very similar to this must take place quite routinely in the dream work. The difference, of course, is that the symbolized thoughts in the dream work are often unconscious latent thoughts instead of a conscious train of abstract thought.

Thus the symbol-making capacity of man is nowhere more evident than in his dreaming processes, and there is something of the artist in every person who dreams. It is interesting that an individual's dream imagery may manifest a great deal more ingenuity and "creativity" than he is ever capable of in waking life. In fact, Freud suggested that artistic creativity relies on essentially the same mechanisms as dreams. He argued that *myths*—collective artistic products—are especially comparable to dreams and may be regarded as the collective dreams of entire cultures.

This tendency of dreams to represent abstract ideas in concrete ways, like the mechanism of condensation, represents a reversal of the tendencies characteristic of normal waking thought. The normal course of intellectual development is usually equated with a process of *abstraction*—of progressing from the processing of raw sensory impressions on their own terms to the efficient codification of experience in terms of abstract categories. The more "intellectual" a person becomes, the further he moves from dealing with concrete experience on its own terms. In dreams, however, this normal sequence of moving from the concrete to the abstract representation of ideas is reversed.

There is still one other feature of dreams that Freud noted in *The Interpretation of Dreams*. In all of the dreams that he encountered the manifest content always contained a fairly direct reference to an experience the dreamer had had in the waking state the day previous to the dream. Freud called this part of the dream the *day residue*. Sometimes the day experiences to which the day residues referred were trivial, scarcely worth any attention at all at the time they occurred. There was no pattern to this, however, because at other times the day residues included highly significant waking events. This suggested to Freud that the factors governing the selection of the day residue for each dream did not have to do with the essential nature of the waking experience per se. Instead, what seemed to be important was the *relationship* between the day experience and the latent dream thoughts.

More specifically, Freud assumed that the day residue is the vehicle that makes possible the first displacement in the dream work and that therefore allows the manifest dream to get started. For an illustration, consider an individual who has an active but unconscious latent thought. Since it is a "dangerous" thought the censorship will not allow it direct expression. Further, suppose that in the preceding day the individual had experiences X and Y, with X being by far the more important from the point of view of his waking concerns. Also assume, however, that Y provides a much more convenient image with which to symbolize disguisedly the active latent thought. In this case Y will always be selected over X as the day residue of a dream. The purpose of the day residue is to provide an excuse, as it were, for the disguised and displaced expression of the latent dream thoughts, and a trivial waking event may thus become the starting point of a dream. Since day residues were *invariable* characteristics of dreams, Freud concluded that they must be *necessary* as well; if there were no memory of a day experience to serve as the target of the first displacement, there could be no dream.

It is now possible to draw together the mechanisms Freud postulated to describe the phenomenon of dreaming. He began with the assumption that dreams are the disguised representation of the fulfillment of wishes, with the essential nature of the wishes remaining unconscious for the dreamer. In the waking state, these wishes are normally allowed little or no expression whatsoever, but the state of relaxed censorship brought on by sleep permits an initial displacement of activation from the unconscious latent wish to the memory of a recent waking experience. This provides the starting point for the dream work, which by the mechanisms of further displacements, condensation, and the concrete symbolization of ideas translates the latent content into its final manifest form. As the manifest content is recalled the next day, it may have to be modified still further in memory because of the more severe censorship demanded by the waking state.

In addition to describing the *process* of dream formation, Freud also expressed views about the *function* of dreams. *Compromise* is the essence of Freud's formulation. On the one hand, he saw dreams as wish-fulfilling fantasies allowing for the partial expression of impulses that would normally be completely repressed in the waking state. If the latent content were not allowed this partial expression in dreams, it is possible that the ideas involved would eventually achieve sufficient intensity to break through even the severe censorship of waking life. The best result would be a "slip," and the worst would be a neurotic or psychotic symptom. Therefore dreams serve as a kind of harmless "safety valve" for unconscious and dangerous impulses.

On the other hand, since the hallucinated wish fulfillment in dreams is not direct but disguised, Freud concluded that dreams serve the further function of allowing sleep to continue in spite of the dangerous ideas that are being activated and gratified. If the latent ideas were expressed directly in dreams, the sleeper would immediately awaken in a paroxysm of anxiety. Not only the latent thoughts but *any* potentially disturbing stimuli tend to be woven into the fabric of the manifest dream and thus rendered less disturbing. It is not uncommon, for example, for the sound of the morning alarm to be incorporated into an ongoing dream in some innocuous way, for example as a train whistle. In general, then, dreams may be described as effecting a compromise between unconscious but active and "dangerous" wishes on the one hand, and a wish on the part of the organism for undisturbed sleep on the other. Both wishes normally receive at least partial gratification in the course of a night's dreaming.

The Revised Model of the Mind

The Interpretation of Dreams was a colossal book, its seven chapters totalling more than six hundred pages. Most of the book is devoted exclusively to dreams: there is a thorough review of the literature published about dreams up to the year 1900, and an extensive explication and documentation with examples of the concepts introduced in the preceding sections of the present chapter. In the last chapter of *The Interpretation of Dreams,* however, Freud attempts to go beyond dreams and to use what he has learned from and about them as the foundation for a new general model of the mind. The aim of Chapter 7 is thus much like the aim of the "Project," and the model itself is the logical extension of the thinking begun there. In spite of the obvious similarities between the two works, however, their terminologies differ considerably. Chapter 7 employs an explicitly *psychological* terminology, and deliberately avoids concepts with neurological connotations; Freud goes so far as to insist that the components postulated as making up the psyche in Chapter 7 not be thought of as having exact anatomical referents.

Because it is complex and frequently speculative, with a fair share of ambiguity and uncertainty, Chapter 7 is extremely demanding for the reader. It is among the most seminal works that Freud ever wrote, however, and some of the best scholars of Freud can truly be said to have devoted their lives to the study and understanding of Chapter 7 of *The Interpretation of Dreams,* without wasting their time. Only the major points of Chapter 7 can be outlined here.

Freud observed that the locus of psychic activity presumed by the model in Chapter 7 cannot appropriately be called the nervous system, since no reference is made to neurons or other distinct neuro-anatomical units. Instead, Freud refers to the mind as a kind of "compound instrument" somewhat analogous to a telescope. The units of this instrument are called "agencies" or "systems" that are without simple relationships to anatomical structures.

Nevertheless, the new model, like the "Project," still takes as its starting point a consideration of the *reflex,* that elementary behavioral unit consisting of an immediate physical response to an external stimulus. Freud argues in Chapter 7 that in conceptualizing a reflex one must assume at the very least the existence of a *perceptual system ("Pcpt"*[9]*)* to receive the external stimulation and a *motor system ("M")* to enact the response. Thus the psychic apparatus as a whole is bounded at one end by *Pcpt* and at the other by *M,* with the normal flow of activity proceeding from *Pcpt* to *M.* A diagram like the one Freud used to illustrate a reflex is shown in Figure 7.[10] The space between *Pcpt* and *M* represents the rest of the psychic

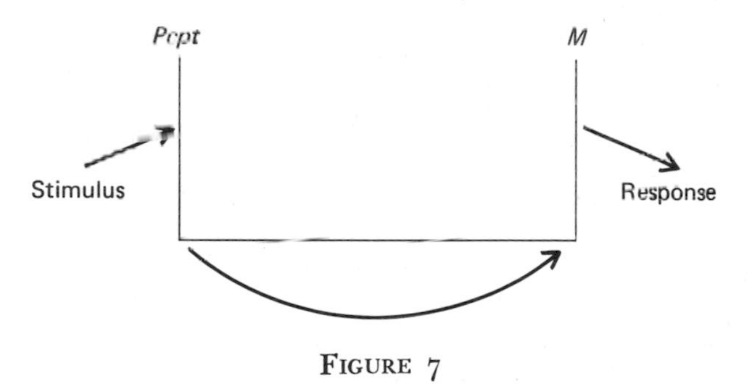

FIGURE 7

[9] Freud consistently used abbreviations to denote the psychic agencies in Chapter 7. Those used here are identical with the ones provided by the translators of the *Standard Edition.*

[10] Adapted from *Standard Edition,* Vol. V, p. 537.

apparatus, though it is left blank here because for the explanation of a simple reflex nothing more is needed beyond these two agencies.

Continuing as he had in the "Project," Freud went on to suggest that most behavior is more complex than the reflex, and that additional agencies must be necessary to account for that complexity. He pointed out that most non-reflexive behavior is *learned,* and that the phenomenon of learning suggests that the psychic system must have some capacity for memory. Therefore Freud postulated the existence of an agency whose function is to store the memories of past events, and he labeled it a *mnemic system ("Mnem").* Since it is usual for memory to come into play after a stimulus has been perceived but before specific action is taken to deal with it, Freud placed *Mnem* between *Pcpt* and *M* in his model.

But *Mnem* is not just a place where memories are stored. In order for memories to have any "meaning"—to be of any use in regulating behavior—they must be *organized.* That is, they must be placed in relationships with one another such that one memory can call up another in an adaptive pattern. For example, when an individual perceives an angry bear running at him, that perception must arouse memories of earlier experiences with angry bears (or of things that have been told him about angry bears), which in turn must call up memories of appropriate corrective actions like running away from the bear. The final appropriate action is therefore the result of a series of memories that have been aroused by the initial stimulus. Thus *Mnem* consists of many discrete memories standing in specific relationships to one another. In general, it corresponds to the pattern of prefacilitated contact barriers that allows for the easy association of one memory with another in the "Project."

The model in Chapter 7 is more sophisticated than that of the "Project," however, because it acknowledges both that there are many different ways in which memories can be interrelated and that some systems of interrelationship are more "advanced" than others. According to Freud, the simplest kind of relationship or association between two memories is based upon simultaneity or near-simultaneity of experience: events that are experienced close together in time are highly likely to be associated with one another. Simultaneity, of course, was the basis of all association in the "Project," and that assumption is thus retained in Chapter 7. But the newer work goes further with an explicit recognition that "higher" mental activity necessitates the association of ideas and memories of things that have never been experienced simultaneously. The process of abstraction entails the formation of new mnemic entities—"concepts"—that are composed of many discrete experiences and memories, but that can be treated as unities themselves. For example, the concept "chair" derives from a series of experiences over a considerable period of time with discretely different objects. High chairs, easy chairs, barbers' chairs, etc., all come to be subsumed under the concept "chair," and as a result become associated with one another in spite of the fact that they are never all experienced together at the same time. Thus abstract concepts are able to transcend simultaneity and may in the course of time come themselves to be associated with other abstractions.

As a result of considerations like these, Freud concluded that the psychic apparatus must have not just a single mnemic system but rather a whole series of mnemic systems arranged hierarchically in order of increasing abstraction. One can imagine a *Mnem* system based entirely on association by simultaneity, a *Mnem* representing a first level of abstraction, a *Mnem* representing a second level, and so on.

Figure 8[11] represents Freud's conception of the psychic apparatus with the addition of the mnemic systems. Stimulation impinging on *Pcpt* is normally processed through a series of memory organizations—i.e., it is thought about at varying levels of abstraction—until an appropriate response is selected. Then the motor system is activated and the response occurs, not as a reflex but as the result of deliberation.

The next factor that Freud took up in his model was that of

[11] Adapted from *Standard Edition*, Vol. V, p. 538.

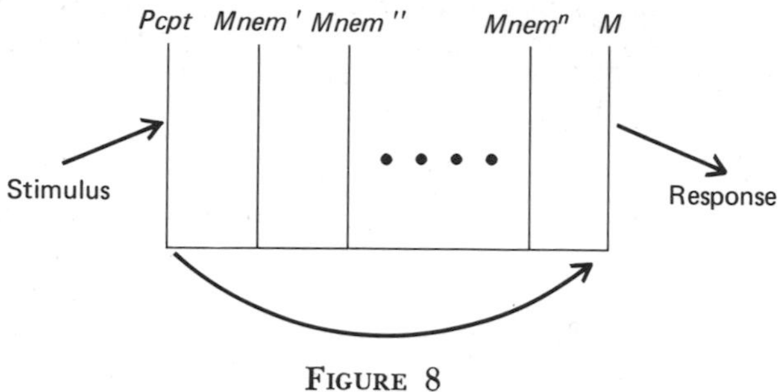

FIGURE 8

consciousness. He had already impressively demonstrated that conscious effort can provide only a partial representation of the factors governing human behavior. An individual is capable of being aware of only a part of his experience, and when such diverse phenomena as slips, neurotic symptoms, and dreams occur he may be completely in the dark as to the real causes of his behavior. In fact, Freud demonstrated that in such cases one actually resists becoming aware of the truth; in other words, lack of consciousness may be a motivated state.

To account for these phenomena in his new model of the mind, Freud postulated a tripartite classification to denote the ease with which specific ideas and memories are available to consciousness. First, there are those ideas that are actively in consciousness at a given moment. These conscious contents are constantly being replaced by new elements in the stream of awareness, of course, and thus what is conscious is highly transient. Indeed, it is unusual for a single idea to remain in consciousness for more than a few seconds at a time.

Because of this highly transient nature of the contents of consciousness, Freud did not postulate the existence of a separate system of conscious ideas. Instead, he designated as a discrete system all of those ideas and memories that are *capable* of becoming conscious and labeled it the *preconscious system* (*"Pcs"*). What is conscious at a given moment is that part of the preconscious of which one happens to be aware. Thus the preconscious consists essentially of all of the memories, ideas, and information that an individual has at his command and that he can bring into actual consciousness quickly and with a relatively small expenditure of effort.

A good example of a preconscious idea is the memory one has of one's own name. When one is asked for one's name, one can reply very quickly and easily as the appropriate information comes into consciousness. After replying, however, one's name becomes replaced in immediate consciousness by something else and recedes back into the preconscious to await the next appropriate time for it to come into awareness. Not all preconscious ideas are so easily accessible as one's own name. An example of a less accessible preconscious idea is any information that one has to think hard about before providing, such as the answer to a difficult examination question. Sometimes a preconscious idea may even be temporarily totally inaccessible to consciousness, only to emerge totally spontaneously at a later time as when the correct answer to the examination question does not come during the examination proper, but flows quickly to mind as soon as the examination is over. Thus preconscious ideas are not all *immediately* accessible to consciousness, but they are all potentially accessible, given a certain amount of time and effort, or the presence of the appropriate memory props.

Standing in contrast to the preconscious is the *unconscious system ("Ucs")*, the contents of which have no direct access to consciousness at all. The contents of the unconscious include memories and ideas that have been repressed, such as the pathogenic ideas of hysterics and the latent content of dreams.

In his diagram of the psychic apparatus, Freud placed the systems *Pcs* and *Ucs* near the motor end of the system. He did not designate consciousness as a separate system at all, but instead conceptualized it as a kind of "lens" placed at the extreme motor end of the system, with a vantage point on the most superficial level of activity in the system. This level is in the preconscious, of course, since consciousness can only observe preconscious ideation. Therefore *Pcs* is placed closest to the motor end, followed by *Ucs*. This structure is shown in

Figure 9,[12] and it nicely illustrates the fact that the contents of *Ucs* have no direct access to consciousness (or to the motor end). In the diagram, the only way for the contents of *Ucs* to become conscious is to pass through the system *Pcs,* thereby undergoing a transformation. This schematic diagram therefore illustrates the relationships Freud had discovered to exist in the dream work, with the latent thoughts (i.e., the thoughts from the *Ucs*) expressing themselves only by attaching themselves to the day residue and to those of its associates that constitute the manifest content (derived entirely from elements in the *Pcs*). The manifest content is that part of the *Pcs* that has been activated by the *Ucs,* according to the rules laid down by the censorship.

There is a certain inelegance to this formulation, arising from the fact that the *Pcs, Ucs,* and *Mnem* systems do not represent mutually exclusive localities in an overall structure of the psyche. That is, an idea's being part of the *Ucs* or *Pcs* at a given moment does not preclude it from being organized by one of the *Mnem* systems. It is thus not possible to "locate" an idea on this diagram, since one idea can be part of two systems at once. Therefore the diagram does not represent a map of the mind, and it can be confusing to think of it as such.

Freud seems to compound this confusion when he goes on to state that *Pcs* and *Ucs* need not be thought of only as agencies or systems; they also can be thought of accurately as *processes*

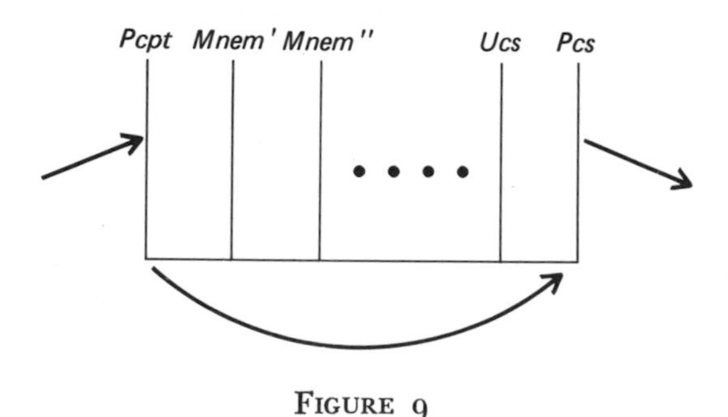

FIGURE 9

[12] Adapted from *Standard Edition,* Vol. V, p. 541.

of excitation of the mental apparatus. Thus the difference between a preconscious and unconscious train of thought may lie primarily in the way each excites the psychic system as a whole. Moreover, as Freud describes in detail the characteristics of unconscious and of preconscious thought, one finds only slightly modified versions of old friends from the "Project": the primary and secondary processes.

Freud states that when a train of thought is dominated by the *Ucs* it behaves according to a series of processes more basic and elemental than those characterizing preconscious trains of thought. Therefore the unconscious thoughts follow primary processes, while the preconscious thoughts follow secondary ones. The primary processes are observable only because the *Pcs* is sometimes taken over by the *Ucs,* as in dreams and neurotic symptoms; the secondary processes are observable by the direct introspection of "normal" thought processes.

When a train of thought is dominated by the unconscious—i.e., when it follows the primary processes—one of its major characteristics is that it seems dominated by the goal of attaining the immediate gratification of wishes. Thus the unconscious ideas lying behind dreams, symptoms, and slips are essentially wishes. These wishes strive for gratification without regard for reality. The term that Freud introduced to denote this wish-fulfilling drive on the part of the primary processes was the *pleasure principle.*

The similarities between the "Project" and Chapter 7 are accentuated once again as Freud describes the *energy* he assumes to be responsible for the primary processes. Even though he has abandoned the neurological context of the "Project," he retains the term *cathexis* to denote the excitation of an idea or memory. A train of thought is described as involving the flow of cathexes from one *idea* to another, instead of from one *neuron* to another, and the basic principles remain the same. Freud states that in the primary process the flow of ideas is characterized by the en bloc transmission of cathexes from one thought to another. That is, if idea A becomes excited with two units of cathexis and then in the course of the train of thought transmits excitation to idea B, it tends to transmit both units at once. When idea B then transmits to idea C, it transmits the two units it has obtained from A as well as any precathexis it may have had itself. In this way the intensities of cathexis tend to increase regularly as a primary process train of thought progresses. One result of this undisciplined transmission of excitation is that *condensations* are especially likely to occur, since a small number of en bloc transmissions to the same idea may quickly hypercathect it and cause it to discharge. Though Freud speaks of "ideas" rather than "neurons" in describing this phenomenon, the psychological results of the primary process are the same as in the "Project."

Still another psychological aspect of the primary process that Freud emphasized in Chapter 7 is that the associations between ideas in its train of thought are likely to seem illogical. Thus, for example, one thought may lead so quickly to its opposite that the opposite may be said to symbolize the original thought. Or, just as commonly, opposites may stand side by side as equal partners in the primary process train of thought, both being acknowledged as true in spite of their logical incompatibility with one another. Even though these primary process characteristics are ludicrous from a logical point of view, they are not without their rationale. It is an obvious fact that opposites are closely related to one another associatively. If we ask a person to say the first thing that comes to his mind upon hearing the word *good,* it is quite likely that he will respond with the word *bad,* indicating that the two opposite concepts are closely associated in his mind. In fact, the very meanings of the two words are intertwined; the whole idea of "goodness" has no meaning except as a contrast to the notion of "badness." It is relatively easy, therefore, to transfer cathexis from one idea to its opposite. And since the primary process does not take reality into account, there is nothing to prohibit the acceptance of two contrary but highly associated ideas at the same time, or the use of one as a substitute for the other. This attribute of the primary process is obviously useful for the censorship, which can see to it that an objectionable unconscious idea is represented in consciousness by its opposite.

In marked contrast to the primary process is the secondary process, characteristic of "normal" mental activity and the system *Pcs.* Preconscious activity, of course, must take into account the demands of reality, and therefore it must operate in a more controlled and disciplined manner than the unconscious primary processes. In the primary processes, intensities of cathexes tend to multiply rapidly and to fluctuate greatly because of the en bloc transmissions of excitation. The more intense an idea's cathexis becomes, the greater the controlling influence it exerts on the train of psychic activity. Thus primary process thought is itself highly variable and erratic, lacking the consistency necessary for dealing with reality. The secondary process, however, is able in large measure to disregard the intensities of individual ideas and to direct attention evenly over a wide field of possibilities. The cathexes of ideas in the secondary process were described by Freud as "quiescent," by which he meant evenly distributed. The flow of psychic energy is achieved in very small units, instead of en bloc transmissions, thus permitting the maintenance of the overall quiescent state. In practice, this means that the train of thought does not become dominated by single hypercathected ideas, but instead may play evenly over a wide variety of possibilities.

The simple example of a hungry man who is lost in a forest without food illustrates this. If the primary process dominates, the idea of "food" quickly becomes hypercathected and all thinking comes to center upon images of food and its consumption. In thinking only about food, however, the man is unable to concentrate upon the intermediate steps that may be necessary to obtain it but that have nothing immediately to do with food themselves—e.g., building a trap, constructing a fishing line, etc. On the other hand, if the secondary process is in control, the man is able to forget about food temporarily and to concentrate instead on the various possibilities for adaptive action. In performing this secondary process thinking the man is able to weigh each thought in terms of its realistic probability of success. Contradictory and illogical lines of reasoning will be ignored or rapidly dismissed.

One more characteristic of the secondary process discussed by Freud in his Chapter 7 was its ability to inhibit the emotion or affect associated with ideas. The primary process, dominated by the pleasure principle, is attracted to ideas that have pleasant connotations, but is repulsed by unpleasant memories. The secondary process, in dealing with reality, must sometimes contemplate unpleasant possibilities. Thus, in addition to sometimes temporarily ignoring ideas that are intensively cathected, the secondary process must occasionally be able to concentrate attention on possibilities that are altogether repugnant.

The primary process thought, characteristic of the system *Ucs*, may now be summarized by noting that it tends to be dominated by ideas connoting pleasure, and that it tends to be undisciplined and "unrealistic" in its utilization of such mechanisms as condensation and symbolization. The system *Pcs*'s secondary process, on the other hand, is dispassionate, evenhanded in its regard for various possibilities, logical, and above all oriented toward reality.

Having now defined these two antagonistic processes, it is necessary to admit that neither one of them is often encountered in its pure state. Most human thought is a combination of primary and secondary process thinking—i.e., the result of a compromise between the unconscious and the preconscious. The phenomena of dreams nicely illustrate both components and thus served as an ideal vehicle for Freud to use in dramatizing the operation of his revised model of the mind.

There are three necessary preconditions for the formation of a dream: a state of sleep must exist, an unconscious thought (wish) must be aroused, and there must be at least a slight cathexis of some ideas in the preconscious as a result of the previous day's experience. All three of these things almost always happen quite naturally at night. The unconscious wish is the latent thought, of course, and in terms of Freud's new schematic model it is denied entry to consciousness because its way is blocked by the system *Pcs.* It does have access to *Pcs* itself, however, and since some of the preconscious ideas are already partially cathected by the previous day's experience they are especially inviting targets. One of these preconscious ideas becomes activated by displaced unconscious excitation, thus forming the dream's day residue according to the rules described earlier. Thus a preconscious thought is "taken over by" energy from *Ucs,* and when this happens it begins behaving like an unconscious thought. That is, the newly activated preconscious thought is the starting point for a train of primary process thinking. The resulting thought processes are therefore characterized by many condensations and illogical sequences.

Once the preconscious idea has been cathected to such a high degree by the unconsciously derived excitation, it naturally presses toward a discharge at the motor end of the system. In the state of sleep, however, this is impossible because of the shutting down of the motor system (*M*). Therefore, the excitation begins a *regressive* flow back toward the perceptual end of the apparatus—an argument taken from the "Project." As the excitation passes along its regressive path in the new model a new dimension is added, however, because it encounters the various mnemic systems along the way. Furthermore, the closer it gets to the system *Pcpt,* the more primitive become the mnemic systems it crosses. The consequence of this for the highly cathected thought is that it comes to be represented in terms of more and more primitive—i.e., less and less abstract—symbolic relationships. When the thought finally reaches *Pcpt* is is therefore expressed in a highly concrete form. In Freud's own terms, "the fabric of the dream thoughts is resolved into its own raw material."[13]

The term *regression* is especially useful in describing this whole process of dream formation. First, it connotes the fact that the direction of the normal flow of thought has been

[13] *Standard Edition,* Vol. V, p. 543.

reversed. Normally, thought processes move from concrete to abstract, whereas in dreams the reverse is true. Second, there is a "backwards" movement in the topographical sense suggested by Freud's diagram of his model. The normal, progressive direction is from left to right, as in a reflex; in a dream, it is from right to left. Third, dreams represent a regression in that a *current* idea from the *Pcs* (the day residue) is taken over by an unconscious wish dating from childhood (the latent thought). This hearkening back to an earlier period of time, also classified as a regression by Freud, was a process that came to play a key role in his developing theory of sexuality.

After the regression has been completed, the system *Pcpt* becomes activated by the excitation, and the manifest dream itself occurs as an hallucination. At this point, of course, it has acquired all of the characteristics it should have according to Freud's dream theory. It is a disguised representation of the latent thought characterized by displacement, condensation, and illogic because of its having been dominated by the primary process. It is also highly concrete because it has undergone the regressive transformation on its journey toward the perceptual system. In other words, the dream work has been completed.

Finally, once the hallucination has occurred, it is experienced and remembered by the sleeper like any other sensory perception. In terms of Freud's model, this means that it must be processed through the psychic apparatus in the normal, progressive direction. As it does this, of course, it becomes subject to the censorship and logical processing that are normal in waking life, and the result is the secondary revision of the manifest content that Freud found to happen in the recollection of every dream. The dream as it is related by the dreamer to another person is therefore the end result of a thought being processed by the psychic apparatus at least twice—once in a regressive and once in a progressive direction.

The basic conception of the psychic apparatus as presented in Chapter 7 was never abandoned by Freud, though it was expanded upon in later years. The study of dreams was therefore extremely useful in enabling him to construct and illustrate a model of the psyche that was to remain the bedrock of psychoanalysis.

SUGGESTED FURTHER READINGS

Freud's letters to Fliess (*The Origins of Psycho-Analysis* [New York, Basic Books, 1954]) during the years 1896 to 1899 provide an intimate look at the development of the dream theory and of the transition from the neurological model of the "Project" to the psychological one of *The Interpretation of Dreams*. Of particular interest are letter 52 (written in December, 1896), which briefly describes a model of the mind intermediate between the "Project" and Chapter 7; and letter 69 (September, 1897), which provides Freud's reasons for abandoning the seduction theory.

The Interpretation of Dreams (New York, Avon Books, 1965), originally published in 1900, is Freud's masterpiece. It contains a richly documented delineation of the dream theory proper, together with the "topographic" model of the mind presented in Chapter 7. A much shorter and highly readable description of just the dream work was given by Freud in *On Dreams* (New York, Norton, 1952), originally published in 1901.

5

Sexuality

Although Freud's study of dreams and neurotic processes constituted his first and greatest theoretical contribution to the understanding of human behavior, he did not receive much immediate public recognition for it. A small number of physicians—including Alfred Adler, Otto Rank, and Carl Jung, all of whom were later to become famous in their own right—were impressed by Freud's work and became his pupils, but the general level of Freud's popularity is reflected by the fact that exactly 228 copies of *The Interpretation of Dreams* were sold in its first two years. By 1910, however, Freud had created a sensation in the intellectual world, and ten years later he was internationally famous.

Freud's enduring fame is based upon all his achievements, but there is little doubt that his initial recognition occurred because he published a number of works between 1905 and 1910 emphasizing the role of sexuality in human life. His views attracted much attention because they shocked a society unaccustomed to dealing frankly with the subject. Much abuse fell upon Freud's head as a result; in 1910, for example, one distinguished Canadian academician accused Freud of seeming to condone "free love, removal of all restraints, and a relapse into savagery." These were unjust accusations, since Freud's personal conduct was always above reproach and his moral standards were quite conventional. What he *was* guilty of was presenting the world with some new ideas slightly before their time had come. His work called into question the view of human nature cherished by the Victorian mentality: that civilized man is an essentially rational creature who is unmoved by all but the most elevating of passions. Needless to say, sex did not qualify as an elevating passion.

That Freud was not too far ahead of his time, however, is shown by the relative speed with which his ideas were finally accepted. Freud had the good fortune to live to see himself acclaimed as a great man; he was an intellectual revolutionary who saw the final success of his revolution. His success was due in part to his consummate skill in formulating and communicating his ideas, but it was also due to his ability to capitalize on tendencies and inclinations that were at the forefront of contemporary thought. Just as he had employed the latest neurological knowledge and assumptions in his construction of a far-reaching model of the mind, so he was able to use current and avant-garde ideas from other intellectual realms as the starting points for his theory of sexuality, illustrating once again that intellectual revolution occurs when a great man makes use of an appropriate *Zeitgeist*.

The Background of Freud's Sexual Theory

The first jolt to the complacent nineteenth century view of man as a strictly rational and enlightened being had been delivered in the middle of the century, when Charles Darwin proposed the theory of natural selection as the key to evolution. The undeniable consequence of his theory was that man, like all other animals, had to be seen as the descendant of a long line of more primitive ancestors. It was not easy to reconcile this idea with the popular view that man was a perfect object created by God's handiwork on a single afternoon.

In the literary and philosophical worlds as well, the latter half of the nineteenth century saw a departure by some thinkers from the idea of man as a perfectly rational animal. The philosophers Schopenhauer and Nietzsche, for example, both saw human beings as guided more by passion than by reason. Their "romantic" views suggested that the tragedy of human existence arises because of a conflict between basic motivating passions and an artificial reason that tries to suppress them. These ideas began to pierce the Victorian armor, making it no longer unthinkable to regard man as an animal among animals, governed by something more primitive than beneficent reason.

Finally, sexuality itself began to be dealt with scientifically by a small group of investigators. In 1886 a prominent Viennese physician named Richard von Krafft-Ebing (1840–1902) wrote a classic medical text entitled *Psychopathia Sexualis,* which described in detail various sexual perversions and malfunctions. It was a courageous act to write such a text, and he was almost expelled from the British medical society when his book appeared because he had not taken precautions to see that it was kept out of non-medical hands. At about the same time an Englishman named Havelock Ellis (1859–1939) was beginning his pioneering study of sexual function and malfunction within an anthropological framework. Ellis, who would devote his entire professional life to such study, was probably the first person to deserve the title "sexologist." His work was just beginning to be known toward the end of the nineteenth century.

In Switzerland, the psychiatrist Auguste Forel (1848–1931) studied sexual problems in the 1890s, and in 1905 he published a much-cited work on that topic. And finally, as a sure sign that studies of sex were beginning to come into vogue—at least among the medical and scientific avant-garde—a scholarly periodical devoted to studies of sex appeared in Germany in 1899.

All of this indicated that Freud was not completely alone in concerning himself with the serious study of sexual factors. He had company even in his area of specialization, since ideas linking sexuality to hysteria were very much in the air. Freud's friend Fliess had already formulated his "nasal reflex neurosis" by the 1890s, and Freud himself cited three experiences that he had had as a young physician-in-training in which people whom he respected greatly made casual but definite allusions to the involvement of sexuality in psychopathology. The first such person was Breuer. At one point when Freud was a very young physician, he and Breuer worked together with a neurotic patient whose husband was impotent. In discussing the case Breuer casually remarked that neurotic behaviors like hers were always associated with the "secrets of the marriage bed." The second person Freud remembered in this context was Charcot, whom he had overheard to comment offhandedly that some nervous disorders were quite regularly caused by *"la chose genitale"* (literally, "the genital thing"). Finally, when Freud was in training one of his favorite teachers, a famous gynecologist named Chrobak, remarked that the only cure for a patient of his—a highly anxious woman whose husband also happened to be impotent—was described in the prescription *"Penis normalis dosim repetatur"* ("Repeated doses of a normal penis").

Thus three of Freud's most revered mentors had intimated that sexuality plays an important role in the genesis of neurotic conditions. None of them went beyond this, however. For each of them the idea was just a passing insight that seemed to have some validity, but that never was raised to the dignity of a formal principle. Wilhelm Fliess had begun to speculate about such things, but it remained for Freud to complete the task, following upon his systematic study of neurotic patients and his discovery of the frequency with which sexual concerns were involved. Once again Freud capitalized on the ideas of the time, using the vague intuitions of others as the starting point for his own intricate theory of the interrelationships between sexual and psychological matters.

The Development of the Sexual Theory

The major immediate source of Freud's discovery of the relationship between sexual ideas and hysteria was, of course, the free associations of his hysterical patients. His early and ill-fated "seduction theory" was his first attempt to account for the fact that so many of his patients culminated their free associations by recalling "memories" of seduction and sexual trauma in childhood. Though it was highly original, there was nothing particularly revolutionary about the seduction theory at the time it was propounded. It relied on the traditional view of sex as an exclusively adult and genital concern, and even added its own characteristically Victorian touch by attributing pernicious effects to the premature exposure of children to sexuality. The only problem with the theory was that it was manifestly incorrect. In formulating a satisfactory substitute, Freud was forced to go substantially beyond the traditional and "safe" view of sexuality held by his colleagues.

The study of dreams was inextricably wound up in Freud's efforts to revise the theory, and he eventually came to see hysterical symptoms, like dreams, as representing wish-fulfillments rather than traumatic memories. This inevitably necessitated a new view of sexuality that was radical from two points of view: it expanded the time span during which the sexual instinct was presumed to be operative, and it expanded the range of activities that can appropriately be called "sexual" beyond the traditional genital acts. A closer examination of Freud's data reveals why these radical changes were necessary.

When Freud found that the hysteric's pathogenic ideas were better conceptualized as wishful fantasies than as actual memories, he was confronted with a logical dilemma so long as he maintained the traditional view of sexuality. The dilemma arose because these fantasies seemed inevitably to be grounded in childhood, and also to have unambiguous sexual connotations. Since the fantasies could not be interpreted as "true" memories, Freud was forced to the conclusion that they must represent sexual wishes that had occurred in childhood. This, of course, implied that the patients must have had sexual feelings as children, contradicting the notion that sexuality is an exclusively adult concern.

It might seem that there was still one plausible explanation of the data that could have enabled Freud to salvage part of the traditional view of sexuality: that only hysterics are characterized by childhood sexuality, and that normal individuals are completely lacking in sexual feeling until puberty. Thus hysteria could be passed off as the result of a malignant precocity of the sexual instinct in a small number of individuals. Unfortunately for the Victorian world view, however, this explanation was not tenable because Freud had also garnered evidence from his study of dreams that completely normal individuals retained traces of childhood sexual concerns just as hysterics did. Since virtually everybody dreams, and since Freud felt that dreams inevitably reflect childhood sexual wishes, he was forced to conclude that everybody must experience sexual impulses in childhood. This *was* a truly revolutionary idea, very difficult to accept because it called into question cherished notions about the essential purity of childhood and, by implication, of the entire human race.

It was a matter of some irony, as well as a mark of Freud's integrity, that the first "normal" person in whom he detected unmistakable traces of childhood sexuality was himself. Beginning almost immediately with his discovery of the dream-interpretation technique in 1895, Freud began the regular practice of interpreting his own dreams. About a year after he had begun doing this, he underwent a personal crisis of considerable magnitude. In response to this crisis, Freud began subjecting his own behaviors as well as his dreams to intense anlysis by free association. In essence, he became his own patient and carried out his now-famous "self analysis."

The event that precipitated Freud's self-analysis was the death of his father in October, 1896. Although his father was by then a very old man, and his death was not unexpected, Freud found that he was extremely shaken by the event—much more than he had ever anticipated. He aptly described his state to Fliess in a single sentence: "I feel now as if I had been torn up by the roots."[1] Shortly after the death he

[1] *The Origins of Psycho-Analysis* (New York, Basic Books, 1954), p. 170.

had a highly disturbing dream in which he was late for his father's funeral, in spite of having made all the arrangements for it himself, because of a delay at his barber's.

During the next year Freud was in an almost constant state of inner turmoil, and, what was even more disturbing to him, he was frequently unable to make himself work productively. One reason for his state of anguish was unquestionably the death of his father. That he was deeply moved by the event is reflected in his later statement that a father's death is "the most important event, the most poignant loss, in a man's life."[2] Another reason was the fact that he persisted in his self-analysis even when he was unable to carry on successfully with his other work, and in the course of this analysis he inevitably stirred up personal conflicts and issues that were most distressing to contemplate. He came to have a firsthand understanding of the resistance that his patients had manifested in *their* free associating. Just as they resisted bringing their pathogenic ideas to consciousness, so Freud tried to resist certain conclusions about himself that his analysis inescapably suggested. It was only after a truly heroic effort at honesty and objective self-scrutiny—with much concurrent unhappiness and anguish—that he came to acknowledge certain very important memories and impulses in himself.

Among the most disturbing of these were some extremely negative feelings toward his father. So negative were they, in fact, that Freud was compelled to admit that he had at various times harbored wishes for his father's death. The full analysis of the dream about his father's funeral, for example, revealed that at some level of his personality he was not unhappy about the death, since it represented the fulfillment of a long-standing wish.

His father was not the only close family member to be the object of disconcerting feelings revealed in Freud's self-analysis; his mother played a major role as well. As his analysis proceeded, mounting evidence forced Freud to overcome tremen-

[2] *Standard Edition,* Vol. IV, p. xxvi.

dous resistance and finally acknowledge the idea that as a child he had experienced definite sexual wishes toward his mother. In fact, he concluded that his death wishes toward his father derived from the more basic wish to be sole possessor of his mother. It is not possible to cite here all of the evidence bearing on these astonishing ideas, but one example will suffice to illustrate the process by which they came to light. In the course of the self-analysis, Freud recalled and interpreted a dream that he had had as a child of seven or eight. He described the dream as follows: "It was a very vivid one, and in it I saw my beloved mother, with a peculiarly peaceful, sleeping expression on her features, being carried into the room by two (or three) people with birds' beaks and laid upon the bed."[3]

Such was only the manifest content of the dream, of course. Free association revealed a startling latent content. One train of associations to the dream followed from Freud's recognition that the beaked figures were very similar to those in an illustration from the family Bible, an edition known as "Phillippson's Bible." This led to the thoughts that he had first learned the slang word for sexual intercourse from a boy named Philipp, and that the word itself was well represented by the bird imagery in the dream. (The German slang word *vögeln* is derived from *vogel,* meaning "bird.") Thus the dream had clear sexual implications.

Further analysis revealed that the expression on Freud's mother's face in the dream was identical to one that his grandfather's face had had shortly before his death. The reclining figure was therefore clearly a condensation representing his mother and his dying grandfather. It was but a short step in the further interpretation to see the figure as a composite representation of a sexually desirable mother and a dead father (derived from its associations with "grandfather"). This dream was just one of many phenomena in Freud's self-analysis which, upon interpretation, provided indications of the

[3] *Standard Edition,* Vol. V, p. 583.

existence of positive sexual wishes toward his mother and death wishes toward his father, dating from childhood.

It occurred to Freud that this pattern of wishes and memories from his own childhood paralleled rather closely the plot of Sophocles' play *Oedipus Rex,* in which the hero, Oedipus, discovers that he has unwittingly slain his father, Laius, and married his mother, Jocasta, Queen of Thebes. Oedipus thus becomes King of Thebes, but at the same time he brings down the wrath of the gods upon his kingdom. The play portrays the agonizing process by which Oedipus realizes the nature of his deeds—a terrifying self-appraisal not unlike Freud's own self-analysis. When Oedipus learns the true nature of his deeds, he is so horrified that he puts out his own eyes. In Freud's view, Oedipus' horror was symbolic of the dread that always accompanies the revelation of repressed ideas and wishes. This dread was the price of self-awareness, and its avoidance provided the *raison d'être* for the phenomenon of resistance he had so frequently encountered. The particular concatenation of impulses and ideas that characterized the Oedipus story, reflected in Freud's own repressed wishes, were conceptualized by him as a psychic unity. The desire of a child to possess his mother and to be rid of his father, together with the feelings of anxiety and revulsion that come to accompany those desires, were designated as the *Oedipus complex.*

Several bits of evidence quickly suggested to Freud that these Oedipal feelings and wishes were not unique to himself; in fact, he concluded that a wish for the elimination of the same-sexed parent and the possession of the opposite-sexed one is part of the psychic legacy of virtually every human child. The first bit of evidence was provided by the typical pathogenic ideas of his hysterical patients, which, as we have seen, frequently involved incestuous seduction scenes dating from childhood. Once Freud began to interpret these ideas as wishes rather than actual memories they quite easily fell into the Oedipal pattern. The general similarity of dreams to hysterical symptoms—particularly the parallels between latent thoughts and pathogenic ideas—further suggested that the Oedipal wishes were not confined to hysterics. Freud himself was the first example of a non-hysteric whose dreams revealed this, and subsequent interpretation of other "normal" people's dreams confirmed the pattern.

Still another type of evidence confirming the existence of the Oedipus complex was derived from the direct observation of children. Young children are often completely unabashed about expressing affection for their opposite-sexed parents. Frequently they state quite frankly their fantasied intention of eventually marrying their mothers or fathers. The negative side of the Oedipal feelings—the hostility toward the same-sexed parent—is usually more indirectly expressed. This is partly because the same-sexed parent is quite realistically seen by the child as being more powerful than he is, and therefore potentially very dangerous. To express the Oedipal hostility directly is thus to risk catastrophic retaliation. The negative Oedipal feelings are also expressed indirectly because they are mixed with strong positive attitudes as well. Freud very early recognized that human emotions need not follow the laws of logic, and that it was common for human beings to both love and hate another person at the same time. He called this mixed orientation toward another person *ambivalence*. Since ambivalent feelings impel contradictory behaviors, they are complicated and frustrating. Because the same-sexed parent is regarded by the child with the most intense ambivalence—he is loved for being a good and benevolent support but hated for being a powerful rival—the expression of Oedipal hostility is often convoluted and disguised. Nevertheless, Freud felt that it is always present, and that it is expressed in one guise or another in the dreams, play, and fantasy of the child.

Additional evidence for the universality of the Oedipus complex, Freud believed, was provided by a paradoxical source: the very vehemence with which Oedipal notions are consciously repudiated by most adults. Most men respond with repugnance and disgust to the suggestion that they have ever coveted their mothers and wished their fathers dead; such thoughts seem too odious to contemplate. Women respond in the same way to their complementary version of the Oedipal thoughts. Freud believed that the reason these thoughts are especially odious, however, is precisely that they are wishes. Unlike "normal" wishes, though, they do not conjure up simple images of pleasant satisfaction. Along with images of satisfaction, they also carry associations to the entire childhood Oedipal situation, with its ambivalence, fearfulness, and complicated emotional patterning. Freud concluded that in childhood these emotional convolutions become so painful that the child can no longer bear to think about them; hence they become repressed. The disgust that adults feel upon contemplating Oedipal wishes is thus in the service of repression and is a kind of exaggerated, "protesting-too-much" response that gives away its defensive purpose by its very intensity and exaggeration. Thus on a conscious level the Oedipal wishes are resisted violently, while on an unconscious level they find symbolic expression through dreams, symptoms, and works of fantasy like *Oedipus Rex*.

Freud's self-analysis and his work with patients convinced him that Oedipal wishes are not the only childhood phenomena to undergo violent repression and subsequently become the objects of conscious feelings of disgust. He found in the analysis of his own and his patients' free associations many images, dating from childhood, in which sexual pleasure was merged with all sorts of "perverse" activity, involving especially the mouth and the anus in addition to the genitals. These thoughts, of course, were expressed only over much resistance, and were responded to by the patient with the same feelings of disgust and indignation that met Oedipal fantasies. On the basis of these observations, Freud concluded not only that sexuality is present in children, but also that it takes forms regarded as perverse by adults. In fact, he argued that these "perverse" forms of sexuality are actually more universal than "normal" genital sexuality, since children are not yet biologically equipped to experience the latter.

Thus Freud expanded the concept of sexuality far beyond its traditional Victorian dimensions. He came to deny the traditional view of sex as an instinct that is dormant until puberty, at which point it arises in a strictly genital guise. His analyses indicated clearly that sexuality is present even in the youngest of children, in manifestations that are most upsetting from an adult point of view. Indeed, children are subject to strong impulses which in later life seem perverted and antisocial, and must be repressed.

Here was the first expression of a basic theme that was to be echoed and re-echoed in Freud's later writings: that the process of human development and civilization entails the suppression of childishness. Human beings are not born pure and then corrupted as they grow older; rather, they are born with "impure" impulses and subsequently fight an only partially successful battle to overcome them. Thus Freud's ideas do not imply that men are degenerate perverts, as first thoughts about them might suggest. Instead, he believed that mature men fight, and partially win, battles against antisocial and disruptive impulses within themselves. In spite of this, Freud's views on childhood sexuality earned him the opprobrium of his colleagues and of almost everyone else who first learned of them. His only consolation was his belief that the extreme violence with which he was repudiated was actually evidence in favor of his theory, since it drew its intensity from the same forces of repression that had made his discoveries so difficult to begin with. His critics protested too much, and in so doing revealed that Freud had learned something important about them.

Thus the theory of childhood sexuality provided Freud with the final secret of hysteria and dreams. Hysteria came to be seen as the result of an only partially successful attempt to repress childhood wishes that had been rendered obnoxious and dangerous by the demands of civilization and maturation. Dreams were conceptualized as the automatic mechanism, available to neurotics and non-neurotics alike, for the "safe" expression of the same kinds of wishes.

After achieving his initial insights about the existence and nature of infantile sexuality, Freud labored to construct a complete theoretical statement about the nature of sexuality. The essentials of this statement had been worked out by 1905, when they were included in a short book entitled *Three Essays on the Theory of Sexuality*. This work, while not so difficult as the "Project" or Chapter 7 of *The Interpretation of Dreams,* was nevertheless one of the most misunderstood of all of Freud's major works. More than any other single work it was responsible for Freud's reputation as a libertine and corruptor of youth. Nevertheless, the book is a model of clarity and logic in exposition, standing among the most important works that Freud wrote. As shall be demonstrated, it covers some of the same ground already covered in this chapter, but from a different point of view.

The Nature of the Sexual Instinct

In the *Three Essays,* Freud conceptualized sexual manifestations as the result of a specfic *instinct,* or drive. In general, his notion of an instinct was derived from his earlier neurological frame of reference, as is made clear by the following definition: "By an 'instinct' is provisionally to be understood the psychical representative of an endosomatic, continuously flowing source of stimulation, as contrasted with a 'stimulus,' which is set up by *single* excitations coming from *without.*"[4] Thus the first step in Freud's new instinct theory was simply the substitution of new terms—instinct and stimulus—for old concepts: endogenously and exogenously originating energy, or *Q*. As in the "Project," the most fundamental difference between an instinct and a stimulus is that a stimulus can be fled from, whereas an instinct cannot. Thus an instinct makes much heavier demands upon the mind.

In describing the operations of the instincts, Freud found it useful to distinguish four different aspects or components of every instinct. First, he noted that every instinct must have a *source* in the organic processes of the body. The source of an instinct is a quantity of excitation originating in a particular organ system within the body.

[4] *Standard Edition,* Vol. VII, p. 168.

Second, Freud asserted that every instinct has a certain *impetus* or *pressure*. This term simply refers to the quantitative strength of the excitation arising at the source. An instinct whose impetus is very great would naturally be expected to have a greater influence on the behavior of its subject than one whose impetus is weak.

Third, all instincts were said to have an *aim;* in the most general sense, the aim is simply the removal of the excitation arising at the source. Maintaining once again the basic point of view expressed in the "Project," Freud still saw endogenously originating excitation as something to be minimized. The psychic consequence of achieving this aim is the sensation of satisfaction.

Finally, the fourth major component of an instinct was said by Freud to be its *object,* which is that thing or person in the external world that satisfies the aim. An instinct cannot be satisfied or "turned off" without some manipulation of the external world—another consequence of the old idea from the "Project" that endogenous *Q* cannot simply be run away from—and the object is the specific aspect of the external world that must be manipulated.

To illustrate the interaction of the four components, consider the "normal" sexual instinct—i.e., the narrow view of sexuality held by most people in the nineteenth century. In this view, sexuality is something that has its exclusive source in the genital apparatus. When the instinct becomes engaged, a certain amount of tension arises in the genital region, its magnitude varying with the impetus of the instinct. In children, of course, the impetus is assumed always to be zero, and in adults it may vary from time to time and situation to situation. The aim of the instinct is the release of the tension and subsequent shutting off of the source, which is to say, orgasm. The normal object of this instinct is a sexual partner of the opposite sex. Such would be a typical definition of the "true" or "natural" sexual instinct in Freud's time, though some proper Victorians might have insisted further that the only normal object was one's legal spouse.

Freud's major discovery with respect to the sexual instinct, of course, was that this traditional formulation was much too restrictive. He came to believe that the essence of sexual pleasure lies in the rhythmic stroking or stimulation of virtually *any* part of the body. Thus a great many different combinations of source, impetus, aim, and object are legitimately considered to be sexual in nature. Some of the initial evidence that led Freud to broaden his definition in this way has already been considered. The *Three Essays* provide additional supporting data.

The first of the *Three Essays* consists of a discussion by Freud of the most obvious deviations from "normal" sexuality: the sexual aberrations or perversions. He first considers deviations with respect to object. The largest group of individuals exemplifying this kind of deviation are homosexuals, or, as Freud refers to them, "inverts." Less common cases include individuals who use children or animals as sexual objects. Most of Freud's discussion is devoted to inverts, though his conclusions are pertinent to the other cases as well.

The major point Freud makes is that the choice of a deviant object may be the result of the same instinct as that which impels the choice of a normal object. One argument in support of this position derives from the fact that in many cases inversion (or other object deviation) may be demonstrated to result from a specific set of developmental experiences. An overly possessive and "seductive" mother who thwarts her son's attempts at independence while lavishing excessive physical affection upon him may provide one such set. This implies that inversion is a "learned" behavior, attributable to environmental influences rather than innate predisposition. Furthermore, many individuals who are labeled "contingent inverts" are capable of *either* normal or inverted sexual satisfaction. In these individuals heterosexual and homosexual objects are largely interchangeable, the latter frequently being sought only in the abesnce of the former. That the same sexual urge may be satisfied by either type of object suggests that it does not make sense to postulate the existence of separate heterosexual and homosexual instincts. Instead, it seems to be a matter of the same instinct being capable of satisfaction by two different kinds of objects.

Freud concluded that the essential nature of sexuality does not lie in the choice of a particular kind of object. The sexual instinct must take *some* object, but the specific type is determined by environmental conditions and learning rather than the innate nature of sexuality. Freud summed up this idea in the following two passages:

> Experience of the cases that are considered abnormal has shown us that in them the sexual instinct and the sexual object are merely soldered together a fact which we have been in danger of overlooking in consequence of the uniformity of the normal picture, where the object appears to form part and parcel of the instinct. We are thus warned to loosen the bond that exists in our thoughts between instinct and object. It seems that the sexual instinct is in the first instance independent of its object; nor is its origin likely to be due to its object's attractions.[5]

> Under a great number of conditions and in surprisingly numerous individuals, the nature and importance of the sexual object recedes into the background. What is essential and constant in the sexual instinct is something else.[6]

A major implication of Freud's argument here is that the sexual instinct is *not* the same thing as an "instinct to procreate." Instead, it is a much broader instinct whose manifestations only coincidentally serve the ends of procreation because in most cases an adult of the opposite sex is eventually taken as a sexual object. Under those conditions biology prevails and procreation results.

Following his discussion of deviations with respect to the sexual object, Freud took up the issue of anomalies in the sexual aim. If we consider that the "normal" aim of the sexual instinct is the union of the genital organs in the act of copulation, then there are two general kinds of sexual activities which can represent significant deviations of the sexual aim. If

[5] *Ibid.*, p. 148.
[6] *Ibid.*, p. 149.

either kind of activity comes to replace completely the normal aim, it should be classified as a *perversion*. The two general kinds of perversions are "sexual activities which either (a) extend, in an anatomical sense, beyond the regions of the body that are designed for sexual union, or (b) linger over the intermediate relations to the sexual object which should normally be traversed rapidly on the path toward the normal sexual aim."[7]

The most commonly observed perversions of the first type—extending the anatomical loci of sexual gratification beyond the genital regions—involve the use of two particular parts of the body: the oral and anal cavities. Freud points out that a common response to the thought of sexual activities involving these regions—particularly activities where the genitals of one partner come into contact with the mouth or anus of the other—is profound disgust.[8] In spite of this response, however, such activities are commonly viewed as sexual in nature. The fact that some individuals achieve pleasure from them indicates as well that they must be considered as some of the varied manifestations of the sexual instinct.

The second classification of perversions, involving the lingering over intermediate activity, is more closely related to "normal" sexual behavior. Freud noted that when copulation is practiced by consenting adults it usually entails a substantial amount of activity prior to the actual act of intercourse. "Foreplay" or "forepleasure" are terms usually applied to this activity, denoting a great variety of specific acts, including touching and feeling, stroking, looking, and showing. All of these acts may provide sensations of great pleasure, though none of them is strictly or necessarily "sexual" in nature. That is, they may all be performed in non-sexual situations and be completely devoid of sexual connotations. In the lovemaking situation,

[7] *Ibid.*, p. 150.

[8] It should be noted that *disgust* is also a common response to deviations of object such as those discussed in the immediately preceding paragraphs, or to the Oedipal wish for the mother. In general, Freud viewed disgust as an emotion whose primary purpose is to inhibit and restrict the expression of the sexual instinct.

however, when they are preliminary to the act of copulation, they clearly come under the sway of the sexual instinct. When this happens, the urges to perform them are said to constitute the *component instincts* of sexuality. The component instincts themselves may sometimes become highly sexualized, and when one of their aims *replaces* the normal sexual aim the result may appropriately be called a perversion.

Many of the component instincts seem to come in complementary pairs, such as the desire to look at (scopophilia) and the desire to be looked at (exhibitionism), or the desire to hurt (sadism) and to be hurt (masochism). People who derive their sexual pleasure mainly or exclusively from one or another of these activities are perverts: voyeurs or "peeping Toms," exhibitionists, sadists, and masochists, respectively. So long as the component instincts manifest themselves in moderation, however, and are subordinate to the aim of copulation, they are within the domain of "normal" sexuality. Nevertheless, their very existence makes it clear that the boundary between perversion and normal sexuality must be drawn very finely. Freud summarized the relationship between the two as follows:

> No healthy person, it appears, can fail to make some addition that might be called perverse to the normal sexual aim; and the universality of this finding is in itself enough to show how inappropriate it is to use the word perversion as a term of reproach. In the sphere of sexual life we are brought up against peculiar and, indeed, insoluble difficulties as soon as we try to draw a sharp line to distinguish mere variations within the range of what is physiological from pathological symptoms.[9]

Thus perverse *tendencies* may be regarded as universal, though technically speaking the incidence of perversion per se may not.

In general, then, Freud's analysis of the sexual aberrations demonstrated that the sexual instinct of a mature adult is not so simple as it might appear on the surface. Even "normal"

[9] *Ibid.*, p. 160–161.

sexuality was shown to involve the complex interplay of numerous component instincts, each of which in isolation is capable of providing the basis of a perversion. The choices of object and aim were shown to be learned and highly variable consequences of a sexual instinct whose scope is thus much broader than the traditional view suggested. Having expanded the conception of sexuality this far, Freud went on to document some surprising relationships that he discovered between sexual behavior and hysteria.

It has already been shown how Freud found the pathogenic ideas underlying hysteria to be wishes of a sexual nature, usually with a deviant quality. Thus, a new way of viewing hysterical phenomena—suggested by the above analysis of the sexual instinct—is as the result of wishes to engage in perverted sexual activities. This is not to suggest that Freud's hysterics were really perverts. In fact, hysterics were found by Freud to respond *consciously* to ideas of perversion with an unusual degree of repugnance and disgust, and it was to just this exaggerated avoidance tendency that he attributed the genesis of the symptoms. That is, he assumed that hysteria was characterized first by perverse sexual fantasies and wishes, and second by extremely strong resistances against conscious expression of the wishes. The presence of the first characteristic was not surprising, since the analysis of dreams and normal lovemaking revealed that normal individuals experienced "perverse" impulses as well. What *was* remarkable about hysterics was the extremity of their defense against the impulses.

Freud thus came to see hysterical symptoms and perversions as representing opposite sides of the same coin. Taking as his starting point the assumption that deviant sexual impulses are universal, he postulated three general kinds of outcomes. First, the deviant impulses may be acted on directly, thus giving rise to the overt sexual aberrations and perversions. Second, they may be subject to a certain amount of restriction and modification but nevertheless permitted partial gratification through the component instincts of normal sexual life and in dreams. This is the most favorable of the three outcomes, and is essentially a compromise between the sexual instinct on the one hand and the restrictions of society on the other. The third kind of outcome is for the impulses to be subjected to massive resistance and permitted only indirect, unconscious expression through neurotic symptoms such as conversions. Thus perversions and conversions were seen as mutually exclusive responses to the same kinds of "deviant" sexual impulses.

Childhood Sexuality

After demonstrating that deviant sexual impulses in one manifestation or another are an inevitable part of the adult human make-up, Freud was faced with the problem of explaining their *origins*. Not surprisingly, he turned to a consideration of *childhood sexuality* for his answer, interpreting the deviant impulses as the residues of childhood sexual experience. A major part of the *Three Essays* is accordingly given over to a specific theory of the sexual instinct's development throughout childhood.

Freud asserted that the sexual instinct is fully operative in human infants from the moment of birth onwards, though at first it is completely undifferentiated. Specific objects and aims come to be selected only with experience. This means that the infant is potentially capable of taking sexual pleasure from the rhythmic stimulation of any part of his body. This potential for sexual gratification anywhere in the body Freud called *polymorphous perversity*. He found general support for its existence in the observation that young infants seem capable of experiencing sensuous delight from the gentle stimulation or stroking of almost any parts of their bodies. As the infant grows and develops, however, and his sexual instinct accordingly becomes more structured, the extent of polymorphous perversity decreases.

Note that this conception is completely consistent with the "Project," according to which the endogenous *Q* entering the undifferentiated nervous system of a very young organism does not have well-established channels of transmission and discharge available to it. Thus *potentially* the *Q* can organize itself in a wide variety of ways, depending upon the patterns of simultaneous cathexes that happen to obtain within the system when the *Q* enters. On the neurological level, then, this is an exact analogue to the state of polymorphous perversity, where the sexual instinct is undifferentiated and capable of many different outcomes and manifestations.

The conception of the sexual instinct in the *Three Essays* represents a refinement and elaboration over the "Project" because in the later work Freud was concerned with a more specialized aspect of psychological function. He was concerned there with the processing of only a certain kind of endogenous stimulation: that arising from sexual sources. He even employed a specific name for sexual instinctual energy: *libido*, a Latin word meaning "desire" or "lust." Thus libido is the energy arising at sexual sources which enters the psychic system and provides the driving force for the sexual instinct. The pressure of the sexual instinct is determined by the amount of libido impinging on the system at a given moment, and the aim and object are determined by the specific ideas and memories that are cathected by the libido. In general, the aim is constituted by the cathexis of memories of specific past sexual satisfactions, and the object by the memory of persons or things that were instrumental in obtaining those past satisfactions.

Freud's theory of childhood sexuality is concerned with describing how the initially undifferentiated psychic system becomes progressively more structured in its processing of libido. In spite of the fact that the initial state of polymorphous perversity offers unlimited *potential* for the development of the sexual instinct, Freud believed that the contingencies of human experience quickly narrow down the possibilities. Since many of the most crucial narrowing experiences are common to all human infants, he further believed it possible to delineate a universal pattern of sexual development. He postulated a series of specific stages to constitute this pattern, which his followers have come to refer to as the stages of *psychosexual development*.

Following the state of polymorphous perversity, the first stage develops out of what is clearly the most important waking activity for all human infants: feeding. The centrality of the feeding situation is attested to by the fact that newborn infants do little more than eat and sleep in a regular, cyclic pattern. The primary disturber of sleep is hunger, and when the child awakes he is likely to become very agitated until feeding is initiated. The feeding situation itself is obviously a great source of satisfaction since its initiation usually ends the child's agitation and distress. The quieting effect of feeding, plus the fact that the infant quickly drops all other activities in order to suck and eat, suggests that it is a genuinely "pleasurable" experience for him.

A major part of the pleasure must be assumed to come from the satisfaction of hunger. But Freud believed that there is more to it than that, citing the observation that simple sucking, even in the absence of real nourishment, serves to satisfy and quiet an agitated infant at least temporarily. Furthermore, an older infant will happily suck his thumb or a pacifier for long periods of time when he is not eating, and so long as he is not overly hungry or otherwise uncomfortable he seems to take great pleasure from the activity. Thus the infant's mouth and the sucking response quite obviously become involved in the obtaining of a pleasure that is not completely nutritional in nature.

On the basis of Freud's clinical experiences with adults the interpretation of this observation was obvious. Since oral responses had already been demonstrated to take on strong sexual connotations in perversions, neuroses, and latent dream thoughts, Freud hypothesized that the non-nutritive component of an infant's oral behavior was sexual in nature. Such a conception was completely consistent with Freud's expanded definition of sexuality, and the infant's experience then would explain the origin of the oral sexuality observed in adults.

Freud suggested that even though the polymorphously perverse infant can receive sexual stimulation anywhere in his body, some organ systems quite naturally come to receive it more frequently than others. Most prominent among these in early life is the oral zone—the mouth and lips. In the course of normal feeding this area receives much rhythmic stimulation, so in addition to providing nourishment the activity incidentally provides sexual satisfaction. Thus, memories centering about the oral zone and oral stimulation become highly associated with sexual satisfaction. This means that on subsequent occasions libido as it arises will come quite automatically to cathect memories of the oral experiences.

This has profound consequences for the psychological development of the infant, because libido impinges on the psychic system almost continuously. Its pressure varies from time to time, of course, but it is nevertheless almost constantly present in at least a small degree; thus the memories of oral experiences are constantly cathected, at least to a small degree. Their precathexis means that new experiences, whether the result of instinctual *or* external sources of excitation, become associated with oral memories. The oral memories assume a centrality in the psychic life of the infant, and new experiences tend to be organized around them. Thus a sense of *orality* comes to pervade the entire experience of an infant, and oral sexuality comes to play a much larger role than one might expect.

An organ system that becomes the subject of this kind of psychic organization was referred to by Freud as an *erotogenic zone*; the mouth, as the first organ to become sharply differentiated as a vehicle for sexual satisfaction, is thus the earliest erotogenic zone. Freud assigned the mouth primacy as the most important erotogenic zone for approximately the first year of life. That period, accordingly, is known as the *oral stage of psychosexual development*. As the infant develops past the first year or so of life the oral region comes to be challenged as the primary erotogenic zone. In time, a new part of the body, also capable of rhythmic stimulation, becomes associated with sexual gratification even more strongly than the oral zone, and thus a new phase in psychosexual development begins. The new erotogenic zone is the anal area, and the new phase is referred to as the *anal stage*.

The whole notion of anal sexuality is frequently greeted by expressions of astonishment and/or disgust. Peculiar as the formulation initially seems, however, Freud was able to marshal a considerable amount of evidence in its support. He noted that as the child gradually overcomes his neonatal state of helplessness and becomes capable of voluntary muscular activity, one of the first important social obligations he is charged with is the control of his body. Usually he undertakes these obligations willingly and seems to take great pleasure in developing mastery of his own body. One of the situations in which this issue of control becomes most intense is toilet training. The necessity for proper bowel habits is usually very strongly impressed upon the child by his parents, and when the child succeeds in his efforts he is lavishly praised.

All of this means that several sources of potential pleasure tend to coalesce around the child's toilet training activities. When he is successful he earns the praise of his mother as well as satisfaction from achieving control over his own body. Added to these important gratifications is the fact that as he learns to control his bowel, he discovers that he is capable of voluntarily stimulating his anal region through the retention and expulsion of his feces. Such stimulation is capable of gratifying the sexual instinct, according to Freud's broadened definition, and since the experience is repeated on a daily basis the anal region comes gradually to be differentiated as a major erotogenic zone that competes with the oral zone.

The circumstances surrounding the development of the anal erotogenic zone are thus quite comparable to those surrounding the oral stage. In the oral stage, sexual pleasure first appears as a by-product of the feeding situation and thus comes to be associated with oral activities. In the anal stage it occurs as a by-product of the urges and rewards for bowel control as well as the child's own tendencies toward bodily control. "Anal" ideas and memories—typically involving such activities as elimination, retention, smearing, or cleaning—come to assume the same psychic centrality that had characterized the earlier oral memories.

After the child has reached the age of three or four and has mastered the tasks implicit in toilet training and the achievement of coordinated body control, yet another important shift in the organization of libido takes place. Freud asserted that certain pressures inevitably arise in this stage of childhood to mitigate against the primacy of the anal zone and bring to light yet another erotogenic zone in its place. First, there are distinct social pressures against the explicit expression of anal sexuality. Excremental functions generally are regarded with disgust by adults, and the lesson of this response is not lost on the child. Secondly, the child of this age has physical coordination much superior to that of a one- or two-year-old, and he is capable of manually manipulating virtually any part of his body at will. Thus Freud assumed that he comes inevitably to discover the pleasures of infantile masturbation. From the very beginning of his life, the child has occasional experiences of pleasurable manipulation of his genitals, but it is only with his newly developed physical abilities that he becomes capable of achieving regular and intense autoerotic pleasure from them. When this happens, the genitals gradually replace the anal zone as the major locus of sexual pleasure. Thus begins the next stage in psychosexual development, the *phallic stage.* Freud stated that the phallic stage is a regular characteristic of the development of both boys and girls, in spite of the exclusively masculine connotations of its name. The aim of the libido for both sexes in this stage is the rythmic stimulation of the genital region.

The phallic stage marks the last overt stage of infantile sexuality. Freud noted that childhood sexual activity reaches a peak at the age of five or six, while the phallic stage holds sway. In response to the controlling phallic organization of ideas, sexual curiosity becomes prominent; children become interested in anatomical differences between the sexes and seek to inform themselves—albeit in childish ways—about sexual matters. Furthermore, Oedipal feelings and attitudes become especially prominent and intense during the phallic stage. The arousal of such intense and conflict-laden issues frequently makes the phallic stage a difficult period for the child. He may show overt signs of anxiety, sleep poorly, and in general be disturbed in his behavior.

Then, at about the age of six, the entire sexual instinct seems to disappear and the child typically enters a period of sexual quiescence that lasts until the onset of puberty. Freud called this period the *latency stage* and noted that it quite conveniently begins at the age when children enter school and begin to receive formal training in the skills required by their society. Without sexual matters to concern them, the children are maximally able to apply themselves to the important tasks of learning. As the name "latency" suggests, however, Freud assumed that the sexual instinct does not vanish but merely goes into a state of dormancy. More specifically, he assumed that the infantile forms of sexuality undergo *repression*. Thus all the ideas and impulses that had been associated with the oral, anal, and phallic stages are pushed into the unconscious. Once unconscious, of course, they are denied the overt expression they had enjoyed in early childhood and on a conscious level they are responded to with disgust. Nevertheless, they exert their indirect influence, and, even more important, the basic sexualized memory organizations of the three stages remain to control future associations.[10]

Thus "perverse" forms of sexuality were said by Freud to be part of the normal early development of every human being. Sexualized interest in the mouth, anus, and genitals characterizes the childhood of every individual, and it is only after repression that these issues come to arouse so much disgust.

[10] Note that this has implications for the model presented in the *Interpretation of Dreams*. The oral, anal, and phallic memory organizations are equivalent to the primitive mnemic systems. Thus the early mnemic systems are sexually organized, as well as concretely based on simultaneous occurrences.

This childhood sexuality, of course, was what Freud had discerned in the perverse fantasies of his patients and dreamers, and in the component instincts of normal adult sexuality.

Psychoanalytic Character Types

As Freud worked with increasing numbers of patients between 1900 and 1910, he gradually came to the conclusion that childhood sexuality has yet another important effect on adult life. He discovered that subtle differences in the sexual experiences of children can have dramatic effects on the formation of their adult character. The first step leading to this conclusion was the finding of consistent individual differences in the kinds of sexual material presented by his patients. *All* patients provided material relating to childhood sexuality, but some produced predominantly oral associations while others were more consistently anal or phallic in their imagery. One of Freud's "anal" patients, for example, was a young man who suffered from a very distressing *obsession* (a thought that he could not voluntarily prevent from entering his consciousness). As a young army officer he had learned of a particularly horrible torture in which ravenous rats were permitted to bore into the victim's anus. The patient's obsessions were persistent thoughts that his loved ones might be subjected to such torture. The thoughts seemed to come involuntarily, out of nowhere, and the patient was powerless to put them out of his mind. Needless to say, his free associations to this symptom revealed a large proportion of anal imagery.[11]

After working with substantial numbers of patients of this anal type, Freud noticed that they consistently reported that their parents had been exceptionally strict in their toilet training procedures. Insofar as he could check on the accuracy of these reports, Freud found no reason to doubt their authenticity. Thus he discovered a reliable relationship between severe toilet training in childhood and the tendency to produce anal

[11] The complete case is reported in Freud's paper "Notes upon a Case of Obsessional Neurosis," in the *Standard Edition*, Vol. X.

(rather than oral or phallic) forms of free associations in adulthood. This finding was not particularly surprising, of course, because as children the patients had had to worry a great deal about anal functions, which therefore came to stand out more than oral or phallic concerns.

More surprising, however, was Freud's observation that his anal patients tended to have certain distinct personality characteristics in common. Specifically, he found that they manifested exaggerated traits of *orderliness, parsimony,* and *obstinancy* in their adult lives. Thus it was apparent that childhood experiences governing infantile sexuality influenced the overt personality characteristics of adults as well as their fantasies.

As Freud considered this triad of anal personality traits, he concluded that he could find distinct prototypes for them in the toilet training experience. For example, toilet training is one of the first aspects of personal hygiene that a child learns for himself, and it becomes the prototype for situations in which he will be expected to keep himself clean and neat. A child who has been trained to be tidy in the bathroom also turns out to be neat, clean and orderly in other aspects of his life.

The trait of parsimony also finds its prototype in the bowel training situation, though the relationship may not immediately be evident. The essence of the toilet training task, of course, is to learn voluntarily to retain or to expel feces. When the child performs properly and gives up his feces at the appropriate time and place, his parents are so delighted, argued Freud, that the child quite naturally comes to think of his feces as a potential *gift.* Thus when the child retains his feces, in his own mind he is retaining something very valuable, and his behavior can be regarded as an early example of willful hoarding. Since strict toilet training calls for an unusually large amount of this behavior, the tendency to hoard willfully becomes emphasized in some children and persists into adulthood in the form of parsimony.

Obstinacy, according to Freud, has its origin in the same matrix of values and wishes. When feces are thought of as the primal gift, capable of pleasing the parents, the child who withholds them excessively is being obstinate or stubborn as well as stingy.

Another way of putting this is to suggest that in the anal stage children quite naturally manifest the juvenile prototypes of the traits Freud found to be characteristic of his adults with anal fantasies and associations. In children these traits are often mixed with their opposites, however, and the anal stage in general is therefore often a difficult one for parents to deal with. They are frequently bewildered by the child's remarkable ability to be cooperative, generous, and orderly at one moment, only to become messy, obstinate, and "impossible" at another. It is no wonder that the period of development is often referred to as the "terrible twos." In time, however, the child develops a surer sense of his own ability to control himself and be cooperative at the same time, and the difficult traits recede into the background. But if the entire situation has been unusually emphasized for the child through severe toilet training, the entire anal organization is strengthened unusually and he retains the traits of orderliness, parsimony, and obstinacy throughout his life as a legacy from the anal stage. Freud accordingly referred to this particular constellation of traits as the *anal character*.

Anal characteristics are likely to be transmitted from one generation to another, though not by genetic means. If a parent is himself an anal character, it is very likely that his own concerns with orderliness and neatness will cause him to be demanding of the same characteristics in his own children. Poor toilet habits are especially likely to upset such a parent, and therefore he will be very strict in the toilet training of his children. This, of course, tends to create anal characteristics in the children themselves, and thus the traits are passed on to a new generation.

Freud speculated that there probably were constellations of personality traits that constituted *oral characters* and *phallic characters* as well as anal characters, though he himself never completely worked them out. Some of Freud's followers, with his concurrence, worked out models of such character types. The oral character, for example, is presumed to result from either overindulgence or underindulgence during the oral stage. As an adult such an individual is likely to engage heavily in such "oral" activities as eating, drinking, smoking, and talking. Furthermore, if he was *over*indulged as an infant he is likely to turn out cheerful and perhaps unrealistically optimistic in adulthood; if he was *under*indulged, he is likely to become envious, acquisitive, and pessimistic. The phallic character has been less thoroughly formulated than the oral or anal characters, though in general the adult traits of curiosity and exhibitionism have been related to unusually strong crises in the phallic stage.

The implications of these psychoanalytic notions about character formation were very startling, because they suggested that many of the most fundamental components of adult character are shaped by the very early sexual experiences of childhood. Infantile sexuality was demonstrated to have a profound effect not only on isolated aspects of adult behavior like dreams, neuroses, or lovemaking, but also on the personality structure itself. Furthermore, since the formative sexual experiences dated back to the very earliest stages of infancy, the process of personality development obviously began much earlier in life than anyone had previously suspected.

None of Freud's views on childhood sexuality were widely accepted at first. It was not comfortable to think that a person's basic character may be already established by the time he is five years old, or that so much of human behavior is related to sexuality and perversion. Even some of Freud's most gifted followers believed that he over-emphasized the importance of sexuality. Alfred Adler and Carl Jung broke with Freud partly on that account and went on to develop their own separate schools of psychology. Freud himself steadfastly insisted on the basic correctness of his views, however, and continued throughout his life to assign sexuality a pre-eminent role in human motivation. As his initial notoriety turned to fame and appreciation, much of the world came to agree with him.

SUGGESTED FURTHER READINGS

The closest thing to a personal account of Freud's self-analysis is provided by his letters to Fleiss dating from late 1896 and 1897 (*The Origins of Psycho-Analysis* [New York, Basic Books, 1954]). Two letters are especially interesting with respect to the present chapter: letter 50 (November, 1896) describes Freud's immediate reactions to his father's death, and letter 71 (October, 1897) is devoted to a discussion of the evidence that led to the postulation of the Oedipus complex.

The sexual theory itself is spelled out in *Three Essays on the Theory of Sexuality* (New York, Avon Books, 1965), originally published in 1905. A famous case history, that of "Little Hans," was published by Freud in 1909 to document the existence of sexuality in children. The case appeared in a paper entitled "Analysis of a Phobia in a Five-Year-Old Boy." Freud's initial formulation of the anal character was included in a 1908 paper entitled "Character and Anal Erotism." The oral character was first conceptualized by Freud's follower Karl Abraham in the paper "The Influence of Oral Erotism on Character Formation." It appears in a collection of Abraham's writings entitled *On Character and Libido Development* (New York, Norton, 1966). More recently, the psychoanalytic notions of character and psychosexual development have been expanded and elaborated upon by Erik H. Erikson in *Childhood and Society* (New York, Norton, 1963).

6
Psychoanalytic Psychotherapy and the Theory of Instincts

It must not be forgotten that psychoanalysis began as a *therapy*, and that even during the years when Freud was developing his elaborate theories about human nature in general he continued to practice as a psychotherapist. Freud's therapeutic activity was always closely related to his theory building, and over the years a number of significant changes took place in his therapeutic technique that had major implications for his general theory.

Until 1900, however, it seemed to Freud that the cathartic method he and Breuer had developed required little modification. The method seemed to offer unbounded promise for the treatment of not only hysteria but other neurotic symptoms as well. *Obsessions* (unwilled thoughts that persistently intrude into consciousness), for example, were found to be caused by unconscious pathogenic ideas, just as conversion symptoms were. Free association was capable of bringing the pathogenic ideas to consciousness and relieving the obsessions. Most neurotic symptoms came to be seen as the products of unconscious pathogenic ideas, and thus the task of a psychotherapist seemed very simple. All he had to do was facilitate the conscious recognition of those ideas.

The first difficulty that Freud noted in the early days of psychoanalysis was the obvious resistance his patients displayed when their free associations began to touch closely upon repressed material. This did not seem to be a really major difficulty, however, since the therapist had only to be persistent in urging the patient to carry on with his associations, no matter how objectionable they seemed, and to be insightful in his *interpretations* of the patient's associations. In making an interpretation the therapist used his superior insight about the nature of mental dynamics to comprehend the "real" or "hidden" meaning of the associations. He recognized the true nature of the pathogenic ideas before the patient did himself, and conveyed this knowledge by means of interpretations.

Thus if a psychoanalyst were a skillful and insightful interpreter, it seemed that neurotic symptoms could be overcome in spite of the strongest resistance. Given enough free associations, the analyst could tell his patients what their real pathogenic ideas were and thus bring these ideas to consciousness "second-handedly." When Freud treated his early patients, then, his method consisted primarily of urging them to persist in their free associations and of frequently interpreting their associations. He literally tried to tell them what was on their unconscious minds.

Experience was soon to show that the therapeutic task was much more complicated than this. It became apparent that the analyst had to do far more than simply lecture his patients about the contents of their unconscious psyches. One of the cases that most forcefully taught Freud this lesson was that of an eighteen-year-old hysterical woman whom he treated at the end of 1900. She has become famous in the annals of medical literature under the pseudonym "Dora," and her case well illustrates the complicated therapeutic puzzles that Freud was finally forced to confront.

The Case of Dora

Dora initially came to consult with Freud at the behest of her father, who had previously been one of his neuropathic patients. There was nothing particularly extraordinary about her presenting symptoms, which were typical of a turn-of-the-century hysteric. Over a period of several years she had suffered from a nervous cough and from a hoarseness that often resulted in complete loss of voice. These symptoms had no obvious organic cause, but periodically appeared and then spontaneously disappeared for no apparent reason. Immediately prior to seeing Freud she had been in low spirits and had gone so far as to write a suicide note, without, however, actually making a suicide attempt. She also was beginning to experience very brief and intermittent amnesic spells. Though these symptoms were certainly troublesome, there was nothing about them to set Dora apart from other hysterics; her illness was neither spectacular nor unusual.

When she first consulted Freud, he was optimistic and felt himself to be at the height of his powers. He had just made his greatest discoveries about the dynamics of the mind and the influence of infantile sexuality. Thus he had a whole new arsenal of material on which to base his interpretations. Furthermore, Dora herself seemed an ideal patient for his method. She was very intelligent and verbally astute, and she readily took to the task of free association. When Freud interpreted her associations to her, she often took issue with him, and lively arguments followed. But nevertheless she always paid close attention to the interpretations, seemed to understand them, and usually was finally won over to Freud's point of view. From the very beginning her therapy proceeded very nicely, and after only a few sessions Freud wrote to Fliess about her, stating confidently that "the case has opened smoothly to my collection of picklocks."[1]

Indeed, in a brief period of time Freud and Dora made amazing progress together in uncovering the unconscious thoughts and impulses behind her symptoms. Her case, superficially so ordinary, turned out to be a marvelously intricate one that beautifully illustrated the phenomena of overdetermination, displacement, and infantile sexuality. A very impor-

[1] *The Origins of Psycho-Analysis* (New York, Basic Books, 1954), p. 325.

tant part of Dora's therapy consisted of the brilliant interpretation of two of her dreams, which were shown to be closely related to her neurosis.

As Dora's case unfolded, it hinged upon her relationship with four major characters: her parents and their closest friends, a couple referred to as "Herr and Frau K." Dora's mother was a drab woman, little given to taking positive enjoyment from life. She had few interests outside of her household, and spent most of her time dusting and cleaning her many possessions. She spent so much time at this neurotically compulsive activity that she had almost no opportunity to use and enjoy her belongings.

Dora's father was a wealthy and successful businessman who, in contrast to his wife, had a breadth of interests. His health was generally very poor, however. Freud had treated him many years before for a syphilitic infection, and in the years when Dora was growing up he suffered from tuberculosis and a detached retina. He spent long periods of time confined to bed, and because of the tuberculosis he had moved his family from Vienna to a provincial town with a healthful climate. It was here that they made the acquaintance of Herr and Frau K., a middle-aged couple with young children of their own. The two families became fast friends, often sharing the same household on holiday trips. All, especially Frau K., were extremely solicitous about the health of Dora's father.

Frau K. was considerably more ambitious and lively than Dora's mother, and she quickly established herself as the chief nurse for Dora's father. As he regained his health and strength, it became obvious to Dora that Frau K. had replaced her mother in more than just nursing duties: she had become her father's mistress, a liaison that was to last for several years. Frau K. and Dora's father went to considerable effort to arrange convenient meetings, and though they made some effort to be discreet about their relationship, the sharp-eyed Dora did not miss a thing. Dora was not ignored by Frau K. either. The older woman became a confidante and kind of big sister, and as Dora matured Frau K. was her chief source of information about worldly matters. She initiated Dora into the world of sex by showing her a number of illustrated medical and physiological textbooks. This was done secretly, because at the time it was considered scandalous for a teen-aged girl to learn about sexual matters even in such an intellectualized way. For a long time Dora was very appreciative of Frau K.'s friendship, but after a while she came to believe she was simply being used by the older woman as a means of getting close to her father. Thus at the time of her analysis Dora spoke deprecatingly of her former friend.

The final member of this psychopathological cast was Herr K., a handsome though rather passive man who never overtly complained about his wife's affair with his best friend but contented himself with occasional amorous adventures with servant girls in his household. Furthermore, as Dora grew up into an attractive young woman, he began to take an appreciative interest in *her*. From the beginning he had been very kind to her and had given her numerous presents, but as she matured his attitude became more than simply fatherly. This was reflected in an incident that occurred when Dora was fourteen. She had met Herr K. at his place of business to accompany him to a joint outing of the two families. Suddenly Herr K. drew all the shades and kissed her ardently. Dora responded with profound disgust, after which Herr K. apologized profusely and begged her not to mention the incident to anyone. Dora did not—not, at least, until much later.

In the years following this incident Herr K. continued to give Dora expensive presents, including an extremely elegant jewel-case. During this period Dora did nothing to discourage his attentions, and they maintained a close though platonic friendship. Finally, during the summer before Dora's analysis with Freud, a crucial incident occurred. The two families were staying together at a resort, and Dora and Herr K. took a walk together around a lake. Suddenly Herr K. launched into an emotional speech, during which he exclaimed (as Dora vividly remembered), "I get nothing out of my wife"! He concluded by proposing to Dora. Dora indignantly and violently rejected his proposal, and ran back to the resort. For two weeks she remained at the resort, in spite of the fact that Herr K. was staying at the same house, and said nothing to anyone about the incident at the lake. Then, as her father was preparing to leave on a business trip, she suddenly announced that she was going with him, which she did. A short while after that she informed her father of Herr K.'s proposal. He confronted Herr K., who vehemently denied the whole thing. Furthermore, Herr K. cast aspersions on Dora by suggesting that her character was warped from reading indecent literature about sex. This meant that Frau K. must have told him about her secret reading, and Dora quite understandably felt betrayed by both Herr K. and his wife. Shortly afterwards she experienced the worsening of her hysterical symptoms that led to her consultation with Freud.

In her analysis with Freud, most of the time was spent in trying to disentangle and clarify Dora's feelings about these four people. As can be imagined, her feelings were very complicated and ambivalent, with many unconscious, repressed currents. This emphasis on her important interpersonal relationships already marked one slight change in Freud's therapeutic technique from the days when he had collaborated with Breuer. In those days, the therapy had been explicitly *symptom oriented,* whereas in Dora's case Freud was more interested in dealing with the *underlying causes* of the symptoms. That is, in the early days therapy was continued only until all of the specific symptoms had disappeared, and then it was stopped. In Dora's case, however, the mere remission of symptoms was not considered sufficient to constitute a "cure." Freud noted that her symptoms had disappeared spontaneously several times in the past, only to recur later. Thus any absence of symptoms might well be only temporary, and in Dora's case a new criterion of cure was adopted. Freud decided to continue her case as long as new unconscious material relevant to the symptoms continued to come to light, regardless of whether or not the symptoms themselves were constantly present. This general tendency to focus attention on underlying conflicts and attitudes rather than on symptoms has remained to this day one of the hallmarks of psychoanalytic psychotherapy.

As Freud and Dora worked together to try to understand her attitudes toward her parents and toward Herr and Frau K., an incredibly intricate yet completely logical pattern emerged. The long paper in which Freud describes the analysis, entitled "Fragment of an Analysis of a Case of Hysteria," reads much like a mystery story, with one unconscious idea after another merging with the already known part of her story to create a gradually sharpening image of the whole. In the space of a very few weeks, Dora began to understand the true depth and complexity of her feelings toward this strange quartet of people who dominated her life.

One of the things that clearly came to light, for example, was that Dora had really been very strongly attracted to Herr K., even though she had repudiated his advances. It became clear that throughout her adolescence she had undertaken many maneuvers to arrange to be near him and to encourage his attention. She realized that she had often been very solicitous of Herr K.'s young children only so that she could be near him, and not because she really liked the children. Thus when earlier in the analysis she had accused Frau K. of paying attention to *her* only so that she could be near her father, Dora had really attributed her own motives to Frau K. At the same time that she was attracted to Herr K., however, she also feared and resented him. She feared him partly because his unexpected kiss when she was fourteen had aroused dangerous recollections of her infantile sexuality (her response of disgust was one sign that such was the case), and she resented him because she suspected that his affection for her was not completely sincere. Shortly before the incident by the lake, Dora had heard stories about how Herr K. had propositioned one of his maids, using the line "I get nothing out of my wife." When he used exactly the same words in his proposal to her, she naturally felt insulted and abused by him.

Dora's feelings about Herr K. were elaborated and clarified further through the interpretation of a dream that she reported to Freud. The dream was a recurrent one which she had had a number of times immediately following the incident at the lake and once again while she was in the midst of her analysis with Freud. The dream was rather short, and it was recorded by Freud as follows: "A house was on fire. My father was standing beside my bed and woke me up. I dressed myself quickly. Mother wanted to stop and save her jewel-case; but father said: I refuse to let myself and my two children be burnt for the sake of your jewel-case. We hurried downstairs, and as soon as I was outside I woke up."[2] The interpretation of the dream revealed an extremely complicated web of latent thoughts, only the main points of which can be described here.

As should perhaps be expected, a number of distinctly sexual allusions emerged in Dora's free associations to the dream. For example, her consideration of the *fire* that threatened the house led to several associations about water and wetness, the antithesis of fire. Among them were recollections of having wet the bed and of masturbating as a child, and of the fact that masturbating causes a moistening of the genital area. There also was a much more direct allusion to sexuality in the dream, in the image of the jewel-case. In German, the word for "jewel-case" (*Schmuckkästchen*) was a common slang term for the female genitals.

The jewel-case was also closely associated in Dora's mind with Herr K., of course, since he had made her a present of such an object. Still other associations linked him with her sexual thoughts. The fire, for example, was also associated with him. *Smoke* was associated with fire via the expression "There can be no smoke without fire," and Dora noted that Herr K. was a heavy smoker. When he had kissed her in his office his breath had smelled strongly of tobacco smoke; as Dora remembered it, the odor had overpowered her and had contributed strongly to her feelings of disgust. Still another allusion to her feelings about Herr K. was found in her dream statement "I dressed myself quickly." Dora recalled that her

[2] *Standard Edition*, Vol. VII, p. 64.

bed at the resort by the lake had been in a hallway close to Herr K.'s room, and that she had worried about his seeing her in a state of undress. After his proposal, she always hurried to dress in the mornings. She also remembered a real incident in which she had awakened suddenly from a nap and had been startled to find Herr K. standing by her bedside looking at her. This scene was also represented in the dream, except that there it was her *father* by the bedside instead of Herr K.

Dora's father was a key figure in some other important associations. When discussing her childhood bed-wetting—one of the recollections that had established the sexual significance of the fire in the dream—Dora mentioned that her father had often waked her in the middle of the night to take her to the bathroom, thus protecting her from her own incontinence. In her dream, therefore, an image of her father as a protective figure from her past was summoned up and represented. In addition, this protective father-figure *replaced* Herr K.—it was her father who was standing by her bedside in her dream instead of the man who was her current source of anxiety. The dream consequently had Oedipal overtones, which provided Freud with the key to comprehending the basic wish that motivated the dream, and that shortly was partially fulfilled in reality:

> The child decided [in the dream] to fly *with* her father; in reality she fled *to* her father because she was afraid of the man who was pursuing her; she summoned up an infantile affection for her father so that it might protect her against her present affection for a stranger. . . . And how much better it had been when that same father of hers had loved no one more than her, and had exerted all his strength to save her from the dangers that had then threatened her! The infantile, and now unconscious, wish to put her father in the strange man's place had the potency necessary for the formation of a dream.[3]

Thus the dream, in a few short lines, expressed Dora's sexual arousal by Herr K., her anxiety as a result of that

[3] *Ibid.*, p. 86.

arousal, her subsequent rejection of Herr K. as a sexual object, and her substitution of her father—the Oedipal object—for him. Shortly after having the dream for the first few times she achieved a partial realization of its wish in reality by leaving the resort with her father (fleeing *from* Herr K. *with* her father), and telling him of the dangerous proposal Herr K. had made to her.

Once Dora had fled with her father she stopped having the dream, and it did not recur until she was in analysis with Freud. The reason for the dream's occurrence while she was at the resort was obvious: she was in an emotion-laden situation where all of the impulses and ideas expressed in the dream were constantly being aroused. As soon as she left the resort with her father the arousing stimuli were no longer so constantly present, and the need for the dream disappeared. The question of why she had the same dream in the middle of her analysis was less easily answered, however. Why should she have the dream again at a time when she was out of the immediate sphere of Herr K.? Freud wondered briefly about this question and asked her about the circumstances of the day immediately preceding the last occurrence of the dream. He discovered a day residue in an innocuous event that had occurred the day before, but he apparently did not probe further than that. As things turned out, he would have been wise to have done so, because in addition to the interpretations that have been described so far the dream had a further message, intended specifically for Freud.

One reason Freud did not pursue the matter further undoubtedly was that Dora's analysis seemed to go exceedingly well for the next few sessions. Dora's feelings toward the important people in her life were explored in depth, and many aspects of her ambivalence toward her father as well as Herr K. were illuminated. It finally came to light that her feelings about Frau K. were extremely important as well, and that a strong unconscious element in her mental life was a homosexual love for her former confidante. While all these feelings were being revealed in the analysis, Dora was experiencing considerable relief from her symptoms. She seemed to be genuinely getting better, and Freud believed that as soon as they had gotten to the bottom of her attitude toward Frau K. she would be largely cured.

Such was not to be, however. Just as Dora's case seemed to be moving into its most productive stage, a dramatic and unexpected event occurred. On December 13, 1900, after less than three months of treatment, Dora began her therapy session with the question "Do you know that I am here for the last time today?"[4] There followed a very productive analytic hour, from Freud's point of view, in which Herr K. was once again the chief topic of discussion. Dora seemed especially receptive to Freud's interpretations and did not argue about them, as was her wont before accepting them. Then, at the end of the session, "She seemed to be moved; she said good-bye to me very warmly, with the heartiest wishes for the New Year, and—came no more."[5] Dora's analysis was suddenly and prematurely terminated by her own wish. She continued throughout much of her life to be troubled by recurrent hysterical symptoms.

Freud was surprised and shocked by this sudden turn of events, since he had not expected to lose his prize patient just as she was on the verge of making her greatest gains. As he thought back on the case, however, he recognized that perhaps her departure had not been completely without warning. With hindsight, he saw that he should have paid even more attention to the interpretation of Dora's dream when it occurred, because in addition to its other meanings it also represented a signal that she was becoming afraid of Freud and the analytic situation. Several facts led him to this conclusion. First, Freud himself was a passionate smoker of cigars, and he smoked almost constantly during the analytic sessions. Second, one of his favorite expressions was "There can be no smoke without fire," and he used it frequently to indicate to his patients that

[4] *Ibid.*, p. 105.
[5] *Ibid.*, p. 109.

even seemingly insignificant details in the analysis could turn out to be very important. Both of these facts could easily have served to implicate Freud himself in the symbolism of Dora's dream, of course. Finally, there were respects in which Freud's relationship to Dora was similar to Herr K.'s. Herr K. was regarded by Dora as dangerous partly because he aroused sexual impulses in her that she could not comfortably acknowledge. Freud spoke openly with Dora about such sexual matters and thus was a stimulus himself for the dangerous sexual thoughts. Also, Dora had been forced to deal with both Freud and Herr K. primarily because of her father. If it had not been for her father's romance with Frau K. she would not have had to put up with Herr K., and if it had not been for her father's initial insistence that she seek psychotherapy she would not have had to see Freud. Thus there were a number of reasons for equating Freud with Herr K. The "stranger" who aroused Dora sexually and whom she escaped from in the dream by fleeing with her father could be Freud as well as Herr K. Her old dream was useful for expressing a wish in a new situation, and just as it had foretold her escape from Herr K., so it foretold her impending departure from Freud. Her dream, in the analytic situation, was overdetermined in a way that came as a surprise even to Freud.

In his experience with Dora, Freud stumbled upon a phenomenon whose theoretical importance he quickly came to appreciate. He realized that in every psychoanalytic situation it was essential to pay strict attention to the nature of the relationship between patient and analyst. He saw that patients inevitably came to invest him, the analyst, with meanings, attributes, and motives that were not objectively his, but that were similar to those of important people from their past lives —just as Dora saw Freud unconsciously as another version of her old admirer. Freud named this phenomenon *transference,* to indicate that attitudes from the past are inappropriately and unconsciously transferred onto the figure of the psychoanalyst. Consideration of transference led to changes in Freud's therapeutic technique and, later, to changes in his general theory.

The Transference Neurosis

In part, the transference phenomenon may be explained on a common-sense basis. Any person's responses to situations in the present are determined by things that he has learned in the past. Each time he confronts a policeman, for example, his response is conditioned by his prior interactions with authority figures, including other policemen, and even more basically, the first authority figure from his life: his father. Therefore it is not surprising that a patient in psychotherapy should respond to his therapist with attitudes and expectations that have been learned through his earlier interpersonal interactions. The psychoanalyst, moreover, is a particularly easy target for various kinds of transferred attitudes. On the one hand he is an authority, and he therefore tends to elicit the feelings that the patient commonly has about his father and other authority figures. He is also defined as a healer, and thus he is also the recipient of attitudes normally directed toward people in nurturant roles—the prototype for whom is usually the mother.

In addition to these two sets of attitudes that he naturally elicits because of his role as doctor and healer, the psychoanalyst is an unusually good target for other transferences. In psychoanalysis the patient constantly talks of emotion-laden issues and expresses ideas that are not commonly spoken of in normal social intercourse. While he does this, the analyst does not respond emotionally or evaluatively. Instead he greets all of the material with an attitude of objectivity and openness, trying to determine what is true and real in the patient's emotional life, rather than what is good or bad. Because of his evaluative neutrality, he seems a kind of blank screen to the patient, whose imagination can then run wild in attributing concealed emotions to him. For example, while Dora was describing her most intimate past experiences to Freud, he remained impassive and objective, neither praising nor condemning the substance of what he heard. His lack of overt emotional response tempted Dora to imagine, both consciously and unconsciously, what his "real" but covert reactions must be. Since Freud provided no concrete clues about such a response, Dora naturally pictured it in terms that had been made especially salient by her past experiences. Thus at one point she imagined Freud as responding to her as Herr K. had in the past.

From his experiences with patients after Dora, Freud recognized that transference phenomena had a significance above and beyond their potential for disrupting the therapeutic relationship. He saw that the most important aspects of the transference, which were largely unconscious, related to the specific conflicts that underlay the neurotic symptoms. His patients tended to re-create in their relationships with him the key features of their neuroses. Accordingly, Freud postulated that psychoanalytic patients construct a kind of "model" of their real neuroses in their relationships with the analyst, with the analyst being assigned the roles of all of the key figures from their lives. In this interaction, which Freud called the *transference neurosis,* the analyst is therefore responded to at one moment as if he were the patient's mother, then as father, then as lover, etc. Most of this takes place unconsciously, and must be interpreted for the patient if it is not to disrupt the progress of therapy.

Transference phenomena thus add a tremendous complication to the psychoanalytic task. The analyst cannot single-mindedly attempt to uncover the unconscious conflicts dating from the patient's *past* history, but must also be constantly attentive to the *present* analytic situation. He must constantly ask himself, "What important person from the patient's past am I being for him now, and what specific conflict is being played out?"[6] When the answers to that question imply that

[6] An understanding of the transference phenomena sheds light on a previously inexplicable aspect of the case of Anna O.: her hallucinated childbirth. This was a manifestation of her transference feelings for Breuer, whom she fantasied as the father of the child. In reality, Breuer was completely respectable and proper, but in Anna's unconscious imagination he epitomized a seductive figure derived from her early experiences and fantasies.

he is being feared and avoided to some degree, he must interpret the transference for the patient. It is likely that Freud could have salvaged Dora's analysis if he had recognized her transference feelings in time and brought them out into the open for discussion.

The transference neurosis not only complicates the psychoanalytic task, but also provides a new criterion for therapeutic success. So long as a patient's pathogenic ideas remain repressed and beyond conscious control, he is literally incapable of responding to the analyst in a completely objective and realistic way. Once the neurosis has been dealt with and the unconscious made conscious, however, the transference phenomena decrease. When the patient consistently shows conscious insight that he is responding *as if* the analyst were a figure from his past, then the analyst knows that the therapy has been successful.

With the adoption of this new criterion of success, the analyst is provided with a new "handle" on his cases. Since the transference neurosis is a replica of the "real" neurosis, he may devote much of his interpretive energy to the transference situation itself, instead of to the patient's outside reality situation. By dealing with issues that appear in the transference the analyst deals with the issues that are most troublesome to the patient generally. Thus the basic therapeutic process comes to be defined as *working through* the transference. This lengthens the course of psychoanalytic treatment considerably, since it takes much longer to work through the transference than it does to deal with a simple pattern of symptoms. Whereas individual symptoms can theoretically be removed relatively quickly, over a period of a few months at the most, it typically takes a number of years to complete an analysis according to the new criterion.

The Compulsion to Repeat

After Freud had isolated transference as a crucial variable in psychoanalytic therapy, he began to see its implications for his general theory of the mind as well. Of particular importance was his gradual realization that the transference neurosis involves a repetition of *traumatic* and *painful* situations from the patient's past. The repetition of pleasant or happy situations was to be expected, of course, since it is natural to wish to recreate such experiences. But the repetition of painful experiences was surprising, from a common-sense point of view. Nevertheless, evidence clearly showed that Dora had unconsciously re-created her convoluted and painful relationship with Herr K. in her transference neurosis, substituting Freud as the new object of her ambivalent feelings. Another patient had suffered frequent severe punishments in childhood at the hands of a brutal father. In his analysis he naturally transferred some of his unconscious feelings about the father to the analyst. More surprising was the fact that he seemed willfully to try to provoke the analyst, to make him so angry that he would punish him. It was as if the patient were asking the analyst to assume the role of a brutal father, thus enabling him to repeat his childhood traumas. None of the repetition was conscious to this patient or to Dora, however; they seemed blindly and unconsciously to be repeating their earlier mistakes in new situations. This surprising general tendency to re-create and re-live earlier traumatic situations was referred to by Freud as the *compulsion to repeat.*

As the years went by, Freud became aware of other situations besides the transference neurosis in which the compulsion to repeat was manifested. The play of children provided one important kind of example. Freud noted that a child who undergoes some unpleasant experience, such as a medical procedure, is likely to re-enact in his subsequent play the various specific operations to which he has been subjected. If the doctor has looked down his throat, the child is likely to carry out the same procedure on himself or a playmate with great accuracy of detail. Freud came to believe that the child's compulsion to repeat such unpleasant activity is in the service of achieving mastery over an emotionally important situation. By imitating and repeating the act over and over again, the child develops a retrospective sense of control.

The clearest examples of all of the compulsion to repeat were provided by a clinical condition Freud encountered frequently during World War I, known as *traumatic neurosis.* Traumatic neuroses are conditions that are clearly precipitated by severe and overt stress of the kind that war experiences frequently cause. Usually they are caused by "close calls" rather than situations resulting in actual physical injury. The death or injury of a close comrade, while the patient himself was miraculously spared, was a frequent precipitating trauma in World War I. The specific resulting symptoms may vary considerably from one patient to another, and range from severe anxiety attacks to hysteric-like conversions or dissociations. A common factor among all patients, however, is an obsession with the trauma that precipitated the illness. All of the patients' associations tend to converge on the traumas, and even their *dreams* tend to center about it. Often they wake up in a state of profound panic after dreaming that they are re-living the traumatic situations. Thus Freud saw that the compulsion to repeat past traumas may extend even to the dream life of some individuals.

All of these manifestations of the compulsion to repeat posed a theoretical dilemma for Freud, since according to his basic theory such phenomena ought not to occur. The dreams of traumatic neurotics were a special embarrassment to his theory, because there was no way that the re-living of traumas in dreams could be construed as wish-fullfillment. The compulsion to repeat in all of its forms violated some of the most fundamental principles that Freud assumed to govern mental functioning.

From his earliest works onwards, Freud had consistently assumed that the *pleasure principle* and the *reality principle* established the two most essential, though contrasting, tendencies in human behavior. The pleasure principle impels the organism toward immediate, impulsive action and primary process gratification. The reality principle, on the other hand, enables the organism to tolerate delay in gratification and to exercise secondary process thought. In the broadest sense, however, the pleasure principle and reality principle are not really antagonistic to one another, since the *final* goal implied by both principles is the same: the discharge of tension. The purpose of the reality principle is to allow pleasure to be obtained, though in accordance with reality and not necessarily as quickly or automatically as the pleasure principle would dictate. Without the pleasure principle to establish the basic goal of tension reduction, there would be no need for a reality principle. Thus Freud saw the reality principle as subordinate to the pleasure principle, and all behavior as in the service of tension reduction.

The behaviors exemplifying the compulsion to repeat clearly did not fit in with this formulation, however. In all cases the compulsion to repeat involves an increase in tension and unpleasure. According to the pleasure and reality principles, such behaviors ought to be systematically and vigorously avoided. In 1920 Freud finally wrote a major work to deal with these anomalous data, to see if he could reconcile them with his earlier theory. Entitled *Beyond the Pleasure Principle,* it has remained to this day one of the most controversial of all of Freud's works.

In attempting to reconcile the compulsion to repeat with the main body of his psychoanalytic theory, Freud was forced to return to a free-wheeling, quasi-neurological approach reminiscent of the "Project." "What follows," he wrote, "is speculation, often far-fetched speculation, which the reader will consider or dismiss according to his individual predilection."[7] He then began his exposition by emphasizing the interesting observation that traumatic neurosis tends to be most severe if the patient has been "surprised" by the trauma that overcomes him, and if he does *not* suffer physical injury in its course. If an individual is anxious or frightened before a trauma occurs, or if he is physi-

[7] *Standard Edition,* Vol. XVIII, p. 24.

cally harmed by it, some other disability besides traumatic neurosis is likely to result.

Next, Freud asked the reader to assume that the physical apparatus is a "vesicle" capable of being stimulated. The part of the vesicle on its outer surface, oriented toward the external world, receives stimulation directly from that source. Subjected to almost constant bombardment by external stimulation, this outer section is "baked through" until it becomes a "crust" that is ideally suited to perceive external reality. This process greatly resembles the development of the Phi system, as described in the "Project." The "outer surface" that becomes "baked through" corresponds to the "exterior neurons" which become "permeable" as the result of steady stimulation.

But a new implication is added by the notion of a "crust," because a major function of the baked-through layer is to *protect* the internal parts of the vesicle. Freud saw external stimulation as potentially damaging if permitted unrestricted access to the vesicle for extended periods of time. The kind of protection afforded by the crust is roughly analogous to that provided by the external surface of a copper rain gutter on a house. When water first comes into contact with the metal, oxidation occurs and a layer of copper oxide forms on the surface. Copper oxide is incapable of being penetrated by water, so once it has formed it prevents future water from penetrating to the deeper layers of the metal and oxidizing them. Similarly, the crust on the psychic vesicle protects the deeper layers from being baked through themselves. Freud assumed that this protection is absolutely essential for the ultimate survival of the psychic apparatus, which he described as "a little fragment of living substance . . . suspended in the middle of an external world charged with the most powerful energies."[8]

As in the "Project," the psychic apparatus in *Beyond the Pleasure Principle* was conceived of as receiving stimulation from the interior as well as the exterior of the organism, with

[8] *Ibid.*, p. 27.

the absolute magnitude of the endogenous energies much less than that of the external stimulation. The endogenous stimulation does not "bake through" the vesicle's tissue, and thus is not so dangerous. Freud assumed that the external crust serves its protective function not by eliminating all incoming stimulation, but rather by reducing its magnitude to the same level as that of the endogenous stimulation. Thus the "normal" state of affairs in the psychic apparatus is for all energies to be at relatively low absolute levels. The endogenous excitation originates at such levels, and the potentially damaging exogenous stimulation is reduced to the appropriate magnitude by the protective crust.

Freud went on to speculate that when all of the energies impinging on the psychic system are within this safe order of magnitude, then the over-all functioning of the system is subject to the pleasure principle and its derivative, the reality principle. That is, it functions according to the ordinary rules of cathexis and discharge. But from time to time the protective crust fails to prevent unreduced amounts of external energy from entering the vesicle. When this happens an actual physical threat has arisen, and the organism suspends its normal functioning. On a psychological level, this threat to the apparatus is experienced as a *trauma* that elicits the suspension of the pleasure principle.

Metaphorically, Freud described traumas as resulting from "breaches" in the protective shield, and suggested that the system must have at its disposal a "second line of defense" to prevent the trauma from being totally destructive. He further suggested that the second line of defense consists of a supply of "quiescent cathexis" which may be called up to surround the breach in the shield. The quiescent cathexis then "binds" the massive incoming flow of energy as it passes the breach. The principle Freud suggested here was identical to one introduced in the "Project," in which bound or quiescent energy was described as causing incoming energy also to be bound. Thus, in the case of a trauma, the cathexes within the system are withdrawn from their normal configurations and assume a defensive, binding posture.

When quiescent cathexes come to "back up" the protective crust as a second line of defense, the psychological result is the development of *anxiety* or *concern.* This accounts for the finding that traumatic neuroses occur only if the patient has been surprised by his trauma. If he has been worried or frightened about a particular event just before it happens, his psyche is "prepared" for it with a second line of defense. But if he is not worried, then the second line of defense is missing and he is likely to be overwhelmed by the trauma. Thus, though the state of fear or anxiety is unpleasant, it nevertheless can sometimes be a safeguard for mental health.

The other factor that Freud assumed to be negatively related to the occurrence of traumatic neurosis—the occurrence of physical injury—was also accounted for in this new speculative system. If a physical injury occurs, the result in the psychic apparatus is a massive "narcissistic cathexis," in which psychic energy is withdrawn from the external world and invested in the injured aspects of the self. Since those aspects of the self are highly associated with the trauma itself, the narcissistic cathexis surrounds the breach in the protective shield and serves a binding function similar to that of anxiety. Thus the physical injury provides a special means by which psychological traumas can be dealt with shortly after they occur.

If an individual is neither anticipatorily worried about a trauma nor physically injured in the course of its occurrence, the second line of defense is not established. The breach in the crust is left unprotected, and the psychic apparatus is subject to a massive flooding of dangerous external stimulation. Freud hypothesized that the organism, in response to this danger, initiates a process by which it becomes "retrospectively anxious" about the trauma. In order to become retrospectively anxious it is necessary to recreate the situation in the imagination and to re-live it again and again until sufficient cathexis has been attracted to it to construct a second line of defense behind the breach. This violates the pleasure principle, of course, since it means that a painful memory is retrospectively aroused in all of its unhappy intensity. The behavioral manifestations of this attempt to become retrospectively anxious are the phenomena of the compulsion to repeat. The compulsion to repeat is thus revealed as a mechanism allowing the organism retrospectively to come to terms with traumatic aspects of the external world, in the course of whose operation the pleasure principle is automatically superseded. In this way Freud succeeded in conceptualizing the apparently anomalous data of the compulsion to repeat in terms completely consistent with his earlier theoretical work.

The Death Instinct

After postulating mechanisms to account for the compulsion to repeat, Freud went on in *Beyond the Pleasure Principle* to use that discussion as the basis for a brand new general theory of instincts. In what many regard as an astonishing conclusion, he asserted that there is a *death instinct* which stands along with the sexual instinct as a prime motivator of human behavior. Before describing Freud's arguments for the death instinct here, however, it is necessary to review briefly the views he had held on the instincts in general prior to 1920, views which were modified in the new work.

In the very earliest versions of psychoanalytic theory, until 1914, Freud assumed that there were two major instincts governing human behavior: the sexual instinct, which was conceptualized as a generalized drive for obtaining physical pleasure, and the *ego instinct,* which strives for the self-preservation of the individual. Hunger, in its purely nutritive aspects, was one manifestation of the ego instinct. Another was fear, because of its role in preventing the individual from approaching threatening or dangerous stimuli. In short, Freud traced any behavior in the service of self-preservation to the ego instinct.

The postulation of twin sexual and ego instincts enabled

Freud to account neatly for many of the psychological phenomena he was most interested in; they were explained as the results of conflict and compromise between the two instincts. The sexual instinct, for example, could be held responsible for the basic wishes contained in pathogenic ideas or latent dream thoughts, and the ego instinct for the recognition that the wishes portend dangerous consequences if they are acted upon. Thus the sexual instinct strives for the expression of the wishes, while the ego instinct demands their suppression. Symptoms and manifest dreams represent compromise solutions to this conflict between the two instincts.

By 1914, however, Freud discovered that he had difficulty in maintaining his conception of the sexual and ego instincts as separate, independent entities. His difficulty stemmed from observation of states of *narcissism,* characterized by excessive concern for the self, or self-love. At first, Freud felt that narcissism should be classified as a manifestation of the ego instinct, since it is so closely tied to self-preservation and aggrandizement. He found that this view was beset with problems, however, when he considered that an excess of narcissism in an individual tends to be associated with a relative lack of sexual libido, and vice versa. This logically should not be the case if the sexual and ego instincts are truly independent of one another.

One clear example of the reciprocal relationship between narcissism and sexuality is provided by a person who becomes ill. In his illness he tends to withdraw his interest from the external world and to become self-centered; in short, the person who is ill or in pain becomes narcissistic. Coincident with his narcissism, of course, is a diminution of his sexual interest. The lover with an upset stomach or an excruciating toothache does not cut a very romantic or sexually effective picture. The obverse relationship is illustrated by the state of "being in love," regarded by Freud as one of the purest manifestations of the mature sexual instinct. An infatuated young lover typically *under*values himself—i.e., manifests the opposite of narcissism—at the same time that he *over*values his beloved. Thus there was ample evidence to suggest to Freud that extreme sexuality and extreme narcissism were incompatible with one another. This meant, of course, that they were not independent of one another, and suggested instead that love for the self and love for external objects must be but alternative manifestations of the same basic instinct.

Accordingly, Freud offered a new conceptualization of the sexual instinct in 1914, in a paper entitled "On Narcissism: An Introduction." There he suggested that sexual libido be subclassified as either *object libido* or *ego libido,* depending on whether it cathects representations of external objects or of the self, respectively. The nature of the libido itself is the same in both cases, the major difference deriving only from the specific memories and ideas it cathects. Libido, then, became virtually synonymous with the undifferentiated endogenous *Q* that was assumed to activate the nervous system from within in the "Project," and the two instincts of Freud's early scheme became reduced to one. The functions that had previously been attributed to the ego instinct were now considered to be the consequences of ego libido. In general, the ego libido contrasted with object libido in the same ways that the ego instinct had earlier been believed to contrast with the sexual instinct. The only major change wrought by the new formulation was that the ego libido and object libido were seen as potentially interchangeable manifestations of the same sexual energy. Of course, the meaning of the word "sexual" was once again broadened, since self-preservative functions now came to be connoted by it.

This view of human behavior as motivated by a single, highly general sexual instinct was the one that Freud maintained until he wrote *Beyond the Pleasure Principle.* He never felt very comfortable with this one-instinct formulation, however, primarily because his multitudinous clinical findings about the importance of conflict and compromise in human psychology seemed to point more appropriately to the existence of at least two clashing, contrasting instincts. Thus it was probably with a sense of relief that Freud found he could use his discussion of the compulsion to repeat as a stepping-off point for a new and revised two-instinct theory. The concluding sections of *Beyond the Pleasure Principle* were devoted to his new formulation.

Freud began there by noting that there is something almost uncanny about the compulsion to repeat—that individuals who experience it have the feeling that their actions are dictated by some alien and "daemonic" irresistible force. This irresistibility lends the compulsion what Freud called an "instinctual"[9] flavor, and he concluded that it must therefore be the direct manifestation of an *instinct* to repeat. Then, in one of the most extraordinary and controversial paragraphs he had ever written, he derived the following hypothesis:

> But how is the predicate of being 'instinctual' related to the compulsion to repeat? At this point we cannot escape a suspicion that we have come upon the track of a universal attribute of instincts and perhaps of organic life in general which has not hitherto been clearly recognized or at least not explicitly stressed. *It seems, then, that an instinct is an urge inherent in organic life to restore an earlier state of things* which the living entity has been obliged to abandon under the pressure of external disturbing forces; that is, it is a kind of organic elasticity, or, to put it another way, the expression of the inertia inherent in organic life.[10]

Thus his consideration of the instinctual nature of the repetition compulsion led Freud to speculate that an essential feature of *all* instincts may be a conservative trend. From this basic position he proceeded to assert that since all living matter is synthesized from non-living, inorganic matter (the mechanist doctrine asserting itself once again), and since the

[9] Freud's translator notes that Freud's German word (*Triebhaft*) connotes a greater sense of urgency than the English "instinctual," so the translation is not precise.

[10] *Standard Edition,* Vol. XVIII, p. 36.

tendency of organic matter is to return to earlier states, then living matter is instinctually impelled to return to an inorganic state. In other words, "*the aim of all life is death.*"[11]

While admitting the highly speculative nature of his arguments, Freud went on to cite evidence in support of his hypothesis. He noted that salmon undergo terrible ordeals in order to return to the place of their own conception, whereupon they spawn and then die. They are instinctually driven to their deaths, and the entire process of their spawning run represents a regressive re-creation of their earlier stages of existence. The migration of birds was cited by Freud to prove the same point. These examples point out an important qualification to Freud's hypothesis. They indicate that the death toward which the organisms are instinctually driven is not just *any kind* of death, but a particular death that satisfies the particular repetition needs of the organism. Thus salmon are motivated to die, but to die in a very specific way. The death instinct—or *Thanatos*[12] as Freud came to refer to it—impels each organism toward a highly specific kind of death.

A paradoxical situation thus arises: the instinctual aspects of behavior tend to be conservative or regressive, while those aspects deriving from the contingencies of external reality are progressive and life-extending. *Anything* that stands in the way of an organism's idiosyncratic path to death contradicts his instincts and thus must be warded off. In the service of maintaining this path to death, the organism must defend against threats of death that are not appropriate to it. External reality presents obstacles to the organism's drive toward a particular kind of death, and those obstacles must be fought off by the instinct. When this happens, the death instinct may temporarily take on the attributes of an "ego instinct" and actually serve to prolong life.

Thus the death instinct was viewed by Freud as capable of manifesting itself in a tremendous variety of specific ways, just

[11] *Ibid.*, p. 38.

[12] Thanatos was the name of the Greek god of death.

as the sexual instinct had been conceptualized earlier. He saw the death instinct as capable of being directed either outwardly or inwardly, for example, just like the sexual instinct, with its object and ego libido. When the death instinct is oriented toward external objects it results in *aggressive* behavior toward them; when it is oriented toward the self it results in self-defeating, masochistic reactions. The formulation of Thanatos thus enabled Freud to postulate an instinctual basis for all the hostile, violent, and self-destructive acts that human beings perpetrate upon each other and themselves. In his later works he was to make much of this conception of Thanatos as a pool of destructive, hostile energy.

Freud concluded *Beyond the Pleasure Principle* by arguing that his earlier work on the sexual instinct was still valid, in spite of the new conception of an instinct as a conservative, regressive force. He suggested that the sexual instinct becomes split off from other instincts, thereby assuming the qualities previously attributed to it. His arguments in this regard were rather complex and difficult to follow, centering about a consideration of the germ cells (reproductive cells) as an independent part of each organism. Freud noted that these germ cells are in themselves an independent though primitive form of life, "surviving" in a fashion beyond the life span of their hosts. That is, it is the germ cells that allow a species to perpetuate itself. Freud argued that the instincts governing the germ cells must be separate from the instincts of the organism proper. The instincts of the germ cells are thus independent of the other instincts, sometimes come into conflict with them, and are, according to Freud, identical with the sexual instincts:

> The instincts which watch over the destinies of these elementary organisms that survive the whole individual, which provide them with a safe shelter while they are defenceless against the stimuli of the external world, which bring about their meeting with other germ cells, and so on—these constitute the group of the sexual instincts. They are conservative in the same sense as the other instincts in that they bring back earlier states of living substance

. . . and they are conservative too in another sense in that they preserve life itself for a comparatively long period. They are the true life instincts.[13]

Thus the sexual instincts, attached to an independent and enduring part of the biological organism, exist side by side with the death instincts that govern the rest of the organism. Both sets of instincts are capable of widely varying manifestations. Sometimes they may cooperate with one another, at other times they may compete, and the results are the behavioral indices of instinctual conflict and compromise that Freud studied in the earlier part of his career. To accentuate his sense of the conflict between the two sets of instincts, Freud provided the sexual instincts with the new name *Eros* (the Greek god of love), to contrast them with Thanatos.

The formulation of the death instincts (Thanatos) to oppose the sexual instincts (Eros) was the last word Freud had to say about the general nature of the instincts. He had returned to a dual theory, with conflicting protagonists. In the new formulation the old "ego instinct" was subsumed partly by each of the two final instincts. The narcissistic manifestations of self-concern were considered to be the result of the sexual instinct, as outlined in his 1914 paper on narcissism. Other, purely self-preservative behaviors, however, were now considered to be the result of the organism's hewing the line on its own appropriate path to death. The sexual instincts themselves remained largely untouched by the new formulation, and Freud was also able to provide an instinctual explanation for the aggressiveness in human behavior by positing multiple and variable manifestations of Thanatos.

The theory of the death instinct was not universally accepted, even among some of Freud's otherwise most dedicated followers. Freud's biographer Ernest Jones, who accepted almost every other aspect of psychoanalytic theory, wrote: "No biological observation can be found to support the idea of

[13] *Standard Edition*, Vol. XVIII, p. 40.

a death instinct, one which contradicts all biological principles."[14] After 1920 Freud himself paid more attention to the generally *aggressive* connotations of Thanatos than to its self-destructive aspects. Nevertheless, *Beyond the Pleasure Principle* was a pivotal work for Freud. It seemed to mark a turning point, after which he became increasingly concerned with the more philosophical implications of his theory. Not surprisingly, given his postulation of a death instinct, those implications were rather somber. They are described in the next chapter.

SUGGESTED FURTHER READINGS

Freud discussed the issues surrounding his psychoanalytic psychotherapy in a series of papers spanning more than thirty years. A brief and highly readable account of his early analytic procedures is provided in "Freud's Psychoanalytic Method" (1904). The case of Dora is extensively described in "Fragment of an Analysis of a Case of Hysteria" (1905). Papers discussing the transference neurosis and methods of working through it are "The Dynamics of the Transference" (1912); "Further Recommendations in the Technique of Psychoanalysis: Recollection, Repetition and Working Through" (1914); and "Further Recommendations in the Technique of Psychoanalysis: Observations on Transference-Love" (1915).

The first published work in which Freud explicitly referred to the opposition between the sexual and ego instincts was a short 1910 paper entitled "The Psycho-Analytic View of Psychogenic Disturbance of Vision." In 1911 his influential paper "Formulations on the Two Principles of Mental Functioning" traced the close connections between the sexual instinct and the pleasure principle on the one hand, and the ego instinct and the reality principle on the other.

[14] Ernest Jones, *The Life and Work of Sigmund Freud*, Vol. 3 (New York, Basic Books, 1957) p. 277.

The topic of narcissism received its most exhaustive discussion in a 1914 paper entitled "On Narcissism: An Introduction." A year later the paper "Instincts and Their Vicissitudes" provided the culmination of Freud's instinct theory prior to the postulation of the death instinct. The death instinct was introduced and the compulsion to repeat extensively discussed in Freud's controversial work *Beyond the Pleasure Principle* (New York, Bantam Books, 1959), first published in 1920.

7

Freud's Final Model of the Mind and the Implications of Psychoanalysis

The reader of Freud's collected works will easily see that his early writings had a flavor and style distinctly different from his later efforts. This difference was partly due to the fact that in the early days of psychoanalysis Freud knew that what he was writing was radically new and different, the result of his own purely personal intellectual labor. Thus he took nothing for granted about the nature of his readers. He assumed at the outset that they would be skeptical about his conclusions, and he therefore took great pains to lead them through very basic arguments designed to lay the groundwork for his theory. *Studies on Hysteria, The Interpretation of Dreams, The Psychopathology of Everyday Life,* and *Three Essays on the Theory of Sexuality* were *basic* books, capable of being read and understood by individuals with no prior knowledge of Freud's work.

The same cannot be said of many of Freud's later works. As he began to attract and train increasing numbers of followers, it was quite natural for him to direct a significant proportion of his writing toward them instead of toward the general reader. This tendency was greatly accelerated in 1908 with the founding of the first psychoanalytic periodical. Thus many of

Freud's later works seem to be more difficult, obscure, and dogmatic than the early works because he took more for granted about the knowledge and sympathies of his intended readers.

Another reason for the difference in the later works was that they were simply not as fundamental as the earlier books. After 1905 new advances in psychoanalysis tended not to be revolutionary new discoveries necessitating completely new views of human psychology. Instead they tended to be modifications and elaborations of existing ideas, the correction of gaps and contradictions in early versions of the theory, or the application of psychoanalytic concepts to hitherto unexplored areas.[1] Though not so theoretically fundamental as the early works, they nevertheless greatly refined the presentation of psychoanalysis, expanded its range of applicability, and greatly increased its impact on the world at large.

Revision of the Model of the Mind: Difficulties with the Old Model

One of the important aspects of psychoanalytic theory to undergo refinement—though not radical revision—in Freud's later works was his model of the mind. In the years from 1900 to 1923, the model Freud consistently assumed was the one he had proposed in Chapter 7 of *The Interpretation of Dreams.* Even while he was formulating new and different theories about sexuality and the instincts, he still regarded the most important *structural* components of the mind to be the unconscious and preconscious systems. The important psychological events that he concerned himself with during this period were viewed as capable of being explained theoretically as the results of conflicts and compromises between the two systems. For example, the "ego-oriented" instincts—whether conceptualized as an independent class of instincts as in the earlier

[1] Major exceptions were *Introductory Lectures on Psycho-Analysis* (1916–1917) and *An Outline of Psycho-Analysis* (1940), which were intended as laymen's introductions to the theory, and *Beyond the Pleasure Principle* (1920), which introduced a radically new view of the instincts.

works or as a subclass of the sexual instincts as in later writings—were seen as originating primarily in the preconscious system, while the "pleasure-oriented" sexual instincts tended to operate in the unconscious. By the early 1920s, however, Freud had become aware of a number of ambiguities in this model, and he sought to revise it. He first published an account of the revision in 1923, in a short but highly influential work entitled *The Ego and the Id*. This new model was the last one Freud proposed, and it is still universally accepted by psychoanalysts today.

The major difficulty with the old model arose because the systems *Ucs* and *Pcs* were each defined in two ways, once with respect to their relationships to consciousness and once with respect to their characteristic mental operations. According to the *Interpretation of Dreams*, ideas in the *Ucs* are unconscious *and* operate according to the primary process; those in the *Pcs* are potentially conscious *and* obey the secondary process. These dual definitions added a degree of sophistication and theoretical elegance to Freud's model, but they also contained ambiguities that Freud was gradually forced to deal with.

Thus in a 1912 paper entitled "A Note on the Unconscious in Psycho-Analysis," Freud pointed out that there was a certain ambiguity in his use of the word "unconscious." To reduce the ambiguity, he specified three distinct ways in which the word is used. In the first place, the word may be used to denote any thought or memory that is not immediately in awareness at a given moment in time. As you, the reader, concentrate on the words in this sentence, you are momentarily unconscious of everything besides the ideas it denotes and their immediate associates. This is a rather trivial use of the word "unconscious," of course; in terms of Freud's model it may be used to describe the entire contents of the system *Ucs*, and all of the *Pcs* except what is immediately conscious. Freud referred to this as the *descriptive* sense of the word. It is a truism to say that at every moment the vast majority of ideas are descriptively unconscious, since the capacity of consciousness at a single moment is very small.

The second use of the term specified by Freud is much more important from the standpoint of psychoanalytic theory. This is the *dynamic* sense of the word, and it refers to ideas that are normally *incapable* of entering consciousness, but that nevertheless exert an observable influence on behavior. A major category of dynamically unconscious ideas are those that have been prevented from becoming conscious by the force of repression. For a time Freud believed that the terms "repressed" and "dynamically unconscious" were synonymous. It is in the dynamic sense that the distinction between "unconscious" and "preconscious" ideas makes sense, of course, since preconscious ideas may be unconscious in the descriptive but not the dynamic sense. When Freud described an idea as unconscious in his major writings, he almost always used the word in its dynamic sense, implying that the idea was normally *incapable* of entering consciousness, and not just that it happened to be out of mind at the time in question.

Freud referred to the third use of "unconscious" as the *systematic* sense of the word. Whereas in the descriptive and dynamic senses the word is an adjective, in the systematic sense it is a noun. The systematic sense is implied when one speaks of "*the* unconscious" or Freud's symbol *Ucs.* The systematic unconscious constituted a structural component of the mind in Chapter 7 of *The Interpretation of Dreams*; its counterpart, the system *Pcs,* may be thought of as the systematic representative of the term "preconscious."

Freud elaborated upon the difference between the dynamic and systematic senses in an important paper published in 1915, entitled simply "The Unconscious." He pointed out there that dynamically unconscious ideas are defined simply by their inability to enter consciousness, while ideas in the systematic unconscious are supposedly characterized by an inability to enter consciousness *as well as* a set of attributes identified with the primary process, thus repeating his point from *The Interpretation of Dreams.* He defined these attributes as 1) exemption from mutual contradiction, since the possibility for contradictory ideas to stand side by side and even to symbolize one another always exists in the unconscious; 2) a motility of cathexis that makes inevitable the occurrence of such processes as displacement and condensation; 3) a disregard for appropriate temporal relationships among events; and 4) a disregard for external reality. The prototype for such an idea is provided by a primitive instinctual urge. The characteristics of ideas in the system *Pcs* were quite logically believed to be the converse of those in the *Ucs*: the ability to enter consciousness; non-contradictoriness; activation by the even dispersal of small quantities of cathexis; concern for appropriate temporal relationships; and a regard for external reality.

In the early stages of his theorizing the distinction between the dynamic and systematic senses did not seem especially important to Freud, because he assumed that all dynamically unconscious ideas also inevitably possessed the characteristics of the systematic unconscious. Thus to denote an idea as unconscious or preconscious in the dynamic sense was tantamount to placing it in the system *Ucs* or *Pcs*. Soon, however, Freud realized that the relationships among the supposed characteristics of the unconscious were not so perfectly laid out as he had thought. He was forced to the conclusion that there exist certain mental products that are unconscious in a dynamic sense—i.e., that cannot normally enter consciousness—yet that bear the other marks of the system *Pcs*. They are highly organized and non-contradictory, entail little condensation or displacement, take into account appropriate time relationships, and demonstrate at least some regard for reality—but at the same time they are dynamically as well as descriptively unconscious.

Some of this anomalous evidence was available to Freud at the time that he wrote *The Interpretation of Dreams*, though he did not completely recognize its significance until many years later. From very early Freud had been aware that highly developed *fantasies* lay behind dreams and neurotic symptoms. These fantasies were emphatically unconscious in the dynamic sense, yet they often manifested secondary process characteristics. The fantasies underlying the Oedipus complex are good examples of dynamically unconscious (repressed) ideas that also show a certain amount of secondary process organization. They involve a realistic appraisal of the same-sexed parent as a more powerful rival, for example, and the recognition that the Oedipal wishes are therefore potentially dangerous. A "pure" representative of the system *Ucs* should theoretically not manifest such a concern for possible realistic consequences or such a high degree of logical structure.

This imperfection in his model became sufficiently clear to Freud to cause him to confess in his 1915 paper "The Unconscious" that consciousness, "the only characteristic of psychical processes that is directly presented to us, is in no way suited to serve as a criterion for the differentiation of systems."[1] Thus in essence he had abandoned the criterion of dynamic unconsciousness as one of the hallmarks of the system *Ucs.*

Yet another serious difficulty with the model arose from a detailed consideration of *resistance* in psychotherapy. The earliest examples of resistance that Freud had noted were the obvious signs of distress, repugnance, and recalcitrance manifested by his hysterical patients as they came close to confronting repressed pathogenic ideas. When similar phenomena were encountered in the course of interpreting dreams, Freud concluded that the resistance was the result of the "censorship." In Chapter 7 of *The Interpretation of Dreams,* this censorship was conceptualized as a kind of barrier set up by the *Pcs* at its boundary with the *Ucs,* serving to protect the *Pcs* against incursion from the unconscious. Thus the censorship was viewed as *part of the preconscious system.* The self-aware and "normal" part of the personality—i.e., the preconscious part—required a defense against the unconscious and dangerous part, and the censorship was the protective agency it depended upon.

With the discovery of the transference neurosis (after *The Interpretation of Dreams* had already been written), Freud was forced to the conclusion that the most important part of the

[1] *Standard Edition,* Vol. XIV, p. 192.

resistance was not the most obvious part. The conscious distress and disgust experienced by a patient was only the most superficial manifestation of his resistance. His deepest resistance was embodied in his transference neurosis, which was a replica of his real neurosis, and of which he was completely unconscious. This suggested to Freud that at the most significant level an individual is unaware of his own resistance and of the real nature of his conflicts. That is, he is as unconscious of the process of repression itself as he is of the content of his repressions.

This meant, of course, that both the repressed content and the repressing force were dynamically unconscious. Since the repressing force, or censorship, had been postulated to be part of the system *Pcs,* however, once again there was a clear conflict between the dynamic and systematic conceptions of the unconscious. Freud's recognition of this complication convinced him that the "topographical" model of the mind presented in *The Interpretation of Dreams* was no longer satisfactory. Thus in *The Ego and the Id* he developed a new model of the mind whose components were not dependent upon their relationships to consciousness for their primary definitions, and whose terminology did not entail so much ambiguity and confusion.

The Id, the Ego, and the Super Ego

In formulating his new model of the mind, Freud adapted several components from his earlier work and added one that was completely new. One component of the new model was assumed to be oriented directly toward external reality, responsible for the functions of perception and consciousness. Freud labeled this component with an abbreviation, translated into English as "*Pcpt.-Cs.*" It is a kind of window on external reality whose purpose is to conduct external stimuli into the psyche for processing, and to orient the attention of the organism toward specific aspects of the external world. Quite obviously, *Pcpt.-Cs.* is a largely unaltered descendant of the Phi-Omega systems of the "Project" and the perceptual system (*Pcpt*) of Chapter 7.

As in the earlier models, Freud assumed that there must be an executive agency in the psyche whose function is to direct and control the behavior of the organism while taking into account the dictates of both reality and instinctual impulse. In naming this agency in the new model, Freud reverted to his terminology of 1895 and called it the *ego*. But he now stressed that the ego tends to be reality-oriented and to make use of the secondary process in its activities, just like the preconscious system of Chapter 7. Unlike the *Pcs,* however, its activities are not assumed to bear a simple relationship to consciousness. Part of the ego is unconscious in the dynamic sense, and is responsible for carrying out such functions as fantasy formation and resistance—those secondary process activities that take place outside the reaches of normal consciousness. Still another part of it is preconscious, and performs relatively disciplined psychic activities like thinking and judgment that are normally accessible to consciousness.

With the ego established as the differentiated, reality-attuned component of the psyche, Freud needed to postulate another component to contrast with it and to produce the conflict he had observed to be so pervasive in human behavior. He had to account for aspects of mental functioning that operate according to the primary process, including those primitive passions and "unknown and uncontrollable forces" that often seem to dominate human behavior. Accordingly, Freud postulated the existence of an unconscious, undifferentiated, and primary process portion of the mind, which he chose to call the *id*.[2] As the psychic source of the instincts and passions, the id constantly sends out impulses that must be "civilized" and directed by the ego.

[2] The term that Freud actually used in his native German was "das *Es*," which when literally translated means "the *it*." As was their habit, Freud's English translators Latinized his original everyday term.

In clarifying the relationships between the ego and the id, Freud returned to a familiar theme. He had always believed human psychological development to be a gradual progression from an initial state of undifferentiation and primitiveness to a final one of differentiation and structure. This was first expressed in the "Project," in which the nervous system at birth was assumed to be an undifferentiated network of interconnected neurons. As a result of increasing experience, it was assumed to develop into a highly structured instrument with specially differentiated systems. A similar point of view was expressed in the discussions of sexuality, where an initial undifferentiated state of polymorphous perversity was said to be transformed by experience into highly structured and individuated sexual manifestations.

Freud assumed that precisely the same kind of development takes place to create the psychic structure he described in *The Ego and the Id.* He stated there that the id is "prior to" the ego, and that in the course of development a certain part of the id becomes structured and forms the ego. Thus, when a human infant is born his psyche is virtually all id. As a result his psychic functioning is primitive and is dominated by the primary process. It is only through repeated interaction with the external world that the ego comes to be formed. In Freud's own words:

> It is easy to see that the ego is that part of the id which has been modified by the direct influence of the external world through the medium of the *Pcpt.-Cs.*; in a sense it is an extension of the surface-differentiation. Moreover, the ego seeks to bring the influence of the external world to bear upon the id and its tendencies, and endeavours to substitute the reality principle for the pleasure principle which reigns unrestrictedly in the id. For the ego, perception plays the part which in the id falls to instinct. The ego represents what may be called reason and common sense, in contrast to the id, which contains the passions.[3]

[3] *Standard Edition*, Vol. XIX, p. 25.

The relationships among the various components of the new model were illustrated by Freud in the diagram reproduced here as Figure 10.[4] In this diagram, *Pcpt.-Cs.* constitutes one end of the system, and should be thought of as oriented toward external reality. At the other end is the id, which is oriented toward the inner world of the instincts. The ego is located between these two systems, as is appropriate for an agency whose function is to mediate between external and internal demands. The diagram, of course, represents a relatively mature system. In a totally immature system there would be no ego at all; there the incoming external stimulation would clash directly with the instinctual impulses of the id. It is out of just such clashes that the ego comes to be formed and to assume its role as mediator. The ego's structure may therefore be thought of as merging with both the id and *Pcpt.-Cs.*

This new formulation combined important features from both the "Project" and Chapter 7. The "endedness" of the system, with one part oriented toward the inner and another part toward the outer world, is highly reminiscent of the "Project." *Pcpt.-Cs.* and the id are analogous to the Phi-Omega and nuclear Psi systems, respectively. Also, as in the earlier work, an initial state of undifferentiation, now conceptualized as the

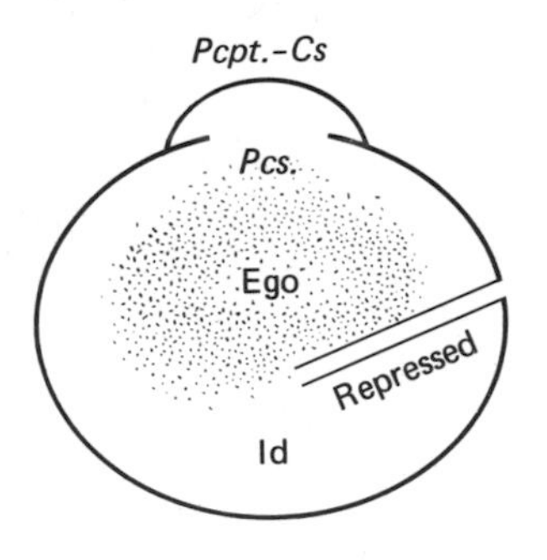

FIGURE 10

[4] *Ibid.*, p. 24.

id, gives rise to almost exclusive primary process functioning in infancy. It is only after an inhibiting and guiding agency, the ego, comes to be formed out of the original undifferentiated mass that secondary process functioning can take place.

Freud retained many aspects of the 1900 model as well. The ego and the id subsume almost completely the earlier systems *Pcs* and *Ucs*, respectively, though Freud retained the terms "preconscious" and "unconscious" in the new model only in their dynamic senses. This permitted him to account for the unconscious fantasies that were so embarrassing to the earlier model. Since they are highly structured and organized they clearly are part of the ego, but since they are also unconscious they are part of its non-preconscious segment.

The other anomalous situation that motivated the creation of the new model—the fact that both the repressed and the repressing force were dynamically unconscious—is also accounted for in the new system. Freud assumed that the repressed material becomes a special part of the id, and that the repressing force or censorship derives from the unconscious part of the ego. To indicate that there is a sharp separation between these two psychic entities, Freud separated them on his diagram by a double line. This differentiates the repressed portion of the id from that portion which merges gradually with the ego. The only way that the repressed part can normally express itself in consciousness is to activate the normal id, from which it is not sharply separated and which then transmits an impulse to the ego. The ego must then find a safe and appropriate avenue for the expression of the impulse. In the course of this indirect path, the repressed idea undergoes all of the distortions and modifications characteristic of the dream work and the neurotic process.

Although the formulations of the ego and the id in Freud's new model helped to reduce the terminological difficulties inherent in Chapter 7, they did not introduce anything that was really new. The major new psychic system Freud introduced in 1923 was a *moral* agency, referred to as the *super-ego*. Freud believed that he had garnered sufficient evidence to postulate the super-ego as an independent component of the psyche, equal in dignity and importance to the id and the ego.

Superficially, it might seem that any moral agency operating in the psyche should be considered to be part of the ego. Moral behavior typically requires the tempering of instinctual passion or impulse, as well a strong degree of discipline and control over thought and action. As such, it would seem to be antagonistic toward the id and consonant with the ego. Furthermore, the moral sense is absent in infancy and grows throughout childhood. Its development thus coincides with ego development. Freud's investigation of moral behavior convinced him that the moral agency should *not* be thought of as part of the ego, however, because many situations arise in which moral considerations seem actively to *oppose* the ego's normal effort to mediate between the demands of reality and the instincts. Occasions frequently arise when an id impulse can be gratified without the slightest danger from external reality but is not acted upon because of "pangs of conscience." As an individual contemplates an id-gratifying action he experiences the unpleasant emotion of guilt and desists from seizing the gratification. This suggests that the moral agency of the psyche must have an enforcing mechanism to see that moral standards are upheld. In Freud's system, the super-ego was accordingly thought of as having an energy supply at its disposal to produce guilt and thus prohibit immoral behavior. Because that energy supply can be turned against the purposes of the ego, the super-ego must be an entity independent of the ego.

The position of the super-ego in the psyche is further clarified by a consideration of the kind of energy it has at its disposal. Freud's thoughts on this matter were heavily influenced by an investigation of a clinical condition strongly characterized by guilt feelings. This condition is *depression,* known in Freud's day as *melancholia.* A clinically depressed individual suffers from feelings of worthlessness, a lack of zest for life, self-accusations, and frequent suicidal impulses—all exaggerations of a normal guilt response.

Freud's analysis of depression was that it is the result of a mourning process that has gone pathologically awry. Mourning is the emotional response to an important loss, and Freud believed that all cases of depression are preceded by the loss of an important object, usually a loved person. Instead of being able to mourn the loss normally, a depressed individual comes to be troubled by strong unconscious feelings of hostility and aggression toward the lost object. At the same time, he *identifies* with the lost object, taking part of him into the ego and unconsciously becoming like him in some respects. Since the depressed person is unable to admit consciously to his hostility, he directs it toward this component of the lost object that has been internalized within himself. When the self-reproaches of the depressed patient are carefully scrutinized, they are therefore seen as directed more appropriately against the lost object than against the patient himself. The feelings of exaggerated guilt are really manifestations of *aggression* that has been directed inwards in a peculiar way.

The following case, though not one described by Freud himself, illustrates the dynamics he postulated for depressed states. The patient was a nineteen-year-old girl at the time of her first psychiatric hospitalization. She had sought the help of a psychotherapist because she had rather suddenly begun to experience strong suicidal impulses, and her attitude toward them was mixed. On the one hand she was frightened of them and experienced them as originating in sources alien to her. On the other hand, she saw them as being somehow justified because of her own worthlessness. She explained that she had engaged in numerous acts of promiscuity and had run around with a "bad crowd." Thus she implied that she was not worth very much as a person, and that perhaps suicide was her only honorable means of expiation. Because the therapist she contacted believed her to be a genuine suicide risk, she was hospitalized for a period of several months. During the period of her hospitalization she made a number of unsuccessful suicide attempts and also engaged in self-mutilative behaviors. One of her most common such acts was to claw terribly at a particular spot on her left arm, sometimes with her fingernails, and sometimes with a knife or razor blade.

Therapeutic interviews with the patient clearly revealed that her symptoms were closely related to her feelings about her mother, who had died some years earlier under highly compromising circumstances: she was murdered by a transient soldier with whom she had been spending a night. She was without identification papers when she was killed, and her body was so badly battered that it was definitively identified only because of a large, distinctive birthmark on the left arm.

Immediately after her mother's death the patient did not seem to react dramatically. On a conscious level she felt more warmly toward her mother than she ever had before, and in family discussions in which negative things were quite naturally said about her mother's character, the patient became her staunchest defender. She maintained that her mother had been badly misunderstood and ill-treated by the family, and that that was what had driven her to carry on with other men. A subtle change soon occurred in the patient's interpersonal behavior, however. She gradually began to drop her relationships with her former friends and to take up new friendships with people who had bad reputations. She began to think of herself as a "bad" person, and as if to satisfy this new self-image she began for the first time in her life to behave promiscuously. These reactions intensified until they developed into the symptoms that immediately preceded her hospitalization.

The patient's drift into promiscuity was clearly the result of an identification with her mother. It represented a radical change in her personality that could have no other logical source. At the same time, this "derived" aspect of her self provided a convenient target for the angry impulses that her mother's death had raised in her. The appropriate object of these impulses was the mother herself; after all, she had brought tremendous shame to the family by the tawdry circumstances of her death. It was only natural that the patient should experience feelings of anger, mixed with her sorrow and love. It is difficult in our society to speak ill of the dead in the best of circumstances, however, and for reasons peculiar to herself the patient was especially unable to express directly the negative side of her feelings toward her dead mother. Instead she expressed them indirectly by hating the part of herself that was derived from, and symbolic of, her mother.

Her promiscuity served in yet another way to express indirectly her hostility toward her mother. Whenever her family or friends were apprised of her "bad" behavior, they usually reacted with an expression like "Well, she certainly is her mother's child," or "What else can we expect when her mother was so disreputable?" or "Like mother, like daughter." Thus, by calling attention to her own bad behavior the patient also called attention to her mother's prior transgressions. Then other people could express blame and hostility toward the mother, and spare the patient the necessity of doing so herself.

The patient's arm mutilation while she was hospitalized was yet another example of the same basic phenomenon. The specific part of her arm that she scratched so terribly corresponded exactly to the location of her mother's birthmark. In scratching herself she thus unconsciously identified with her mother, seeing to it that she too had an ugly disfigurement of the left arm. At the same time she expressed aggression toward the image of her mother through the hostility of her act.

Therapy with this patient was directed towards helping her to acknowledge *consciously* her feelings of anger toward her mother. The crisis in the case was reached when she underwent an extremely violent hallucinatory experience and smashed with her fist every pane of glass in a combination door. She afterwards explained that at the time she had had the sensation of hitting not a door, but an image of her mother. Discussion of this incident helped her to realize that she really did harbor feelings of intense rage toward her mother. With the conscious acknowledgement of these feelings, the need for the indirect expression receded, and gradually her feelings of worthlessness and self-hatred disappeared.

This case clearly illustrates the close relationship between guilt—which is a kind of shorthand term to denote all of the unhappy feelings the patient experienced about herself—and feelings of rage and aggression. Guilt is most simply conceptualized as *aggression turned inward.* Thus, as soon as an external object is found for the aggression the guilt ceases. This implies, of course, that the super-ego, as the originator of guilty feelings, must have at its disposal a supply of energy from the aggressive death instinct, i.e., from Thanatos. The psychic "home" of the instincts, including Thanatos, is the id, and therefore this suggests that the super-ego must have close relations with the id. This is another reason for postulating it to be a separate component of the psyche, independent of the ego.

In summary, then, the super-ego is partly like the ego in that it is a differentiated and structured component of the psychic apparatus that develops with experience. It is also partly like the id, because it has at its disposal a quantity of aggressive instinctual energy that it can employ to oppose the ego in seeing that its standards are met. Super-ego "impulses" may join with id impulses and with the constraints of reality in placing extremely difficult burdens upon the ego. Because of the super-ego, mature human beings must not only strive to be *realistic* as they set about meeting their instinctual needs; they must strive to be *moral* as well.

The Development of the Super-Ego and the Psychological Difference Between the Sexes

In the years following the postulation of the super-ego, Freud devoted considerable effort to elaborating the specific developmental events that cause it to be instituted in the psyche. Some of his theorizing along this line was startling, and it has recently become the subject of bitter dispute because it suggests a basic psychological difference between the sexes. It has been vehemently attacked by feminists as prejudiced against women.

Freud noted that a sense of morality is completely lacking in infants and young children. Thus they must be assumed to lack super-egos. It is only after they achieve a certain maturity that they may be said to possess a "conscience," and to experience control over their behavior by internalized standards of right and wrong as well as by the constraints of reality. Typically, it is at about the age of five or six that children first seem to experience strong sensations of guilt; i.e., their moral transgressions are punished from within themselves as well as by external authority figures. This is also the age at which infantile sexuality ends and the latency stage begins. Since the beginnings of conscience and the end of infantile sexuality occur at about the same time, Freud hypothesized that both of these phenomena may be achieved by the same thing—the institution of the super-ego.

The final stage of infantile sexuality preceding the super-ego is the phallic stage, when the Oedipal impulses reach their maximum intensity before finally being repressed. Thus Freud frequently referred to the super-ego as the "heir" to the Oedipus complex; the Oedipal impulses disappear, and in their stead one finds a super-ego. Freud believed that the impetus for the formation of the super-ego is the extreme intensity of the Oedipal conflicts. The anxieties and fears surrounding them become so great that a massive defensive effort is required to allow the child to retain his equilibrium. The general result of the defensive effort is the establishment of the super-ego, whose standards prohibit the expression or acknowledgment of Oedipal wishes.

Freud postulated that there are major differences between boys and girls in the specific circumstances surrounding the institution of their super-egos, though in both cases Oedipal wishes are directly involved. For the young boy, the most important figures in his life are unquestionably his parents. Because both of his parents meet his needs and play supportive roles in his life, he loves them both. However, the mother assumes greater centrality in his life because of her larger role in his caretaking, and usually she comes to be the first differentiated object of the child's sexual instinct. The father, according to Freud, is dealt with primarily by identification. Thus the general orientation of a boy toward his parents typically consists of a desire *to have* his mother (as a love object) and *to be like* his father. This orientation develops gradually during the infantile stages and is especially pronounced by the time the boy enters the phallic stage.

It has already been noted that one of the most prominent behavioral characteristics of the phallic stage is a heightened curiosity, in particular about sexual differences. This curiosity leads to an attitude of comparison and competition; other people are constantly compared with the self, and the child is greatly concerned with knowing how he personally stacks up against others. Because of the controlling general cathexis of the genital zone, differences in different people's genitals become a source of interest. The little boy thus discovers that his father's penis is much larger than his own, and he is much impressed by the fact. It reinforces his naturally developing awareness that his father is a much larger and more powerful figure than himself. At the same time, the child is aware of the fact that his father is a *rival*. His Oedipal wish is to possess his mother, but he now must recognize that his much more powerful father also has claims on her. His feelings toward his father thus become highly conflicted and ambivalent. He loves his father and identifies with him, but he also hates him for being a rival and fears him because he is so powerful.

The little boy's sexual curiosity leads to an intensification of this conflict when he notices that there are some people—little girls—who have no penis at all. Just as his father seems so superior to him with regard to his sexual organ, so little girls seem greatly inferior. The boy can draw no comfort from his superiority over girls, however, because their condition suggests a terrifying possibility to him: they may have once possessed penises but subsequently been deprived of them. Since the phallus is so important to the boy with his phallic libidinal organization, such a possibility is unspeakably horrible to him. And since it happened to someone else, he reasons that very possibly it could happen to *him,* especially since he sees himself as engaged in a mighty rivalry with his powerful father. The father might decide to punish him for his audacious Oedipal strivings by depriving him of his most prized possession: his penis. Thus Freud suggested that *castration anxiety* becomes an important and agonizing aspect of the young boy's Oedipus complex.

The castration anxiety finally makes the Oedipal conflict so intolerable that it must be resolved once and for all. What typically occurs, according to Freud, is a massive repression of the dangerous impulses—so massive that it includes not only the specifically dangerous wish for possession of the mother, but all other sexual wishes as well. Thus the sexuality of childhood comes to an apparent end. All of its oral, anal, and phallic aspects succumb to repression, and the latency stage begins.

Freud conceived of this massive repression as a truly extraordinary psychic event requiring an extraordinary psychological mechanism to allow it to take place. This mechanism, according to Freud, is an extreme intensification of the boy's identification with his father. During the most conflict-ridden phase of the Oedipal stage the father has been the major external force inhibiting the child's expression of sexuality. By increasing his identification with the father the boy makes his inhibiting power a part of himself. All of this takes place unconsciously, and the result is a new component in the boy's psyche consisting of inhibitions derived from the father by identification. Furthermore, all of the aggression that had previously been both directed toward and represented by the father remain associated with this internalized aspect of him. In other words, the repressive mechanism results in the formation of the super-ego. The moral agency in the boy's psyche is thus directly instigated by his fear of castration and effected by an identification with the prohibitive and aggressive aspects of his father.

Since the boy's super-ego development is assumed to be so directly related to his masculine anatomy, it is obvious that the identical process cannot be ascribed to the young girl. The girl's development is the same until the early phallic stage, in which the mother is fully developed as the primary object. From that point onward the girl's course must diverge from the boy's, because the events that give rise to castration anxiety in the boy cannot do so in the girl. When she observes that little boys have penises while she does not, her inference is not that she might be castrated in the future, but that she has *already* been castrated. Thus the observation of the anatomical difference between the sexes does not inspire fear, as in the boy, but resentment and envy instead. She feels that she has suffered a grievous narcissistic wound and consequently develops a compensatory wish to acquire a penis of her own. Freud called this attitude *penis envy*.

Part and parcel of penis envy is a sense of having been cheated, and according to Freud the blame for this is placed squarely on the person the girl knows "made" her in the first place: her mother. The little girl's relations with her mother now become complicated, as her primary love object becomes the object of resentment as well. As the girl seeks compensation for her deficiency, Freud asserted that she develops a new wishful fantasy of having a child by and for the father. Wishes of this type were the sources of the seduction fantasies that Freud uncovered in his early female hysterics.

Once this fantasy is established, the father replaces the mother as the little girl's primary sexual object, and the mother then quite naturally is seen as the chief rival for the father's love. The Oedipal pattern of the girl therefore comes to be established as the complement of the boy's. In the girl's case, however, this extreme attraction for the opposite-sexed parent and rivalry with the same-sexed one comes about after a more complicated developmental process than the boy's.

A further difference arises because the girl cannot experience castration anxiety or its equivalent. From her point of view she has already been castrated and has nothing further to fear along that line. Her mother may be respected and feared as a larger and more powerful rival, but she does not have the ultimate power to strike at the heart of the libidinal organization. Therefore the conflict engendered by the girl's Oedipal wishes is not as great as it is for the boy, and the motive for identification with the same-sexed parent is not as intensified as in the boy.

Following this reasoning, Freud put forth the controversial hypothesis that girls do not develop strong super-egos. The super-ego may develop to a certain extent, but on the average it is much weaker than that of the boy. "Anatomy is destiny,"[5] according to Freud, and the destiny of females is less desirable than that of males in his evaluative scheme. Females, with relatively weak super-egos, lack the stern moral sense that often characterizes men. Freud stated his opinion in the following passage from a 1925 paper entitled "Some Psychological Consequences of the Anatomical Distinction between the Sexes":

> I cannot evade the notion (though I hesitate to give it expression) that for women the level of what is ethically normal is different from what it is in men. Their super-ego is never so inexorable, so impersonal, so independent of its emotional origins as we require it to be in men. Character-traits which critics of every epoch have brought up against women—that they show less sense of justice than men, that they are less ready to submit to the great exigencies of life, that they are more often influenced in their judgements by feelings of affection or hostility—all these would be amply accounted for by the modification in the formation of their super-ego which we have inferred.[6]

Freud's arguments about the factors underlying the development of the super-ego have struck many critics as being fanciful, not to say highly biased. Freud himself admitted that his formulations were based on the free associations of "a handful of cases," and might therefore be misleading. Nevertheless, he never changed his mind about their probable validity. In

[5] *Standard Edition,* Vol. XIX, p. 178.
[6] *Ibid.,* pp. 257–258.

assessing this part of Freud's theory, it is important to recognize that his ideas about how the super-ego develops are logically independent of his arguments for the *existence* of a moral agency like the super-ego. One can accept Freud's conceptual notion of the super-ego and the tripartite model of the mind but at the same time reject the view that the super-ego develops primarily as the result of castration anxiety.

Ego Psychology and the Defense Mechanisms

The overall effect of Freud's final model of the mind was a clarifying one. In particular, the new model illuminated the terms of the basic conflicts that constantly beset human beings and determine their behavior. From the earliest days of psychoanalysis Freud had viewed almost all behavior as the result of some sort of conflict between wish and reality. In the new model he explicitly recognized a third party to the conflict: the moral demands of the super-ego. With the recognition of this added complexity, it was inevitable that special attention should be paid to the psychic *mediator* of conflict. Thus in the years following *The Ego and the Id* increasing theoretical attention was paid to the role and function of the ego.

Whenever three independent entities make conflicting demands, there is seldom a solution that will be completely satisfactory for all three. The major function of the ego is therefore to effect reasonable *compromises.* Its most common problem occurs when an instinctual impulse arises in the id and presses for an immediate gratification that would bring the organism into realistic danger and/or violate the moral demands of the super-ego. The ego processes must result in a compromise whereby the id gratification is either delayed or modified so that the dictates of reality and conscience can be recognized. Many different kinds of compromise are possible, of course, and they may vary considerably in the degree to which they favor the three parties to the conflict. Thus some may permit fairly direct gratification of impulses while merely paying lip service to the constraining forces; others may allow only the slightest and most highly disguised of instinctual gratifications to occur.

The notion of compromise was closely related to that of *defense* from the earliest days of psychoanalysis. Neurotic symptoms were first conceptualized as compromises between sexual and ego-preservative impulses, allowing for the symbolic expression of sexuality but removing its dangerous consequences. Similarly, the dream work was demonstrated to modify the instinctual nature of latent thoughts while at the same time permitting them disguised expression. With the new emphasis on the ego and its processes, it became apparent that many other human behaviors that occurred in waking life and in completely normal individuals were also the results of compromise mechanisms. In fact, several distinctively different strategies of compromise were discerned. Because of the close relationship between compromise and defense, these ego operations were referred to as *defense mechanisms.* The systematic specification of the defense mechanisms was begun by Freud in a 1926 work entitled "Inhibitions, Symptoms and Anxiety" (also published under the title *The Problem of Anxiety*) and continued by his daughter, Anna Freud, who worked as a close collaborator. Other psychoanalytic theorists have also been active in elucidating defense mechanisms.

The name of one of the commonest defense mechanisms is already familiar from the discussion of hysterical symptoms and dreams. In fact, the defense mechanism of *displacement* is very similar to the process of the same name as it occurs in dreams and symptom formation. When displacement as a defense mechanism takes place, a substitute object, related to the original object by some associative link, becomes the target of an instinctual impulse. A simple example of displacement is provided by an individual who is unfairly disciplined by his superior at work but makes no obvious response until he arrives at home and yells at his wife and beats his dog without real cause. In this case he has displaced his aggression, originally directed toward his boss, onto the "safer" targets of his wife and dog. The aggressive impulse toward the superior may have been regarded by the ego as dangerous because of reality factors—the worker might lose his job if he expressed his anger toward his boss—or because of super-ego demands—he may have internalized a moral precept prohibiting the expression of aggression against authority figures. At any rate, the expression of aggression against the wife and dog is a compromise that allows for the discharge of aggression but avoids the negative consequences that would follow from attacking the boss.

Another use of displacement is often made by people when they select marriage partners. It is often obvious that a man's wife bears distinct similarities to his mother, or a woman's husband to her father. In these cases it is likely that the marriage choices were made partly because of displaced Oedipal wishes. In choosing a spouse who is similar to the Oedipal object, the taboo sexual impulse is permitted partial gratification in a manner acceptable to the super-ego as well as to the law. The whole defense process is unconscious, of course, since a general function of defense mechanisms is to keep the nature of the conflicts they resolve out of conscious awareness.

One of the more primitive defense mechanisms, often serving to favor instinctual expression at the expense of reality, is called *denial.* It occurs when a person is unable to accept the reality of something that has happened and simply denies its existence. A couple may have a violent quarrel in private but begin behaving in the friendliest of fashions as soon as they know they are being observed. After a time they may "forget" that they ever quarreled in the first place, thus succeeding in denying the reality of angry impulses that they had expressed.

Denial may be directed against aspects of external reality as well as against instinctual expression. It is a frequent defense in periods immediately following catastrophic events. A woman whose husband has died may continue to behave for a time as if he were still alive. She may keep his easy chair and smoking table in just the fashion that he liked them and continue to prepare his favorite meals. Her behavior, implicitly expressing the expectation that her husband will soon return and take up his customary activities, represents a denial of the fact of his death.

A defense mechanism that is in some respects a more sophisticated version of denial is *rationalization*. Like that of denial, the goal of rationalization is to blunt the effect of something that has really happened. Rationalization occurs when a person constructs a plausible but false rationale for something that he has done or experienced. A person who has cheated on his income tax, for example, may rationalize that the tax laws are written so that intelligent citizens may take advantage of certain loop-holes. It is not that he is dishonest; he is just doing what is expected of him. A much grimmer example of rationalization is provided by a soldier who enthusiastically participates in war crimes, giving full vent to all of his violent and sadistic impulses. Afterwards, he rationalizes his behavior by insisting that he only did what he was ordered to do, that his victims were really enemy soldiers who would gladly have done the same thing to him, and so forth. This excuse may have a certain degree of truth to it, but it also may serve to hide the real nature of the soldier's behavior from others and, even more importantly, from himself. Rationalization is successful as a defense only when it disguises reality for the rationalizer, since only then can it prevent the anxiety that would be aroused if the truth were squarely confronted.

Another common defense mechanism is *projection*, which occurs when a person unwarrantedly attributes to someone else an impulse that he unconsciously experiences himself. According to Freud the extreme suspiciousness characteristic of "paranoid" individuals is the result of extreme use of projection. The paranoid individual experiences intense aggressive impulses which he cannot consciously accept. He projects his hostility onto others, with the result that he perceives them as very dangerous and threatening. Hence he regards the world with exaggerated suspicion.

Projection is a very common defense mechanism in hostile or competitive situations. In wartime, for example, it is typical to attribute all sorts of unworthy motives and acts to the enemy, while never even imagining the possibility of the same on one's own side. In daily life projection is a convenient means of avoiding the unpleasant truth that one's own motives and impulses are less than completely honorable by attributing those motives primarily to others.

Introjection or *identification* is an important defense mechanism that has already been considered, though in another context. This mechanism is the reverse of projection, since it involves taking the attributes of another person and making them part of the self. The suicidal girl who identified with her dissolute mother used identification as a defense against her hostile feelings. She internalized parts of her mother and then directed her aggression against those "derived" components of her personality. Thus the hostile impulses were permitted expression via the patient's self-destructive and guilt-ridden behaviors, but their real target did not have to be consciously recognized.

Another defensive use of identification is made in the establishment of the super-ego. The conflict-creating Oedipal impulses are finally dealt with by a massive internalization of parental constraints. These internalized constraints prevent even the contemplation of the Oedipal impulses and thereby reduce the child's sensation of conflict. At the same time, identification with the same-sexed parent allows for the vicarious gratification of the Oedipal impulses. Identification thus turns out to be one of the most important of all the defense mechanisms, since it is through its effects that the third major component of the psyche comes to be formed.

Yet another important defense mechanism is *reaction formation*. When this occurs, a dangerous unconscious impulse receives expression in a conscious perception of its opposite. Usually reaction formation takes place when a person's attitude is ambivalent to begin with, and when only one side of the ambivalence may be comfortably expressed. Situations that appropriately call for the unacceptable side of the ambivalence elicit intensified manifestations of the opposite, more comfortable impulse. The suicidal girl made use of reaction formation, in addition to identification, in dealing with her aggression toward her mother. Her real attitude toward her mother was ambivalent, consisting of hatred for bringing disgrace upon the family, as well as love. The hatred could not be expressed consciously, however, and situations such as family discussions that would be expected to elicit the unconscious hatred brought on a reaction formation. The *conscious* experience of the girl was then an intensification of her positive feelings for her mother, whom she defended in the discussions.

A defense mechanism of a rather different type from those discussed so far is *isolation*, sometimes referred to as *isolation of affect*. When isolation occurs, an instinctually aroused thought is permitted to reach consciousness, but only after it has been stripped of the emotion or affect that should normally accompany it. Usually ideas and affects go hand in hand, particularly if they derive fairly directly from the id. Thus some thoughts quite literally send chills up and down the spine, others inspire surges of happiness, and still others inspire less intense emotion. When isolation occurs, however, the emotion appropriate to a thought does not occur. The process is a compromise, in that only a part of a thought-emotion complex is permitted expression. Individuals who make extensive use of isolation are usually described as cold-blooded, because they are capable of thinking about all sorts of emotionally charged things without becoming emotionally aroused. The stereotype of the cold-blooded military planner exemplifies such a person. He is able to think comfortably about "casualties" and "losses" as they occur in combat, and even to categorize them as "light," "moderate," or "heavy" without recognizing emotionally that his subject matter is human death and suffering. "Kill-ratio" and "mega-death" are two very recent examples of concepts that owe their existence to the defense mechanism of isolation.

Sometimes, however, isolation as a defense is highly adaptive. A surgeon, for example, must employ isolation at least temporarily if he is to work effectively. If he allows himself to be overcome with emotion because of the thought that his work involves the cutting of real flesh and blood, his efficiency may suffer and there will be a real risk to his patients on the operating table.

A defense closely related to isolation is *intellectualization,* which denotes an attempt to deal with an instinctual conflict in an explicitly and exclusively intellectual way. A teenager who is upset by his sexuality, for example, may attempt to deal with his conflict by reading medical and technical books about the physiology of sex. Students who take courses in abnormal psychology because they hope to learn something about their own conflicts, and thereby bring them under control, also make use of intellectualization. While they gain technical information in great detail, they suppress their emotional responses. Intellectualization may sometimes be a highly adaptive defense, enabling people to gain real mastery over their conflicts. If it is carried to extremes, however, the intellectualizer is likely to be considered pedantic, cold, and highly detached by persons who are in closer contact with the emotional side of life.

These are some of the principal mechanisms that the ego employs in its efforts at compromise and defense. Each defense mechanism allows for some kind of instinctual expression while at the same time modifying the instinct to accommodate the demands of reality and the forces of conscience. Sometimes defenses occur after the fact and modify only the recollection of the impulse. Thus mechanisms like denial and rationalization load the compromise in favor of the instinctual expression and against reality. Other defenses alter the instinct itself (reaction formation) or change its object (displacement, projection, and introjection). Still others deal with impulses by stripping them of their emotional accompaniments, as in isolation and intellectualization. In all cases, however, the result is a creative act on the part of the ego. Sometimes the result is highly effective, resulting in maximal satisfaction to all the three parties to the intrapsychic conflict; at other times it severely neglects one or more of the demands, and its consequences may be labeled psychopathological. Whatever their outcome, ego-defense mechanisms are now recognized as dominating a great deal of human activity. Their discovery and elucidation is one of the major achievements following from Freud's final model of the mind.

The Implications of Psychoanalysis

Toward the end of his life, Freud turned his attention partly away from clinical issues and theory construction, and attempted to derive the lessons that his final version of psychoanalytic theory had to teach about the human situation in general. He addressed himself to questions about the development and future of human civilization, and to the "ultimate questions" men have long asked about the purpose and meaning of life. Consistent with his view that the essence of human existence is conflict among the id, reality, and the super-ego, and that the best result one can hope for is a tolerable compromise or effective defense mechanism, his answers to the questions were hardly very optimistic.

Traditionally, questions about the purpose and meaning of existence have been within the domain of religion. Freud, however, did not put much stock in the pronouncements of the orthodox religions. In fact, he analyzed the institution of religion with the same scrutiny he had applied to neurotic patients, and found that it came out little better. From early in his career he had been cognizant of some striking similarities between religious practices and the symptoms of some neurotic patients. The *obsessive compulsive* individual is often beset with compulsions to perform ritualistic acts like repeated handwashing; if he does not perform them he is overcome with anxiety and guilt. Similarly, the religious faithful are often required by their religions to participate regularly and carefully in rituals and ceremonies. Often the religious person feels driven to participate especially enthusiastically because of a sense of sin and guilt, which is alleviated through his religious activities. Descriptively, the only difference between such a person and an obsessive-compulsive neurotic is that his ritualized activity is shared by many people, whereas the neurotic's is usually idiosyncratic and private.

For many years Freud withheld from publishing anything really negative about organized religion out of respect for a close friend of his who was a Protestant minister. Finally, however, Freud spoke his mind fully. In 1927 he wrote a work devoted exclusively to religion, *The Future of an Illusion*, in which he pointed out that the most important articles of faith for the great Western religions are by definition incapable of empirical proof. Furthermore, on the basis of concrete experience, and judged by the reality principle, they are highly implausible. Freud suggested that these ideas are *illusions*—notions that are based primarily on wishes and that do not take into account the nature of reality.

The common religious belief that Freud thought was most patently an illusion was the notion that there exists a benevolent God who watches over the life of each individual and sees that he is compensated in the afterlife for his sufferings on earth.

> These [religious beliefs], which are given out as teachings, are not precipitates of experience or end-results of thinking: they are illusions, fulfilments of the oldest, strongest, and most urgent wishes of mankind. The secret of their strength lies in the strength of those wishes. As we already know, the terrifying impression of helplessness in childhood aroused the need for protection—for protection through love—which was provided by the father; and the recognition that this helplessness lasts throughout life made it necessary to cling to the existence of a father, but this time a more powerful one. Thus the benevolent rule of a divine Providence allays our fears of the dangers of life; the establishment of a moral world-order ensures the fulfilment of the demands of justice, which have so often remained unfulfilled in human civilization; and the prolongation of earthly existence in a future life provides the local and temporal framework in which these wish-fulfilments shall take place.[7]

The best that Freud could say about religious illusions is that they are not *necessarily* false, since they are independent

[7] *Standard Edition*, Vol. XXI, p. 30.

of reality and not necessarily contrary to it. The odds against their being true are great, however, and Freud did not believe that they constitute a very firm basis for adaptive behavior. He placed a much higher value on illusions of another type: artistic and literary creations that present artists' views of the world as they would like to see it. These are very different from religious beliefs in that they are consciously recognized as illusions, while religious ideas are accepted as reality. Freud's personal evaluation of the idea of a loving, paternalistic God is summarized in a single sentence: "The whole thing is so patently infantile, so foreign to reality, that to anyone with a friendly attitude to humanity it is painful to think that the great majority of mortals will never be able to rise above this view of life."[8] For Freud, it was always better to apply the criterion of reality to *any* idea, no matter how pleasing or repugnant its implications might be. The reality principle should prevail as often as possible.

After rendering such a negative verdict about the truth of the traditional answers to ultimate questions, Freud attempted to pose some answers of his own. In an influential work entitled *Civilization and Its Discontents*, published in 1930, Freud stated categorically that the major goal in life is simply the gratification of instinct. The sudden discharge of dammed-up tension from within the psychic system constitutes the most positive instance of "happiness." To put it another way, the most basic purpose of life is to achieve the aims of the pleasure principle. The very nature of the human psyche, however, makes constant intense pleasure impossible. The gratification of the pleasure principle can occur only as an "episodic phenomenon." Freud stated "When any situation that is desired by the pleasure principle is prolonged, it only produces a feeling of mild contentment."[9] The rationale for this assertion dates back to the "Project" and Freud's assumptions about the summation of stimuli; the "experience of satisfaction"—the

[8] *Ibid.*, p. 74.
[9] *Ibid.*, p. 76.

prototype for pleasurable experience—was assumed to occur only as the result of the discharge of large amounts of accumulated *Q*. Such discharges could not occur constantly, but only after sufficient quantities of energy had been stored in the nervous system. Thus the summation-of-stimulation hypothesis returned in 1930 in a philosophical form: "Our possibilities of happiness are already restricted by our constitution."[10]

Although the attainment of happiness by instinctual gratification is a difficult enough task in itself, the human situation is further complicated because life presents almost constant threats of *un*happiness; i.e., of pain. These threats come from three sources—man's own body, his physical environment, and his social environment—which may be thought of as constituting "reality." Thus an added burden is placed upon the human being, in that he must try to minimize painful stimulation from reality as well as to maximize his instinctual gratification. The one goal may be thought of as the minimization of unhappiness, the other as the maximization of happiness. To complicate things still further, the two goals, if pursued absolutely, are mutually exclusive. The hedonist, who seeks nothing but sensual pleasure from life, is highly vulnerable to the slings and arrows of harsh reality; his opposite, the extremely security-minded person, is so consumed with his fear of reality that he is unable to take any pleasure from life. Thus once again we encounter the familiar Freudian theme of conflict, and, as usual, the only solution is to find a workable compromise.

There is nothing really new in Freud's treatment of human happiness so far. Essentially, it is simply a restatement of the idea that human nature is defined by a fundamental conflict between wish and reality—between internal and external sources of excitation. This notion dates back as far as the "Project," and Freud's discussion of happiness is also easily translatable into the terms of his 1923 model of the mind. The source of the need to maximize happiness is the id, and it is the ego

[10] *Ibid.*, pp. 76–77.

that must try to avoid unhappiness from the real world. It is also the ego which must try to find compromise solutions.

In discussing the compromise strategies commonly employed to resolve this dilemma, Freud describes some ego mechanisms referred to as *sublimations*. Sublimation occurs when the energies of an instinct are used to initiate behaviors that are adaptive to reality and socially appropriate. In principle, a sublimation is identical to a defense mechanism, since it is a psychic compromise between conflicting demands. In fact, several psychoanalytic scholars have listed sublimation as one of the defense mechanisms, along with displacement, projection, denial, and the rest. Sublimation has slightly different connotations from the other defense mechanisms, however, because it is always associated with "normal" or "healthy" processes, while the defense mechanisms often have psychopathological connotations. To some degree the two concepts overlap, since whenever a defense mechanism is used for good, adaptive purposes—as when the surgeon isolates his affect in order to work effectively—the result is indistinguishable from sublimation.

One important means of sublimation is to exert one's energies toward the mastery of nature—i.e., to *work*. When work is directed toward a goal that has been freely chosen, and when it is effective, it results in definite feelings of pleasure as well as a degree of control over external reality. Highly productive and effective people, who "live for their work" and receive genuine gratification from it, employ sublimation successfully. Freud regarded his own scientific contributions as the result of sublimation of this type, but he pointed out that the pleasures derived from work are highly refined sensations that are not sufficiently gratifying for many people. They seem somehow "higher and finer," and "their intensity is mild as compared with that derived from the sating of crude and primary instinctual impulses; it does not convulse our physical being."[11] Thus work is a *possible* means to happiness, but to be such it requires an innate aptitude for effective achievement

[11] *Ibid.*, pp. 79–80.

—which many people possess only to a moderate degree—and the willingness to settle for relatively mild feelings of satisfaction.

Another means to happiness by sublimation is to employ instinctual energy to effect a mild and conscious loosening of the bonds with reality. The prototype of this kind of activity is the *play* of children, which is dedicated to the purpose of constructing controllable and pleasurable fantasy worlds. A mature version of the same tendency is practiced by the artist, who, in effect, creates his own miniature universe. There is no doubt that the artist takes great joy in the act of creation, though it, like the joy from work, is mild and refined when compared to purely instinctual gratification. Both the child's and the artist's creative play makes use of illusion, which has been discussed in the context of Freud's views on religion. Participation in the illusions of religion is still another way of solving the happiness problem by loosening the ties with reality. But we have seen that Freud did not value this solution highly because of the failure of conscious understanding to accompany most religious experience. Freud greatly preferred consciously adopted illusions, either playful or artistic, as the road to happiness.

Still another route to happiness—in most ways the best one of all—is *love*, the establishment of permanent affectional ties with external objects. An obvious advantage of this solution is that it sometimes allows for the overt and "pure" gratification of the sexual instincts, thus resulting in experiences of intense positive pleasure. Genuine love also entails a considerable amount of sublimation, however, because it involves a real concern for the loved object and the willingness to undergo sacrifices for it. A certain portion of sexual instinctual energy must be deflected from its original aim of immediate, indiscriminate gratification in order to effect the permanency and depth of the loving relationship. Love would seem to be the ideal compromise to the dilemma of maximizing happiness and minimizing unhappiness. It permits the overt gratification of some instinctual impulses, and by linking people together in relationships where they help and care for each other it serves their reality needs as well. The only problem with love as a solution is that it puts a person at the mercy of his love object and leaves him extremely vulnerable to its loss or desertion. ". . . we are never so defenceless against suffering as when we love, never so helplessly unhappy as when we have lost our love object or its love."[12] Individuals who have already "lost at love" may be very reluctant to choose love as a path to happiness again.

Thus in Freud's view the three "positive" solutions to the human dilemma are effective work, creative play, and enduring love. Of those the greatest, though also the most dangerous, is love. Not one of them is a perfect solution, because all of them are compromises. In general, however, they are *good* compromises, and the person who can regularly employ all of them in his life is fortunate indeed.

A factor common to the three sublimated routes to happiness is that they are all regarded as "civilized," and in fact are possible only in an ordered social setting or civilization. Work is almost always directed toward communal goals, even though parts of it may be executed in isolation, and the mastery over nature it achieves is the result of many people's working together or building upon each other's accomplishments. Artistic activity and religion are "civilized" almost by definition, and neither would be meaningful outside a social context. Love is the quintessential permanent social relationship, and the interpersonal bonds that it creates help to hold organized societies together. Thus Freud concluded that the ego is granted considerable flexibility in its search for happiness by the fact that human beings live in civilized societies. Without civilization or culture, the options for sublimation would never occur. Conversely, of course, there could be no civilization in the absence of sublimation.

Freud could not conclude that all of the effects of civilization are positive, however. He had witnessed the immense car-

[12] *Ibid.*, p. 82.

nage of World War I, perpetrated by, and even in the name of, "civilized" societies. And even as he wrote *Civilization and Its Discontents* the specter of Hitler and National Socialism was beginning to rise in Germany. It was clear to Freud that there exist daemonic, destructive forces in civilized societies, forces which he could interpret only as manifestations of Thanatos, the death instinct. As he tried to understand the origins of civilization's self-destructive impulses, a gloomy possibility, derived from his speculations about the super-ego, suggested itself.

These speculations began with the observation that the ego pays a price for operating in a social environment that offers it opportunities for sublimation. Any civilized society places restrictions on its members at the same time that it provides them options. These restrictions and rules constitute demands for morality, the intrapsychic agent of which is the super-ego. The super-ego performs a very valuable social function by ensuring that citizens will heed the moral prohibitions necessary for the maintenance of their society. Furthermore, the super-ego exists *because* human beings live in civilized societies. If it were not for the conventions of family structure, dictated by society and maintained by the binding power of love between husband and wife, there would be no Oedipal conflict and hence no super-ego. Thus the super-ego may be seen as the price modern civilized man pays for his social nature.

The super-ego was assumed by Freud to have special links with the pool of aggressive energy in the id, as we have seen, and this was the root of his most pessimistic thoughts about human civilization. The effect of the super-ego is to pit the two great instincts against each other; its aggressive energy is employed to combat and repress the infantile urges of the sexual instinct. Thus a paradox arises: civilization provides the circumstances that make possible the effective and creative deployment of the erotic instincts, but at the same time it severely restricts those instincts by means of the super-ego. It provides greater opportunities for sublimation, but less available energy with which to sublimate. Opportunities for happiness are both increased and reduced at the same time.

The super-ego's harnessing of aggresive energy also tends to divert that energy from its original aim of guiding the organism along its appropriate path to death. Instead of being used to ward off external impediments to that path, the aggression becomes mobilized in the service of morality. It may express itself inwardly and result in feelings of guilt, or outwardly in manifestations of moral outrage against the enemy who transgresses against one's own moral code. Here, of course, is the source of the destructive and nihilistic impulses which seemed to Freud to plague civilized societies.

The thought that most disturbed Freud was that with increasing "progress" in civilization, there may occur an increase in the power of the super-ego to enforce civilization's more difficult demands. This would mean that the sexual, "life instincts" become increasingly restricted, while the potentially destructive capacity of the death instincts is greatly enhanced. The future of man and his civilization are dependent upon their maintaining a proper balance between the strength of the two great classes of instincts. Whether they will be able to do so or not was a moot question for Freud. Accordingly, he concluded *Civilization and Its Discontents* with the following famous lines:

> Men have gained control over the forces of nature to such an extent that with their help they would have no difficulty in exterminating one another to the last man. They know this, and hence comes a large part of their current unrest, their unhappiness and their mood of anxiety. And now it is to be expected that the other of the two 'Heavenly Powers', eternal Eros, will make an effort to assert himself in the struggle with his equally immortal adversary. But who can see with what success and with what result?[13]

Ever the great realist, Freud was no more sanguine about the future of human civilization than he was about the ultimate probability of finding perfect happiness.

[13] *Ibid.*, p. 145.

A Concluding Word

This survey of Freud's thought has sought to show that its character and scope changed gradually but dramatically over the years, even while certain themes and ideas remained constant. In the early stages Freud was concerned with relatively circumscribed and technical problems centering around the neuroses. With the first insights about hysteria and the development of the free association technique as a tool, the tone of his writing was buoyant and optimistic, and he dealt with increasingly general and significant problems. The investigations of dreams and slips revealed much about human sexuality, which knowledge in turn led to a consideration of the most basic instincts that motivate humanity. By the time the great duality of Eros and Thanatos was postulated, Freud was on the threshold of a profoundly philosophical view of man as a creature whose most basic characteristic is intrapsychic conflict. This view was expressed in his final model of the mind, which portrayed the psyche as an arena for the clashing and compromising of divergent forces and impulses.

Freud did not shrink from the logical consequences of his conception of man as a creature in conflict. In his later years his thought took on a somber tone as it analyzed the potential effectiveness of civilization as the means to human happiness. Faithful to his own reality principle, he concluded that the best that men can hope for in life is to achieve a satisfactory compromise among their conflicting urges and requirements. Though this may seem an unduly pessimistic assessment of the human situation, it is perhaps worth reflecting that in our present age of division, conflict, and strife, the idea of realistic and just compromise is not altogether unattractive.

SUGGESTED FURTHER READINGS

The principal works in which Freud described the different uses of the word "unconscious" and which reflected his growing disenchantment with the model of Chapter 7 are a 1912 paper entitled "A Note on the Unconscious," a 1915 paper entitled "The Unconscious," and the first chapter of *The Ego and the Id* (New York, Norton, 1962), first published in 1923. A brief historical survey of these issues is provided by James Strachey's "Editor's Introduction" to *The Ego and the Id,* and a more extensive account is included in *Topography and Systems in Psychoanalytic Theory* by Merton M. Gill (New York, International Universities Press, 1963).

The new model of the mind was introduced by Freud in *The Ego and the Id,* and a later, more complete account of it is found in Chapter 3 of his *New Introductory Lectures on Psycho-Analysis* (New York, Norton, 1933).

Freud's views on the formation of the super-ego and his controversial opinion of female psychology are expressed in a series of four papers: "The Infantile Genital Organization of the Libido" (1923), "The Passing of the Oedipus-Complex" (1924), "Some Psychological Consequences of the Anatomical Distinction Between the Sexes" (1925), and "Female Sexuality" (1931).

Systematic elucidation of the defense mechanisms was begun by Freud in a work entitled *The Problem of Anxiety* (New York, Norton, 1936). His daughter, Anna Freud, wrote another pioneering work on the same subject entitled *The Ego and the Mechanisms of Defense* (New York, International Universities Press, 1935).

A paper written in 1907 entitled "Obsessive Acts and Religious Practices" marked the first linking of religion with psychopathology, but it was in 1927, in *The Future of an Illusion* (New York, Anchor Books, 1964), that Freud presented his most devastating critique of organized religion. His major analysis of human civilization and its relation to happiness was *Civilization and Its Discontents* (New York, Norton, 1962), written in 1930.

Index

Abreaction, 52, 59
Abstraction, 117–18, 123
Adler, Alfred, 134, 163
Affect, 55, 56, 221–22
Aggression, guilt and, 207–10
Ambivalence, 143
Amnesia, 35, 37, 42–43, 53
Anaesthesias, hypnotic, 43
Animal magnetism, 40–41, 42*n*
Anna O., case history, 47–51, 59, 93, 178*n*
Anti-Semitism, 21–22
Anxiety, 185
Aphasia, 31
"Art of Becoming an Original Writer in Three Days, The," 11–12
Associations, 51, 120
see also Free association

Baquet, 41
Behavior, selectivity in, 71
Bernheim, Hippolyte, 45–46, 52, 53–54
Beyond the Pleasure Principle, 182 ff., 186, 188–89 ff., 193
Bisexuality, 28
Bois-Reymond, Emil du, 15–16
Börne, Ludwig, 11–12
Braid, James, 44
Brentano, Franz, 14
Breuer, Josef, 25–26, 47–51, 52, 54–57, 59, 137, 165, 170, 178*n*
Brücke, Ernest, 14–16, 18–19, 21, 22, 25, 66

Castration anxiety, 213, 214, 215
Cathartic method, 50–51, 52–53 ff., 165
Cathexis, 66–67 ff., 95–96, 154, 199
  dream theory and, 101–2, 104–5, 110
  ego and, 83–85, 86–92
  endogenous stimulation and, 67–68, 70–72
  exogenous stimulation and, 67, 68–70
  hysteria and, 92–95
  inter-neuronal flow and, 72–75; effect on mental activity, 75–77
  mental growth and, 77–78, 80–83
  narcissistic, 185
  need, 80
  Omega system and, 83–86
  perceptual, 80, 81, 82, 84–85 ff.
  Phi and Psi systems and, 79–83
  quiescent, 184–86
  revised model of the mind and, 127–31
  wishful, 82, 83–85 ff., 89–90, 101–2
Censorship, 114–15, 118, 200, 201, 205
Charcot, Jean, 24–25, 45–46, 137
Chroback, Rudolf (gynecologist), 137
Civilization and Its Discontents, 225, 231
Cocaine, 24

Index

Compulsion to repeat, 180–86, 189
Condensation, 115–16, 128, 130, 131, 199
Consciousness, 123–24
  final model of the mind and, 200–1
Conservation of energy, law of, 16–17
Conversions, 55–56
Copernicus, 7

Darwin, Charles, 7, 135
Death instinct, 186, 188–93, 210
  aggression and, 191
  civilization and, 230–31
Defense hysteria, 57–58
  seduction theory and, 59–60
  therapy for, 58–59
Defense mechanisms, 217–23, 227
  see also individual mechanisms
Denial, 218–19, 222
Depression, 206–10
Disgust, sexual instinct and, 150
Displacement, 96, 199, 217, 222
  dream theory and, 112–13, 118
  first model of the mind and, 93–94, 95
Dissociation/dissociative reactions, 34–36
Dora, case history, 166–76, 177–78, 180
Dreams/dream theory, 96, 181
  dream-work process, 112–19
  free association and, 104, 106–7*n*, 111
  function of dreams, 119–20
  latent and manifest content, dream-work process and, 111–20, 126; censorship, 114–15, 118; condensation, 115–16; consideration of representability, 116–18; day residue, 118; displacement, 112–13, 118; secondary revision, 113–15
  origin of theory, first model of the mind and, 98–105; Freud's own dream, 103–5
  psychopathological theory and, 105–11; hysteria, 108, 109–10; neurotic processes, 107–8; seduction theory, 108–9
  revised model of the mind and, 130–32
  sexuality and, 106–10, 112, 113, 138, 139–40, 141, 143, 145
  symbolism in, 112–13, 116–17
  wish fulfillment and, 99, 101–2, 106, 110, 112, 119; psychic reality, 110–11
  see also Mind, revised model of
Du Bois-Reymond, Emil, 15–16

Ego, 83–85, 96, 202–6, 226–27, 229
  defense mechanisms and, 216–23
  depleted, during sleep, 100, 102, 103
  dream theory and, 115*n*
  hysteria and, 92, 94–95
  neural mechanisms of, 86–88; primary and secondary processes, 88–92, 94–95
  strong and weak, *see neural mechanisms of*
Ego and the Id, The, 197, 203
Ego instinct, 186–88, 190, 192
Ego libido, 188
Electrotherapy, 38, 51–52
Ellis, Havelock, 136
Endogenous stimulation, 67–68, 70–72, 80–81, 82, 83, 100, 101–2, 110, 147, 153–54, 184, 188
  see also Mind, first model of
Eros, *see* Instinct, sexual
Erotogenic zones, 156, 157
Esdaile, James, 43–44
Exhibitionism, 151, 163
Exogenous stimulation, 67, 68–70, 80, 81, 82, 83, 99–100, 101, 102, 103, 110
  see also Mind, first model of

Fantasy, 54, 199, 202, 205
Fliess, Wilhelm, 26–28, 63–64, 99, 104, 108, 136, 137, 139, 167
Forel, Auguste, 136
"Fragment of an Analysis of a Case of Hysteria," 170

Index

Free association, 1–6, 11–12, 54, 108, 137–38, 140, 165, 166
  dream theory and, 104, 106–107*n*, 111
Freud, Amalia, 9–11
Freud, Anna, 217
Freud, Jakob, 9–11
Freud, Martha Bernays, 22, 25
Freud, Sigmund, 8–9
  academic scientific career, discrimination and problems, 21–22
  education/intellectual development, 10–20
  enters Vienna General Hospital, 22–23
  family background, 9–10
  later writings, change in, 195–96
  neurological studies, 23–25
  private practice, friendship with Breuer and Fliess, 25–28
  self analysis, 139–43
  transition from neurological to psychological level of analysis, 98–99
Fugue states, 35, 37
Future of an Illusion, The, 224

Goethe, Johann Wolfgang von, 13, 27
Great man theory, 8
Guilt, 206–10, 211

Hallucinations, 43
  see also Dreams/dream theory
Helmholtz, Hermann, 15, 16–17, 18, 66
Herbart, Johann, 12
Hitler, Adolf, 230
Homosexuality, 148–49
Hydrotherapy, 38, 51, 52
Hypnosis/hypnotic phenomena, 38–39
  early use and investigation of, 39–44
  hysterical phenomena and, 44, 45–51; Anna O., case history of, 47–51; Freud's early study of, 51–54, 60
  Nancy school, 45–46
Hysteria, 32, 33–39, 105, 112, 115, 136
  ancient Greek concept and treatment of, 37–38
  childhood sexuality, 137–39, 145
  defense, 57–60
  Freud's early study of, psychoanalytic theory and, 51–61
  hypnoid, 56–57, 59
  hypnotic phenomena and, 44, 45–51; Anna O., case history of, 47–51
  perverse sexuality and, 152
  primary process and, 92–95
  retention, 56, 57, 59
  symptoms, 33–37; dissociative reactions, 34–36; paralyses, 33–34
  therapy for in Freud's time, 38
  see also Psychopathology

Id, 202–6, 210, 216, 221, 226, 230
Identification, 220
Illusions, 224–25, 228
"Inhibitions, Symptoms and Anxiety," 217
Instincts, 196–97, 204
  death, 186, 199–93, 210, 230–31; sexual instinct and, 191–92
  ego, 192; sexual instinct and, 186–87
  to repeat, 189–90
  sexual, 230; death instinct and, 192; ego instinct and, 186–88; germ cells theory, 191–92; nature of, 147–53; object or ego libido, 188
  term defined, 146–47
Intellectualization, 222
Interpretation of Dreams, The, 96, 111–12 ff., 120–21 ff., 134, 146, 195, 196, 197, 198, 199, 200, 201
Introjection, 220, 222
Inversion, *see* Homosexuality
Isolation, 221–22

Jewish mysticism, 12
Jones, Ernest, 26, 192–93

Index

Jung, Carl, 134, 163

Krafft-Ebing, Richard von, 136

Learning, 122
Libido, 154, 155, 158, 187
  object or ego, 188
Liébeault, Ambrose-August, 45–46, 52
Life force, 15–16
Love, 228–29
Ludwig, Carl. 15, 16
Lueger, Karl, 21

Masochism, 151
Masturbation, infantile, 158
Mechanists/mechanist doctrine, 16–20, 23, 31, 63 ff., 189
  see also Mind, first model of
Melancholia, 206
Memory
  mnemic system and, 122–23
  Psi system and, 79–80, 95
Mesmer, Franz Anton, 39–42, 43
Mesmerism, 42
Meynert, Theodor, 23, 66
Mind, final model of
  ego, 202–6, 210; defense mechanisms and, 216–23
  id, 202–6, 210, 216, 221
  Pcpt.-Cs., 201–2, 203, 204–5
  relationship between components, 204–5
  repression, 205
  super-ego, 205–10, 216, 218, 220; development of infantile sexuality and, 210–18
  unconscious and preconscious systems, fallacies in previous model of, 196–201
Mind, first model of
  assessment of, 94–95
  biographical background, 63–65
  differentiation of neural network: anatomical considerations, 78–79; ego, 83–85, 86–88; mental growth and, 77–78, 80–83; Omega system, 83–86; Phi and Psi systems (permeable and impermeable neurons), 79–83
  dream theory and, 98–105, 110
  neurons/neural network: cathexis, 66–67; endogenous stimulation, 67–68, 70–72; exogenous stimulation, 67, 68–70, inter-neuronal flow, 72–77; *see also* differentiation of neural network
  primary process, 88–92; hysteria and, 92–95
  secondary process, 88–92
Mind, revised model of, 120–21
  cathexis, 127–30
  condensations, 128
  consciousness, 123–24 ff.
  mnemic systems, 122–23, 131
  perceptual and motor systems, reflex and, 121–22
  preconscious system, 124–26; dream formation and, 130–32; as process of excitation, 126–27; as secondary process, 129–30
  unconscious system, 125–26; dream formation and, 130–32; as primary process, 127–29; as process of excitation, 126–27
Mnemic systems, 122–23, 131, 159*n*
Motor system, 121–22, 131
Müller, Johannes, 15
Multiple personality, 35–36
Myths, 117

Nancy school, 45–46, 52
Narcissism, 187–88, 192
Nervous system, 17–20
  see also Mind, first model of; Neurology
Neuro-hypnotism, 44
Neurology, 61, 98
see *also* Mind, first model of
Neuropathology, 23
  Freud's work in, 30–32
  see also Hysteria
Neurophysiology, 17–20, 23, 30

Index

Neurosis, *see* Hysteria; Psychopathology
New physiology, 13–20
Newton, Isaac, 16
Nietzsche, Friedrich, 135
"Note on the Unconscious in Psychoanalysis, A," 197

Object libido, 188
Obsessions, 165
Obsessive-compulsive type, 223–24
Oedipus complex, 10, 141–44, 159, 199–200, 218
  development of super-ego and, 220; female, 214–15; male, 211–13
Oedipus Rex (Sophocles), 142, 144
Omega system, 83–86, 202, 204
"On Narcissism: An Introduction," 188
"On the Physical Mechanism of Hysterical Phenomena," 55
Overdetermination, 58, 59, 92, 94, 105, 109, 115

Paralysis, 31, 33–34, 37, 43
Paranoia, 219
Parapraxis, 61
Pathogenic idea, 57
Pcpt-Cs., 201–2
Penis envy, 214
Perceptual system, 121–22, 202
Perversion(s), 148–53
Phi system, 79–83, 102, 202, 204
  see also Mind, first model of
Physiology, *see* New physiology
Pleasure Principle, 90, 91, 127, 130, 181–82, 186
  gratification of 225–26
Polymorphous perversity, 153–54, 155–56, 203
Preconscious system, 124–27, 129–30, 202, 205
  see also Mind, final model of; Mind, revised model of
Pressure technique, 54
Primary process, 197, 198, 202, 203, 204–5
  dream theory and, 102, 103, 105
  hysteria and, 92–95
  revised model of the mind and, 127–29, 130 ff.
Problem of Anxiety, The, 217
"Project for a Scientific Psychology," 63–65
  see also Mind, first model of
Projection, 219–20, 222
Psi system, 79–83, 101, 102, 204
  see also Mind, first model of
Psyche, *see* Mind, final model of; Mind, first model of; Mind, revised model of
Psychic determination, 6, 20
Psychic energy, 70, 96
Psychoanalysis, 30, 111, 133
  see also Psychoanalytic psychotherapy
Psychoanalytic psychotherapy, 165–66
  compulsion to repeat, 180–81, traumatic neurosis and, 181–86
  Dora, case history, 166–76, 177–78, 180
  symptoms, underlying conflicts and, 170–71
  transference, 177–80; Freud's discovery of, 175–76
Psychoanalytic theory
  implications of: civilization, 229–31; pleasure principle, gratification of, 225–29; religion, 223–25; sublimation, 227–29
  origins of, Freud's study of hysteria and, 51–61
  see also all related entries
"Psychology for Neurologists," 63–65
Psychopathology
  dream theory and, 103, 105–11, 107, 109; hysteria, 108, 109–110; neurotic processes, 107–8; seduction theory, 108–9
  hypnosis and, 45–51
Psychopathology of Everyday Life, The, 61, 195

Psychosexual development, 154–59
Puysegur, Marquis de, 42–43

Rank, Otto, 134
Rationalization, 219, 222
Reaction formation, 220–21, 222
Reality principle, 90, 91, 181–82, 184
Reflex, 68–70, 71, 81, 121–22
Regression, dream formation and, 131–32
Religion, 223–25, 228
Repression, 57, 59, 95, 108, 144, 159, 198, 201, 205, 213
Resistance, 106, 140, 142, 166, 200–1, 202

Sadism, 151
Schopenhauer, Arthur, 135
Scopophilia, 151
Secondary process, 88–92, 96, 103, 129–30 ff., 197, 199–200, 205
Seduction theory, 59–60, 95, 108–9, 138
Sexuality/sexual theory, 7, 22, 28, 132, 203
  background of theory, 135–37
  childhood sexuality, 144–45; anal stage, 156–58, 160–62; castration anxiety, 213, 214; development of sexual instinct, 153–60; effect on adult life, 160–63; Freud's self-analysis and, 139–43; hysterics and, 137–39, 142–43, 145; latency stage, 159; Oedipus complex, 141–44, 159; oral stage, 155–56; penis envy, 214; "perverse" forms, 144, 159–60; phallic stage, 158–59; polymorphous perversity, 153–54; 155–56; super-ego, development of and, 211–15
  civilization and, 230, 231
  development of theory, 137–46
  dream theory and, 106–10, 112, 113
  initial recognition of Freud and, 134–35
  instinct and, 153–60; libido defined, 154
  love and, 228–29
  narcissism and, 187–88
  perversions, 148–52; childhood sexuality and, 153–60; hysteria and, 152
  psychoanalytic character types: anal, 160–62; oral and phallic, 162–63
  seduction theory, 59–60, 95, 108–9, 138
Simultaneity, 123
Sleep, state of, 99–103, 115, 130
Slips, Freudian, 61
"Some Psychological Consequences of the Anatomical Distinction between the Sexes," 215
Somnambulism, 36, 37
Sophocles, 142
Strangulated affect, 55, 56
Studies on Hysteria, 55, 195
Sublimation, 227–28, 230–31
Substitutes, 58
Suggestion, 38, 43
  see also Hypnosis/hypnotic phenomena
Summation-of-stimulation hypothesis, 19, 66, 69, 226
Super-ego, 205–10, 216
  civilization and, 230–31
  development of, 210–11, 220; female, 214–15; male, 211–13
Symbols/symbolism, 58, 130
  dream theory and, 112–13, 116–17
  hysteria and, 29–93

Thanatos, *see* Death instinct
Three Essays on the Theory of Sexuality, 146, 148 ff., 153 ff., 195
Three Faces of Eve, The (Thigpen and Cleckley), 35–36
Toilet training, 157–58, 160–62
Transference neurosis, 175–80, 200–1
Traumatic neurosis, 181–86